The BOOK
of ACTS

THE BOOK
of ACTS

Form, Style, and Theology

MARTIN DIBELIUS

Edited by K. C. Hanson

FORTRESS PRESS

MINNEAPOLIS

THE BOOK OF ACTS
Form, Style, Theology

An earlier edition of this work was published by SCM Press, London, 1956.

Translated from the German by Mary Ling. Chapter 2 translated by Paul Schubert.

Scripture is from the Revised Standard Version of the Bible, copyright © 1946, 1952, 1971 by the Division of Christian Education of the National Council of the Churches of Christ in the USA. Used by permission. Some passages have been modified to conform to Dibelius's more literal rendering of the Greek.

Cover image: Busts of the Apostles Peter and Paul, profiles turned toward each other. Early Christian. Bas-relief (unfinished) 4th C.E. Museo Archeologico Nazionale, Aquilea, Italy. © Erich Lessing / Art Resource, N.Y. Used by permission.

Author photo and portrait: Used by permission of Ulrich Dibelius.

Library of Congress Cataloging-in-Publication Data

Dibelius, Martin, 1883–1947.
    The Book of Acts / Martin Dibelius ; edited by K. C. Hanson.
    p. cm. – (Fortress classics in biblical studies)
    Includes bibliographical references and index.
    ISBN 0-8006-3644-9 (pbk : alk. paper)—ISBN 0-8006-6090-0 (hc : alk. paper)
    1. Bible. N.T. Acts—Criticism, interpretation, etc. I. Hanson, K. C. (Kenneth C.) II. Title. III. Series.

BS2625.52.D53 2004
226.6'07—dc22   2004014292

ISBN 0-8006-6090-0 (hc)
ISBN 0-8006-3644-9 (pbk)

The paper used in this publication meets the minimum requirements of American National Standard for Information Sciences — Permanence of Paper for Printed Library Materials, ANSI Z329.48-1984.

Manufactured in the U.S.A.

09   08   07   06   05   04   1   2   3   4   5   6   7   8   9   10

Contents

PART III: THE TEXT OF ACTS

Editor's Foreword

MARTIN DIBELIUS WAS BORN the son of a Lutheran pastor September 14, 1883 in Dresden, Germany, a year before his colleague, Rudolf Bultmann (1884–1969), with whom he shared many influences and many interests. The year 1883 was notable also as the year that Krakatoa exploded; Italy signed a military pact with Austria-Hungary and Germany; Dvorák, Strindberg, and Brahms all debuted major works; the Orient Express began railroad service between Paris and Istanbul; and Adolf von Harnack published *Texte und Untersuchungen zur Geschichte der altchristliche Literatur.*

Dibelius studied theology and philosophy in Neuchâtel, Leipzig, Tübingen, and Berlin. He took his first theological exams in Leipzig in 1905. His two dissertations (for the PhD and the ThD) were both history-of-religion works—on the ark of the covenant (*Die Lade Jahves*, 1906) at Tübingen, and the spirit-world in Paul (*Die Geisterwelt im Glauben des Paules*, 1910) at Berlin. He also received his licentiate in theology in 1908 in Berlin. He was Privatdozent in Berlin during the years 1910–1915. And in 1915 he became Professor of New Testament in Heidelberg, where he taught for thirty-two years until his untimely death at the age of sixty-four.

Along with Bultmann, Dibelius was heavily influenced by three of the giants in biblical and theological studies at the beginning of the twentieth century: Hermann Gunkel, Adolf von Harnack, and Johannes Weiss. Studying the form-critical method with Gunkel, Dibelius and Bultmann adapted it to the study of the Gospels, and they each published a major work on the method: Dibelius, *From Tradition to Gospel*; and Bultmann, *The History of the Synoptic Tradition.* Following Gunkel, both of them were interested in the oral tradition and its development into the Gospels; and they also followed Gunkel in his association with the History-of-Religion School (*Die Religionsgeschichtliche Schule*). This shows in their broad-ranging use of especially Greco-Roman traditions in the interpretation of the New Testament. But while Bultmann was a contributor to the *Theological Dictionary of the New Testament,* Dibelius was not—although his students, such as Heinrich Greeven, were.

Dibelius fit in well at Heidelberg, since his immediate predecessor in the New Testament chair was Johannes Weiss. Weiss, too, was associated with the *Religionsgeschichtliche Schule*; and Weiss's work foreshadowed the use of form criticism with the New Testament, developed by Dibelius and Bultmann. Dibelius was also prolific as a writer of commentaries, almost as soon as he began teaching: on all the Pauline epistles and the *Shepherd of Hermas* for the HNT series, as well as the book of James for the KEKNT series. His students also revised several of these, and two of them—on the Pastoral Epistles (revised by Conzelmann) and James (revised by Greeven)—were translated for the Hermeneia series (published by Fortress Press).

As an integral part of his New Testament studies, Dibelius was very much a theologian. His theological interests appear in his works on christology and ethics and his search for the most ancient sources of the Jesus tradition. He was also an enthusiastic participant in the ecumenical movement, like his older cousin, Otto Dibelius (1880–1967), the Bishop of Berlin-Brandenburg, who later became head of the World Council of Churches (1954–60).

In 1926, Dibelius was invited to lecture in Oxford, and in 1933 in Manchester (where C. H. Dodd was professor), as well. In 1937, he visited the United States and delivered the prestigious Schaffer Lectures at Yale University on the Sermon on the Mount (published in English in 1940). This invitation came on the heels of three of his major works having been translated into English: *From Tradition to Gospel* (1934), *Gospel Criticism and Christology* (1935), and *A Fresh Approach to the New Testament and Early Christian Literature* (1936). These publications and lectures created more interest in his work in the English-speaking world, since his writings had already influenced such scholars as C. H. Dodd and Vincent Taylor in England.

Among his students, several became renowned New Testament scholars, including Ernst Lohmeyer, Heinz-Dietrich Wendland, Werner Georg Kümmel, Heinrich Greeven, and Hans Conzelmann. Dibelius was granted an honorary doctorate from the University of St. Andrews, Scotland. He died on November 11, 1947 in Heidelberg.

The legacy of Dibelius lives on in numerous ways. His form-critical work was foundational for Gospel studies, which moved on after the war to redaction criticism. His focus on literary aspects of the book of Acts was a precursor to much of the work in New Testament literary criticism today. And questions of setting in life (*Sitz im Leben*) were important for laying the foundation of current emphases in social history and social-scientific criticism. But like other great scholars, (such as Wellhausen, Gunkel, and Bultmann), his work is not only of interest for historical reasons—his insights and groundbreaking analyses remain standards for contemporary research. And while the exegesis of the book of Acts continues, it does so on the shoulders of Dibelius and the work presented in the essays included here.

Note that I have edited Dibelius's essays in a number of ways. Most importantly, I have (1) added footnotes (marked by square brackets) and bibliographies in order to bring the reader up-to-date in the discussions; (2) employed the RSV for most biblical translations; (3) added a few citations that were unclear in Dibelius's text; (4) added translations for many of the Greek and Latin quotations; and (5) I have arranged the essays topically (the original edition arranged them in chronological order of publication). The editorial notes from the original collection were added by the late Prof. Heinrich Greeven. Those notes are marked at the end with his initials, "—H. G."

I am grateful to SCM Press for their cooperation in rights for the translation and to Vandenhoeck & Ruprecht (the publisher of the original German collection) for their assistance. But most of all, I am deeply grateful to Dr. Ulrich Dibelius, the son of the author, who not only granted the rights for this new edition of his father's writings but also provided the photo for the back cover and the photo of the painting in the frontispiece; this project could not have been done without his gracious help.

K. C. HANSON

Acknowledgments

Chapter 1 was not published prior to the first German collection of Dibelius's essays. It is titled in German "Die Apostelgeschichte im Rahmen der urchristlichen Literaturgeschichte," and is the only chapter produced for the *Urchristliche Literaturegeschichte*, which Dibelius proposed to write for Neue Theologische Grundrisse, edited by Rudolf Bultmann.

Chapter 2 was first published as "Der erste christliche Historiker," *Schriften der Universität Heidelberg* 3 (Heidelberg: Springer, 1948), 112–25. Dibelius delivered it as the "University Lecture" in Heidelberg on February 14, 1947.

Chapter 3 was first published as "Die Apostelgeschichte als Geschichtsquelle," *FF* 21/23 (1947) 67–69.

Chapter 4 was first published as "Stilkritisches zur Apostelgeschichte," in *Eucharistērion: Studien zur Religion und Literatur des Alten und Neuen Testaments. Hermann Gunkel zum 66. Geburtstage, dem 23. Mai 1922 dargebracht von seinem Schülern und Freunden*, 2 vols., edited by Hans Schmidt, FRLANT 36 (Göttingen: Vandenhoeck & Ruprecht, 1923) 2.27–49.

Chapter 5 was first published as *Die Reden der Apostelgeschichte und die antike Geschichtsschreibung*, SHAW.PH 1949 (Heidelberg: Winter, 1949).

Chapter 6 was not published prior to the first German collection of Dibelius's essays. It is the only completed part of a larger work Dibelius planned on Paul (not to be confused with the small Göshen volume which he published in 1951), which had the projected title *Paulus der radikale Christ* (Paul the Radical Christian).

Chapter 7 was first published as *Paulus auf dem Areopag*, SHAW.PH 1938–39 (Heidelberg: Winter, 1939).

Chapter 8 was first published as "Paulus in Athen," *FF* 15 (1939) 210–11. The same essay appeared as "Paul in Athens" in the English publication *Research and Progress* 6 (1941) 3–7, in a version with an extended conclusion (included here).

Chapter 9 was first published as "Die Apostelkonzil," *TLZ* 72 (1947) 193–98. That issue was a Festschrift for Walter Bauer on his seventieth birthday.

Chapter 10 was first published as "Die Bekehrung des Cornelius," in *In Honorem Antonii Fridrichsen Sexagenarii*, ConNT 11 (Lund: Gleerup, 1947), 50–65.

Chapter 11 was first published as "The Text of Acts: An Urgent Critical Task," *JR* 21 (1941) 421–31, and translated by Paul Schubert. In appeared in his German *Aufsätze* as "Der Text der Apostelgeschichte (Die nächste Aufgabe)."

Abbreviations

Ancient

ℵ	Codex Sinaiticus
A	Codex Alexandrinus
Appian	
Bell. civ.	*Bella civilia* (Civil Wars)
Hisp.	*Hispania* (Spain)
Hist. rom.	*Historia romana* (History of Rome)
Sam.	*Samnites*
Syr.	*Syriaca* (Syria)
Athenaeus	
Deipn.	*Deipnosophistae* (The Learned Banquet)
Athenagoras	
Suppl.	*Supplementum* (Supplement)
Caesar	
Bell. gall.	*Bellum gallicum* (Gallic Wars)
Callimachus	
Epigr.	*Epigrammata* (Epigrams)
Cicero	
Fam.	*Epistulae ad familiares* (Letters to Relatives)
Nat. d.	*De natura deorum* (On the Nature of the Gods)
Opt. gen.	*De optimo genere oratorum*
Republ.	*De republica* (On the Republic)
Tusc.	*Tusculanae disputationes* (Tusculan Disputations)
Clement of Alexandria	
Strom.	*Stromata* (Miscellanies)

Clement of Rome
   1 Clem.   *1 Clement* (First Epistle to the Corinthians)
Const. apostol.   *Apostolic Constitutions*
Corp. Herm.   *Corpus Hermeticum*
d   Latin text of Codex Bezae
D   Codex Bezae (Cantabrigiensis)
Didasc.   *Didascalia apostolorum* (Syriac)
Dio Chrysostom
   Or.   *Orationes* (Orations)
Dionysus of Halicarnasus
   Pomp.   *Epistula ad Pompeium Geminum* (Letter to Pompey)
E   Codex Basiliensis
Euripides
   Herc. fur.   *Hercules furens* (The Madness of Hercules)
Eusebius
   Hist. eccl.   *Historia ecclesiastica* (Ecclesiastical History)
   Praep. evang.   *Praeparatio evangelica* (Preparation for the Gospel)
gig   Codex Gigas (13th cent.)
Homer
   Od.   *Odyssey*
Ignatius
   Eph.   *Letter to the Ephesians*
   Philad.   *Letter to the Philadelphians*
Iranaeus
   Haer.   *Adversus haereses* (Against Heresies)
Isidor of Pelusium
   Ep.   *Epistulae* (Letters)
Josephus
   Ant.   *Antiquities of the Judeans*
   C. Ap.   *Contra Apionem* (Against Apion)
   War   *Judean War*
Julian
   Or.   *Orationes* (Orations)
Justin Martyr
   Ap.   *Apologia* (Defense)
Lactantius
   Divin. instit.   *Divinarum institutionum*
LXX   Septuagint

Philo
   Abr.   *De Abrahamo* (On Abraham)
   Cher.   *De cherubim* (On the Cherubim)
   Dec.   *De decalogo* (On the Decalogue)
   Det.   *Quod deterius potiori insidari soleat* (That the Worse Attacks the Better)
   Deus   *Quod Deus sit immutabilis* (That God is Unchangeable)
   Leg.   *Legum allegoriae* (Allegorical Interpretation)
   Mos.   *De vita Mosis* (On the Life of Moses)
   Opif.   *De opificio mundi* (On the Creation of the World)
   Post.   *De posteritate Caini* (On the Posterity of Cain)
   Sacr.   *De sacrificiis Abelis et Caini* (On the Sacrifices of Abel and Cain)
   Spec.   *De specialibus legibus* (On the Special Laws)
Philodemus
   Piet.   *De pietate* (On Piety)
Plato
   Apol.   *Apologia*
   Repub.   *Republic*
Pliny the Elder
   Nat. hist.   *Naturalis historia* (Natural History)
Sallust
   Bell. Cat.   *Bellum catilinae* (Catiline War)
   Bell. Jurg.   *Bellum jugurthinum* (Jugurthine War)
Seneca
   Ep.   *Epistulae* (Letters)
   Q. nat.   *Quaestionis naturalis* (Natural Questions)
syr[h]   Syriac version (Heraclean text)
Tertullian
   Adv. Marc.   *Adversus Marcionem* (Against Marcion)

MODERN

AB   *Anchor Bible*
ABD   *Anchor Bible Dictionary*, 6 vols., edited by D. N. Freedman, 1992
ABRL   Anchor Bible Reference Library
ACNT   Augsburg Commentary on the New Testament

AKGWG	Abhandlungen der Königlichen Gesellschaft der Wissenschaften zu Göttingen. Philologisch-historische Klasse
ANET	*Ancient Near Eastern Texts Relating to the Old Testament*, 3d ed., edited by James B. Pritchard, 1969
ANRW	*Aufstieg und Niedergang der römischen Welt*
ANTC	Abingdon New Testament Commentaries
ARU	Arbeiten zur Religionsgeschichte des Urchristentums
ARW	*Archivs für Religionwissenschaft*
BETL	Bibliotheca ephemeridum theologicarum lovaniensium
BEvT	Beiträge zur evangelischen Theologie
BFCT	Beiträge zur Förderung christlicher Theologie
BGU	Ägyptische Urkunden aus den königlichen Museen zu Berlin
BHS	*Biblia Hebraica Stuttgartensia*
BHT	Beiträge zur historischen Theologie
BibIntSer	Biblical Interpretation Series
BibKon	*Biblische Konfrontationen*
BK	Biblischer Kommentar
BTS	Biblisch-theologische Studien
BTZ	*Berliner theologische Zeitschrift*
BUS	Brown University Studies
BWANT	Beiträge zur Wissenschaft vom Alten (und Neuen) Testament
BZ	*Biblische Zeitschrift*
BZAW	Beihefte zur Zeitschrift für die alttestamentliche Wissenschaft
BZNW	Beihefte zur Zeitschrift für die neutestamentliche Wissenschaft
CC	Continental Commentaries
ConNT	Coniectanea Neotestamentica
CTL	Crown Theological Library
DLZ	*Deutsche Literaturzeitung*
EB	Echter Bibel
EBib	*Etudes bibliques*
[Ed.]	editor's note
EKKNT	Evangelisch-katholischer Kommentar zum Neuen Testament
ESEC	Emory Studies in Early Christianity

ET	English translation
EvTh	*Evangelische Theologie*
FAB	*Für Arbeit und Besinnung*
FCBS	Fortress Classics in Biblical Studies
FF	*Forschung und Fortschritt*
FOTL	Forms of the Old Testament Literature
FRLANT	Forschungen zur Religion und Literatur des Alten und Neuen Testaments
GBS	Guides to Biblical Scholarship
HAT	Handkommentar zum Alten Testament
HAW	Handbuch der Altertumswissenschaft
HBT	*Horizons in Biblical Theology*
HNT	Handbuch zum Neuen Testament
HTIBS	Historic Texts and Interpreters in Biblical Scholarship
HTKNT	Herders theologischer Kommentar zum Neuen Testament
IBC	Interpretation: A Biblical Commentary
ICC	International Critical Commentary
IDBS	*Interpreter's Dictionary of the Bible, Supplementary Volume,* edited by Keith Crim, 1976
ILCK	International Library of Christian Knowledge
Int	*Interpretation*
IRT	Issues in Religion and Theology
JBL	*Journal of Biblical Literature*
JHS	*Journal of Hellenic Studies*
JR	*Journal of Religion*
JSNTSup	Journal for the Study of the New Testament: Supplement Series
JSOT	*Journal for the Study of the Old Testament*
JSOTSup	Journal for the Study of the Old Testament: Supplement Series
JSS	*Journal of Semitic Studies*
JTC	*Journal for Theology and the Church*
KAT	Kommentar zum Alten Testament
KBL	Ludwig Koehler and Walter Baumgartner, *Lexicon in Veteris Testamenti libros*
KeH	Kurzgefasstes exegetisches Handbuch zum Alten Testament
KEKNT	Kritisch-exegetischer Kommentar über das Neue Testament

KHAT	Kurzer Hand-Commentar zum Alten Testament
KNT	Kommentar zum Neuen Testament
LCBI	Literary Currents in Biblical Interpretation
LD	Lectio divina
LXX	Septuagint
MDAIA	*Mitteilungen des Deutschen archäologischen Instituts*
MT	Masoretic text
NDF	Neue Deutsche Forschungen
NEBKNT	Neue Echter Bibel
Neot	*Neotestamentica*
NGWG.PH	Nachrichten der Gesellschaft der Wissenschaften zu Göttingen
NKGWG	Nachrichten von der Königlichen Gesellschaft der Wissenschaften zu Göttingen. Philologisch-historische Klasse
NKZ	*Neue kirchliche Zeitschrift*
NovTSup	Novum Testamentum Supplements
NTAbh	Neutestamentliche Abhandlungen
NTC	New Testament in Context
NTD	Neue Testament Deutsch
NTS	*New Testament Studies*
NTT	New Testament Theology
OBT	Overtures to Biblical Theology
OGIS	*Orientis graeci inscriptiones selectae*, 2 vols., edited by W. Dittenberger, 1903–5
OrChr	*Oriens christianus*
ÖTKNT	Ökumenischer Taschenbuch-kommentar
OTM	Oxford Theological Monographs
OtSt	*Oudtestamentische Studiën*
QD	Quaestiones disputatae
RHPR	*Revue d'histoire et de philosophie religieuses*
RNT	Regensburger Neues Testament
SDAW	Sitzungsberichte der deutschen Akademie der Wissenschaften zu Berlin
SacPag	Sacra pagina
SAT	Die Schriften des Alten Testaments
SBL	Society of Biblical Literature
SBLAB	Society of Biblical Literature Academia Biblica
SBLDS	Society of Biblical Literature Dissertation Series
SBLMS	Society of Biblical Literature Monograph Series

SBLSBS	Society of Biblical Literature Sources for Biblical Studies
SBLSS	Society of Biblical Literature Semeia Studies
SBLSymSer	Society of Biblical Literature Symposium Series
SBS	Stuttgarter Bibelstudien
SBT	Studies in Biblical Theology
SBTS	Sources for Biblical and Theological Study
SDAW	Sitzungen der deutschen Akademie der Wissenschaften zu Berlin
SEÅ	*Svensk exegetisk årsbok*
SG	Sammlung Göschen
SHAW.PH	Sitzungsberichte der Heidelberger Akademie der Wissenschaften, Philosophisch-Historische Klasse
SHBC	Smith and Helwys Bible Commentary
SNTSMS	Society for New Testament Studies Monograph Series
SNVAO	Skrifter utgitt av det Norske Videnskaps-Akademi i Oslo
STU	Schweizerische theologische Umschau
SUNT	Studien zur Umwelt des Neuen Testaments
SWJT	*Southwestern Journal of Theology*
TDNT	*Theological Dictionary of the New Testament,* 10 vols., edited by Gerhard Kittel and Gerhard Friedrich, 1964–76
TEH	*Theologische Existenz Heute*
ThBü	Theologische Bücherei
THKNT	Theologischer Handkommentar zum Neuen Testament
ThSt	Theologische Studiën
TLZ	*Theologische Literaturzeitung*
TQ	*Theologische Quartalschrift*
TRE	*Theologische Realenzyklopädie,* edited by Gerhard Krause and Gerhard Müller, 1977–
TRu	*Theologische Rundschau*
TSK	*Theologische Studien und Kritiken*
TU	Texte und Untersuchungen zur Geschichte der altchristlichen Literatur
TZ	*Theologische Zeitschrift*
VGTB	Van Gorcum's Theologische Bibliothek
VT	*Vetus Testamentum*
VTSup	Vetus Testamentum Supplements

WBC	Word Biblical Commentary
WMANT	Wissenschaftliche Monographien zum Alten und Neuen Testament
WUNT	Wissenschaftliche Untersuchungen zum Neuen Testament
WZMLU	Wissenschaftliche Zeitschrift der Martin-Luther-Universität
YOS	Yale Oriental Series
ZAW	*Zeitschrift für die alttestamentliche Wissenschaft*
ZBK	Zürcher Bibelkommentare
ZDPV	*Zeitschrift für die deutschen Palästina-Vereins*
ZdZ	*Die Zeichen der Zeit*
ZNW	*Zeitschrift für die neutestamentliche Wissenschaft*
ZTK	*Zeitschrift für Theologie und Kirche*
ZWTh	*Zeitschrift für wissenschaftliche Theologie*

Part I

History and Style in Acts

1

Acts in the Setting of the History
of Early Christian Literature

The Acts of the Apostles is unique in style not only in the New Testament but also in great literature. It is distinguished from the New Testament and many other early Christian writings by its literary character, and from the work of the historians by what we may call a theological purpose. But it is primarily the content of the book which makes it unique: as far as we know, no one undertook—before, near the time of, or after the writing of the canonical Acts—to tell in a consecutive narrative the story of the first Christian community and the decisive expansion in the spread of the Christian belief to the West; such was not the aim, for example, of the Apocryphal Acts of the Apostles.

With regard to the question of authorship, it has already been shown that in the Lukan writings the tradition of the Church since Irenaeus and the Muratorian Canon should be taken more seriously than in other instances.[1] Here, in Acts, we shall have to consider the question of whether someone who belonged to Paul's circle could have written a book which is sometimes found to contradict Paul's epistles.[2] But the foremost consideration is that of its style and content.

SCOPE

The book portrays events from the Ascension of Jesus to Paul's arrival in Rome. One distinct section is found preceding 13:1. From here onwards the author tells only of Paul and no longer of the mother-communities in Jerusalem and Antioch—with the sole exception of the so-called Apostolic Council (15:1-35), which is reported because of its bearing on Paul's mission. The first half (1–12) contains the portrayal of the life of the earliest community (1–5); this is followed by an account of the martyrdom of Stephen, with which the author has linked in his own way both the conversion of Paul and the stories of Philip and Peter and the results of their mission, and finally the story of

Peter's imprisonment and release (6–12). In the second half the book relates the evangelizing of Asia Minor and Greece by Paul, and then the story of his long imprisonment (or rather, of the countless trials), including finally his transportation and accommodation in Rome.

Although the division into two parts is so clear, it is difficult to find exactly where the author himself envisaged the break. According to form, the caesura seems most likely to come after the stay in Caesarea, in 21:14, before the departure for Jerusalem. But with regard to content, it might well come after Paul's reception there (i.e., after 21:26); the author, however, has given no indication on this matter.

It is not immediately clear why Luke selected and restricted his material as he did. At the end of Acts we have still to ask why Luke's narrative did not continue any further, and, if he limited himself entirely to Paul in the second half, why he did not tell about the end of the mission and of the apostle's life. At the beginning, the question is raised of the relationship with Luke's Gospel, in that the Ascension of Jesus was related quite briefly in the Gospel, whereas the Acts opens with a detailed account of the Ascension. There is, however, an explanation for the repetition, since here the Risen One not only, as in Luke 24:49, again promises the imminent pouring out of the Spirit, but also says: "You shall be my witnesses in Jerusalem and in all Judea and Samaria and to the end of the earth" (Acts 1:8b). This sentence is certainly stylized in the interests of the author's literary intention; it contains the program for the book: chaps. 1–5 Jerusalem; chaps. 6–12 Judea and Samaria; chaps. 13–28 to the ends of the earth. We should observe here that references such as these, which give a literary significance to events within the book itself, are to be found several times in Acts and are a clear indication of the author's literary purpose.

Further peculiarities are to be seen, however, in the choice of material. Chapters 6–12 deal with Stephen, the evangelist Philip, Paul, and Peter; chap. 13 onwards deal only with Paul (with Peter and James). But even in ancient times the book was called "Acts of the Apostles." Where now are the apostles? We hear nothing of the acts and experiences of the disciples of Jesus, apart from those of Peter and of John[3] (whose role, beside Peter, is rather like that of a mute in a play). And while Paul's journeys are related consecutively, so that it is at least possible to form some idea of the chronology, we hear nothing at all about the duration and sequence of the events reported in Acts 1–12. As a result, the interval of time, for example, between the conversion of Paul and Jesus' death is variously estimated even today, with estimates varying by months or years. Luke obviously had no information about many events, but we must also remember that there were many events about which he did not desire to tell. Both the circumstances in which he acquired his material and the author's literary intention have made the book of Acts what it is.

The Gospel and Acts

The essential difference between this book and Luke's Gospel also emerges here. They have the dedication to Theophilus in common. This fact, together with the style, indicates a conscious literary intention. But while the dedication of the Gospel shows an objective, impartial attitude, in Acts 1:1-2 the author speaks in retrospect of "all that Jesus began to do and teach, until the day when he was taken up." This allusion to the subject-matter of the first book is entirely in accordance with literary custom;[4] the omission, after this retrospective note, of any proposed plan for the present work, and the immediate commencement of the narrative in 1:3 are not without parallel.[5] In this very first chapter the difference from the Gospel begins to show. It contains what is perhaps an older story of the Ascension of Jesus,[6] a list of the apostles, and an account of the choosing of Matthias, an event that is embellished with a speech by Peter. Whatever tradition may be contained in these three passages, all three have in any case been revised by the author, and obviously more drastically than appears to be the case in the Gospel. And the whole book confirms the impression gained here. It has been put together in quite a different way from Luke's Gospel. The evangelist Luke connected fragments of tradition as did Mark and Matthew—only he linked them together better than they, stylized them more richly, revised them more critically. Nevertheless, in spite of these improvements in the interests of history, Luke's Gospel did not as a result constitute a movement forward to "great" literature.

The Acts, however, does. This is shown by the introduction of speeches, the independent treatment of the sources, the artistic linking together of one action with another. The Acts of the Apostles thus implies an epoch in early Christian writing; a book has come into existence here that can count as literature—however this "advance" may be assessed. And this book was written by one who had only just (or years before) composed another that, in spite of certain peculiarities, was on the whole not of a literary nature at all. The difference can be understood. In Luke's Gospel, it was a question of making available to the communities in a well-thought-out composition and in good style the essentials of the tradition concerning their Lord. Above all, this book was to be a Gospel like the others. But here, in Acts, the same author has ventured upon something new. Without models, with gaps in the tradition, as will be shown, certainly without written sources, he describes a portion of early Christian history and must necessarily form a consecutive and essentially convincing narrative out of what he knows and what he can learn. He can use his talents and his inclination quite differently from when he was composing the Gospel, the literary type of which was determined by an obligation to abide in tradition about Jesus. Here, the new literary freedom and the style that resulted from it are determined by the new task itself.

And what a task it was! A number of people had found themselves together in their belief in Jesus Christ and in the expectation of his coming again and were leading a quiet—and in the Jewish sense "pious"—life in Jerusalem. It was a modest existence, and nothing but the victorious conviction of the believers betrayed the fact that from this number would go out a movement that would transform the world, that this community would subsequently become the center of the Church. Gradually, differences developed both with the Jewish authorities and among the believers themselves. But belief in Christ spread across the provinces of Syria, laying hold also of the non-Jewish population, and was proclaimed by the apostle Paul in Asia Minor, Macedonia, and Greece. That belief spread to other parts of the world is an historical development that cannot be explained simply. For a generation or so the followers of Jesus had preserved words or stories about his life. When these were put together they made a picture of the Master's work. The story of the formation and development of these communities, however, was not one that could be transmitted by popular tradition in the same way. The incidents involved were too complicated; moreover, they were concerned with too broad a field, and could not be put together to form a unified action. It is quite probable that the communities did preserve stories of individual events which had taken place among them, stories of healings, conversions, and martyrdoms, especially if extraordinary events made God's protection and power particularly evident. But an author who wished to write history and not simply to relate stories could not be content with collecting, sifting, and linking together such fragments of narrative. He had to try to mould them into a significant sequence and—as the most important task—to bring to light a certain "meaning" indicated in the events.[7] But here too he was dependent upon the material that was at his disposal.

SOURCES

This brings us to the much-discussed question of the sources of Acts.[8] The most obvious hypothesis is the one that concerns itself with the narrative of Paul's journeys. Constant reference has been made to one fact in particular: that in several sections of this account the story is told in the first person plural. This "we account" includes, however, only Paul's journey from Troas to Philippi (16:10-17); the journey which took place years later from Philippi to Miletus (20:5-15), and from there to Jerusalem (21:1-18); and finally, the journey made by Paul, as a prisoner, from Caesarea to Rome (27:1—28:16). If we take the "Western" text of Acts as the original, an isolated note from Antioch

(11:28) would have to be included. If we wish to restrict ourselves to the "we passages" for the source of the missionary journeys, we find only thirty-seven verses.[9] If, on the other hand, the "I" which lies behind the "we" is intended to mean the author of other or even of all the accounts of journeys or of the whole book, the "we" has lost its value as a means of determining the source.[10] In contrast to many scholars I therefore disregard the "we" straight away and instead start with the following observations on the account of the journey in Acts 13:4—21:18:

1. It is inconceivable that Luke should have included insignificant and unimportant stations in his account of the journey if he had not had a description of the route at his disposal. In support of this we may quote the mention of Attalia in 14:25 (where, characteristically, the "Western" text completes the information by noting an evangelizing venture), of Samothrace and Neapolis (16:11), Amphipolis and Apollonia (17:1), Caesarea and, probably, Jerusalem (18:22). The sentence in 20:13-14, which is completely unimportant for both the story of the mission and for the biography of Paul, belongs here as well: "But going ahead to the ship, we set sail for Assos, intending to take Paul aboard there; for so he had arranged, intending himself to go by land. And when he met us at Assos, we took him on board and came to Mitylene." Reference is made even to the "early disciple," Mnason (21:16), of whom nothing further is said. Of the six passages mentioned as examples, half belong to the "we-account." There is thus no difference between it and the rest of the narrative with regard to the mention of "neutral" places or persons. So we may suppose that Luke had a written account for 13:4—21:18 (except 15:1-35).

2. The speeches do not belong to this account and will later be discussed together.[11] As they stand in the text, they are Luke's own compositions—whether he used older formulations in composing them or not. Four speeches by Paul are involved in the account of his journeys: in Antioch of Pisidia (13:16-41), at Lystra (14:15-17), in Athens (17:22-31), and at Miletus to the elders of Ephesus (20:18-35). Three times it is clear that they have been inserted from the fact that doublets or unevenness occur in the narrative when the author departs from the source or returns to it again.[12]

3. The isolated stories, also, do not belong to the source, in so far as the way in which they are rounded off before and after indicates that they were already current in the community as isolated stories. Of these, there are five. First, there is the story of Elymas (13:8-12); the original form of the opening of this story has certainly not been preserved.[13] Next there is the healing in Lystra (14:8-18), where the opening words

clearly show the marks of insertion; for in the source (14:6-7) the apostle has already been brought to "Lystra and Derbe and the surrounding district" and is recorded as preaching in those places; but now Luke must lead the reader back to Lystra, in order to tell the story that belongs to that place.[14] The third story deals with the conversion of the prison guard in Philippi (16:25-34); here it is clear that it has been inserted from the fact that, in what follows in 16:35, the earthquake that had taken place in the meantime is not mentioned at all; and only the Western text has bridged the gap.[15] Next there is the little story of the sons of Sceva (19:14-16); the beginning of this has been lost, as we can see from the reference in 19:16 to the house that had not come into the story at all.[16]

The many discrepancies referred to under (2) and (3) are sufficient proof that the speeches and stories cannot be ascribed to that account of the journeys that underlies the whole narrative. What does belong to it is the list of stations—both important and unimportant—with details about hosts, the success of the campaign, and other brief information. The limits of the source cannot be established exactly.[17] A relatively plain account, containing only the bare facts, such as, according to (2) and (3), we must suppose that this was, is in fact the probable thing in that unliterary generation. An itinerary of this sort, in the form of a list of stations, might well have been used on such journeys for the practical reason that, if the journey was made on another occasion, the route and the same hosts might be found again. It is unlikely, however, that any of these five stories was included in this list for a practical purpose. It seems to me quite impossible, for example, that the artistically composed parting speech in Miletus (20:18-25) was included in this account of the journey merely on the grounds that the narrative before and after is in the "we-style."

But Luke did not adopt this itinerary without some revision. There are examples of certain phrases of an "edifying" nature concerning the relationship of believers to the grace of God, and concerning admonitions and straightforward testimony to be found both within the itinerary and outside it;[18] and in both cases they are attributable to Luke. But the author has also abbreviated his source. In the verses shortly preceding the appearance of the "we" (16:1-10), Paul's journey through Asia Minor is related in barest outline only. Paul first visits the communities of Lycaonia that have already been evangelized by him, and then proceeds through the interior of Asia Minor, Phyrgia, and the land of Galatia, since he is "prevented by the Holy Spirit" from preaching in Asia. The cities of the west coast of "Asia" had thus been his real objective. Now he wants to go across Phrygia and the "land of Galatia"[19] to the north, to Bithynia. Again the Holy Spirit prevents him, so that he is even-

tually urged, one might say, to go to Troas. And there a third divine intervention takes place. In a vision in the night he sees a man from Macedonia, who
makes the request: "Come over to Macedonia and help us." This order also he
obeys, and so reaches Macedonia and Greece. What a strange way that is of
writing history! We are told neither how the intervention of the Holy Spirit
manifested itself nor whether Paul evangelized on the way (see the previous
note above); we are told no names of stations or of persons. All the material
that Luke elsewhere has taken from the itinerary is missing here. Did the
source fail here? Was not the old form of the theory of the "we-source" perhaps
correct in maintaining that the author's knowledge was most exact where the
"we" began, and that in the verses before this the author's knowledge was
incomplete? This theory could also appeal to chap. 20, where Paul's last journey through Macedonia and Greece is dealt with summarily in vv. 1-3, while
from vv. 4-5 onwards (in v. 5 the "we" begins again) names and other details
are given.

But there is certainly no lack of actual knowledge in 16:1-10. The author
tells of the strange journeying back and forth of the missionaries in the
provinces of Asia Minor. But if he was able to give the names of the provinces,
he must also have known the names of the places. It is not in order to provide
a survey of the work of evangelism in the individual districts of Asia Minor that
he describes the traveling to and fro of the missionaries. In this section (16:6-
10) his story has only one aim, which is to show how divine intervention on
three occasions had caused the important re-directing of the mission toward
Macedonia and Greece. It does not matter whether it was visions, persecutions, illness, or the destruction of roads that caused Paul to alter the plans for
his journey; it is important only to show that it is divine power that guides the
apostle's steps. Nor is it essential for this narrative that we should know
whether Paul evangelized at all in Galatia on his way through Asia Minor; what
is vitally important is that he did so in Greece.

The apostle's last journey through Greece, however, receives only the
briefest notice in 20:1-3. This is understandable when we see how Luke's portrayal of the journey to Jerusalem has given way to prophecies of suffering and
of separation from the work that Paul has done so far. In Miletus, Tyre, and
Caesarea this theme prevails. From this point of view, the last journey through
Greece has no significance. It was undertaken in order to visit established
communities—and we know from the second letter to the Corinthians how
necessary such visits were—and perhaps in order to found others as well. But
details of such a journey as this do not come within the scope of what Luke
now wishes to portray. Once more, therefore, we may say that the brevity of
the narrative is not due to lack of information but to intentional selection
from material available in the source.

MEMOIRS

Harnack has shown from his lexicographical findings that the "we passages" in the book are not insertions of foreign elements but are similar to the surrounding parts of the book.[20] At the same time, he has shown the Lukan character of the whole work, which excludes the possibility that a separate source was taken word for word into the author's text. Not even literary analogies are able to weigh against this. For we cannot a priori decide about the significance, in these analogies, of the narrative form in the singular or plural—whether it is the vestige of a catalogue or a literary art form. When the Alexander romance combines narrative and letters of Alexander, Eduard Norden sees as presupposed the conjunction of personal (in this case fictitious) account and third-personal report.[21] But there was at that time a lively manufacture of fictitious letters, which is a rather different matter.

A much clearer example of the literary application of memoirs seems to me to be given by Norden in his comparison between Livy's presentation of Cato's Spanish campaign (in the third person), 34.8.4-5, and his course, that is the *Oratio* I of Cato, preserved only in fragments, into which he introduced the narrative (in the "we-style").[22] In the Acts of the Apostles we are concerned, however, with the elaboration of a narrative, not this kind of editing of one, a process that eliminates the "we." A better analogy is the *Periplus Ponti Euxini* by Arrianus, in the Greek language, in which (no doubt because of the official Latin report which had just been delivered to the emperor) is portrayed his voyage to the Cappadocian coast, in a book which is destined for the reading public and dedicated to the emperor. In this case the writer has left the original "we" and "I" in the story, or perhaps occasionally even made use of the first person in his own additions. This autobiographical account has, however, been extended by him in the description of two stretches of the route taken from older sources, which complete his journey so that, taken as a whole, the account of the voyage combines autobiographical writing with reporting in the third person.

As an example from Jewish literature we must first consider the Book of Ezra-Nehemiah, which was later divided into two parts. It includes a passage in the "I" or "we-style" (Ezra 7:11—9:5), which is generally regarded as an excerpt from Ezra's memoirs. But there are those who oppose this as well, and consider either the use of the "I-form" or the alleged author to be fictitious.[23] Nehemiah 1:1—7:5 is usually regarded as an autobiographical account, written in the "I-style." "I" or "we" then appears again in chaps. 12–13, and is understood as an indication that these sections also came from the memoirs of Nehemiah. The "we-style" in Nehemiah 10, on the other hand, is not unanimously explained in this way, but is traced by many to a document that reached the author from some other direction.

Among the Jewish apocryphal writings, the Book of Tobit contributes something to the "I" problem. Here the previous history of Tobit is told by himself (1:2—3:6), perhaps for reasons of style, in order to give the book a personal introduction—at any rate, not because a particular source was being used. In the Latin version of Jerome, however, as in the Aramaic text of the book, which was probably equally late, the first person singular does not appear, and the story begins straight away in the third person. Here style was obviously the primary consideration, for it was found that the "I-style" at the beginning destroyed the smoothness of the narrative.

Of the Christian texts we might mention here, the so-called apocryphal *Protoevangelium of James* is most appropriate. In it Joseph himself tells in 18:2 how, in the hour of the birth of Jesus, he observed that the world stood still. Some scholars have tried to prove that this fabulous description is an insertion. But the extent of the "I-narrative" is not definable; it extends beyond that description of the world, although it does not include the whole story of the birth.[24] We can thus scarcely use the appearance of the first person as a means of distinguishing sources. What we have here, it seems, is not an insertion but simply a naïve need on the part of the author to enliven his account.

The appearance of the first person in the *Gospel of Peter*, of which we possess only a fragment, is more problematical. In this text, which extends from the judgment of Jesus to the resurrection, and thus offers little opportunity for Peter to appear independently, "I-" and "we-narratives" occur in two passages: in §§26-27, when the disciples remain in hiding after the crucifixion of Jesus; and §§59-60, where the disciples ("we, however, the disciples of the Lord") went home and "I, Simon Peter and Andrew, my brother" go fishing. We do not know from what point in Jesus' ministry this Gospel commences, so that we cannot tell whether Peter's denial or the scene in Gethsemane was described in the "I-style." Certainly no particular value is to be ascribed to the "I-evidence" of this Gospel. If we consider how, in the *Ebionite Gospel*, the disciples say, "He chose us,"[25] and how, in a Gnostic work, John is spoken of in the third person, but the account then continues: "When I had heard this, I turned away to the temple,"[26] we cannot help wondering whether the words in the first person were really always the remains of an original text.

Complicated though the situation is, it still seems possible that the "I" is rather a sign of literary elaboration. And when the *Acts of John* and the *Acts of Philip*, from the apocryphal Acts of the Apostles, contain occasional instances of the use of "we,"[27] that need not necessarily be relics of an old text, but may possibly be attributable to an author who wanted to lend clarity, color, and the appearance of authenticity to his story. Thus the finding of this survey is that the occurrence of "I" or "we" may equally well indicate either an old source or a new literary work. It is not Mark's, but Peter's Gospel that contains first-person reporting!

VOYAGE TO ROME

In our book of Acts, the principles arrived at so far can also be applied to what is, perhaps, the strangest part of the book, which consistently uses the form "we"; namely, the report of the voyage to Rome. Although the story is told in the "we-style," it does not have the same character as the other "we-passages" or as the whole itinerary. In the latter, Paul's journeys are described, but his missionary activities have pride of place. Here, on the other hand, the "I," who is implied in the "we," tells of a sea-voyage with a shipwreck; the nautical details have always won the admiration of experts in these matters, but of Paul, who takes the leading place in the action in the chapters concerning the missionary journey, we are told very little. The journey from Caesarea to Malta (27:1-44; 28:1-2) and from Malta to Rome (28:7-14) is described in fifty-four verses;[28] only eighteen of these verses deal with Paul's activities. There are five references to Paul of which we can say that some certainly and others probably have been inserted into a report that was already available. The clearest case is in 27:43. The soldiers want to kill the prisoners when the ship is wrecked so that none will escape; but the centurion wishes to save Paul and so arranges that first those who can swim shall jump overboard and also that the non-swimmers shall then reach land on pieces of the wreckage. Only we do not hear what Paul does, on whose account the measure is said to have been taken. The story of the centurion's apt decision thus, obviously, has nothing to do with Paul; it belongs to the description of the voyage, and, by the introduction of four words, has been made into an account concerning Paul.

The first of the passages about Paul is also seen to be a foreign element. The travelers come to "Fair Havens" in Crete (27:8) and apparently want to spend the winter there; at least, nothing is said at first of their traveling any further. But when it transpires that the harbor is unsuitable, the voyage is continued (27:12). In between comes a suggestion by Paul that they should not set sail again, and the centurion's rejection of this proposal (27:9-11). Without these verses, the sequence is clear and continuous in meaning. Again, we must consider as an insertion into the account of the voyage the short section 27:21-26, in which Paul encourages his fellow-voyagers and assures them, on the strength of his vision in the night, that their lives are safe. For he refers here to the advice which he gave in 27:9-11. In the third passage concerning Paul (27:31), he points out to the centurion that the sailors want to leave the wrecked ship secretly. Here again it is possible that v. 32 should follow immediately after v. 30, and this reading is perhaps to be preferred. Since we have already discussed 27:43, only the section 27:33-36 remains: in the presence of the weary ship's company Paul takes food and persuades the others to do the same. We can see very clearly from v. 37 that there is a lack of continuity here also for, wedged in between eating and being satisfied, the number of the ship's company is given as 276. This is obviously a relic of the old literary account, which has no connection with Paul.

This analysis shows, then, that a secular description of the voyage and shipwreck served as a pattern, basis, or source for the account of the journey, and that the writer inserted into this description a few short references to Paul (because he had some special knowledge?). This does not affect the character of the composition, which remains distinctly literary. And after examining the list of antecedents to which Norden has drawn attention,[29] the impression is strengthened that the sea-voyage is one of the most literary sections of Acts. It is a secular composition with insertions concerning Paul. The "we" is not at all remarkable in such descriptions of travel, and so is not in the least an indication that this is a non-literary account of a journey that originated from among Paul's associates. It is simply the normal usage in a literary description and indicates that the author was present on the journey. It does not turn the description of the voyage and shipwreck into a personal document; the account remains a literary composition of a secular kind.

The First Christian Historian

THE PROLOGUE AND PLAN

Among the writings of the New Testament one book occupies a special place, a fact which often receives too little attention. This is the book of Acts, which tradition attributes to Luke, the author of the third Gospel. There are some things to be said against this tradition, but far more in favor of it, so that we may call the author by the name of Luke.

Luke begins both writings—the Gospel as well as Acts—with a literary dedication to one Theophilus who is evidently a distinguished person. On each occasion we have to note not only the fact of the dedication as a sign of conscious literary intention but also the style of these dedications. The choice of words and the construction of sentences at the beginning of the Gospel betray the educated author; the text of this dedication does not, however, betray the Christian at all, but sounds like the prologue to a secular book.

It is somewhat different in the case of the Acts, in so far as its prologue at least mentions Jesus' name. There, we read: "In the first book, Theophilus, I wrote abut all that Jesus did and taught from the beginning until the day when he was taken up to heaven" (Acts 1:1-2a); but this reference to the preceding book, the Gospel, corresponds entirely with literary custom.[1] And if the continuation of the text also disappoints us in that Luke proceeds straight from this apostrophe to Theophilus to the story, we can still see that the account of this first chapter has been consciously fashioned and fitted together out of a perhaps older narrative, which contained an account of the ascension of Christ, a list of the twelve disciples, and an account of a gathering of the community that included a speech by Peter. Even in this passage we are given an impression, which is constantly reaffirmed throughout the whole book, that accounts are found in Acts that could not possibly be contained in any Gospel. Thus there is an essential difference between the literary type of the

Gospel on the one hand and that of Acts on the other—it exists although the evangelist Luke is also the author of Acts.

How is this to be explained? In writing his Gospel Luke wanted, as his foreword says, by telling Theophilus of the "things which happened amongst us," to convince a distinguished man of the truth of the Christian doctrines, with which he was already acquainted; but he achieved this by following the same principle as the other evangelists, that of recording a succession of traditional stories, allegories, and sayings in order to form a consecutive narrative. Luke, however, linked these fragments together more skillfully, gave them a somewhat richer style and elaborated them rather more critically. It is this last factor that betrays the author who wishes to write history rather than to relate stories. Even so, in spite of these small corrections made in the Gospel in the interests of history, he still cannot be said to have entered the field of "great" literature.

He does so, however, with the Acts of the Apostles. His capabilities and inclination can this time be employed in a different way, because he has to write here without predecessors, sometimes probably even without literary sources, and to see how to make a consecutive account of what he knows and what he can discover. The *new style* is conditioned by the *new task*.

And what a task it was. A band of people had been gathered together in a common belief in Jesus Christ and in the expectation of his coming again, and were leading a quiet, and in the Jewish sense, "pious" existence in Jerusalem. It was a modest existence; and nothing but the victorious conviction of the believers betrayed the fact that from this company a movement would go out which was to change the world, that this community was to become the center of the Church. There were known to have been a few incidents that had aroused a stir, such as conversions, healings, the first martyrdom. The community probably preserved in the form of short stories such things as were a perpetual reminder to them of the reason for their existence. Thus they had, for about a generation, kept faithfully any information about the life of their Lord and Master. Only there was a difference in the amount of material available; far more material had been preserved about the life of Jesus than about the experiences of the early community. The first seven or eight chapters of Acts show that comparatively little was preserved and handed down on the latter subject. We have only the stories of the Ascension and the Whitsun miracle, the healing of the lame man at the gate of the temple, the death of Ananias and his wife by means of a sort of curse by Peter, and finally the martyrdom of Stephen—that is, five stories. And further, the book is called by its Greek title "Acts of the Apostles," but how few such acts (apart from Peter) it can report! The succeeding chapters (8–12) again contain only five stories: the conversion of a distinguished Ethiopian by Philip and the conversion of the centurion Cornelius by Peter, two miracles of healing done by Peter, and Peter's miraculous release from prison. But what is told in the second half of the book, from chap. 13 onwards, is concerned almost exclusively with the deeds and experiences of Paul, who was, indeed, the most successful apostle, although not a direct disciple of Jesus. As we hear nothing more of the deeds of the disciples of Jesus, a host of difficult problems results: Did these disciples also evangelize, and, if so, where? Did Peter die in Rome, and how long was he there? Did John, the Galilean fisherman, suffer a martyr's death in Palestine, or is he the same John who appeared suddenly in Ephesus toward the end of the century? These are all questions that can receive many different answers if we study the whole of the ancient tradition of the Church, but which cannot be answered at all from the Acts of the Apostles. There were evidently some subjects on which Luke had no information and others about which he did not *wish* to write. With this surmise we approach the real object of our examination, the individuality of the book from the literary point of view. It is this that entitles us to call the author the first Christian historian.

TURNING STORIES INTO HISTORY

The historian's art is not limited to collecting and framing traditions, however many he may have at his disposal. He must endeavor to illuminate and somehow to present the meaning of events. He must be impelled by a desire to know and to understand. If Luke had had more traditions at his disposal, but had linked them together only as he does in the Gospel, he would not qualify for the title "historian." We ascribe this title to him only because he did more than collect traditions. He tried to combine in his own way, into a significant, continuous whole, both the tradition current in the community and what he himself discovered. Secondly, he tried to make clear the meaning that these events contained. Both this continuous whole, and its meaning, we must now consider.[2]

Establishing continuity was simplest in the second part of Acts (chaps. 13–21), which deals with Paul's missionary journeys, for here Luke evidently had an account of the stations before him. For practical reasons an account of this kind would have been used on such journeys, in order that, if the journey were to be repeated, the way and former hosts could be found once more. That Luke used such a source is clear from the fact that he also mentions unimportant stations on the journey, of which there is really nothing further to tell. The following sentence serves as an illustration: "But going ahead to the ship, we set sail for Assos, intending to take Paul aboard there; for so he had arranged, intending himself to go by land. And when he met us at Assos, we took him on board and came to Mitylene" (Acts 20:13-14). The content of this sentence was neither conceived in legend nor handed down as an anecdote; it can only be understood as a note taken from a list of stations, from an itinerary.

It seems to me to be a mistake, however, to conclude that because, as we have seen, there was a source for Paul's journeys, there was, similarly, a source for the first part of Acts (chaps. 1–12).[3] If there had been a source for these chapters, giving a continuous portrayal of the development of the early Christian community and of the first missionary activities of the disciples, we should, in this first part of Acts as well as in the second, receive some rough idea of the course and duration of events. But that is not at all the case. While in the second part we always hear something of the chronology of Paul's mission, in the first part we hear so little concerning the duration of the events described that we cannot tell whether months or years (two, three, or five years) intervened between the death of Christ and the conversion of Paul. The text of Acts gives us no indication. Whatever sequence is to be seen in the events has not been derived from any source, but was evidently arrived at by Luke himself; when we consider how little information was passed on to him, the achievement appears by no means small.

Let us take one example: to the story of the martyrdom of Stephen, which Luke adopted and elaborated, he added two sentences. These sentences tell how the young man Saul (Paul's Jewish name) was present at the stoning of Stephen and approved of his death. And between the stories of the missionary activities of Philip and those of Peter the author places one more conversion, the story of the conversion of this same Saul at Damascus. By what is promised to Saul, or Paul, in this story the reader, who has known Paul since the death of Stephen, is prepared for this man's becoming, as we read, "a chosen instrument of mine to carry my name before the Gentiles and kings and the sons of Israel" (9:15). Thus the second part of the book, which deals with Paul's journeys, is anchored in the stories of the first part.

Another means of establishing continuity is offered by the so-called narrative-summaries that are to be found throughout the first part of Acts.[4] In order to understand them, we must appreciate that Luke, in writing a history of the early community, had no material of a truly "historical" kind. There were those stories of a popular type, which have already been mentioned— stories such as one could only expect to find among "uneducated and ordinary men" (4:13). But they were about individual cases; most of them showed how God helps individual Christians, protects them in danger, affords results to their preaching and miraculous power to their words. This material did not constitute history. It did not touch such subjects as the growth of the community, its inner development, its discords, and the full extent of community life. This deficiency is supplied by the narrative-summaries; these are little cross-sections of a general nature that, for the very reason that they are of this type, must have originated with Luke. Popular tradition dealt only with what was individual. What is general, or typical, is described in this way only by one who is looking at the situation as a whole, by a writer who sees history or pattern behind the events.

In connection with this, we must constantly bear in mind the principle with which the new type of research into early Christian tradition, so-called form criticism (*Formgeschichte*), begins. The principle is that, since the early Christian tradition is neither learned nor literary, we have to imagine as its origin not a biography of Jesus or a chronicle of the community, but small units, the individual saying, or the story that is complete in itself. Anyone combining such elements into a whole, as Luke did, was forming a mosaic, and had to fill in any gaps that were left between the stones of the mosaic. In Acts, the narrative-summaries serve that purpose. Before Luke records the martyrdom of Stephen we read: "And the word of God increased; and the number of the disciples multiplied greatly in Jerusalem, and a great many of the priests became obedient to the faith" (6:7). Or, after the conversion of Paul: "So the church throughout all Judea and Galilee and Samaria had peace and was built up; and walking in the fear of the Lord and in the comfort of the Holy Spirit it was multiplied" (9:31). In this way individual stories found in tradition were elaborated to become descriptions of situations.

This distinction between individual elements of tradition and the narrative-summaries is important in our attempt to solve what is a controversial historical problem, the question of early Christian communism. We read in Acts 2:44-45: "All who believed were together and had all things in common; and they sold their possessions and goods and distributed them to all, as any had need." Similarly we are told in Acts 4:34-35: "There was not a needy person among them, for as many as were possessors of lands or houses sold them, and brought the proceeds of what was sold and laid it at the apostles' feet; and distribution was made to each as any had need."

This sounds like organized communism, which requires that every property-owner shall give up his possessions; but both passages are in a narrative-summary, and the function of the narrative-summaries is, as we have seen, to make general statements. In the story relating to this subject, however, we are told that Ananias kept back part of the proceeds and that he was reproached on the grounds that he should have brought all the money or none at all, since the surrender of goods was voluntary. And when, a little earlier in the text, Barnabas is praised for putting the proceeds of the sale of this field at the apostles' disposal, we can see that he did so of his own free will and not in accordance with some rule which was binding for all.

In the early community, there was thus, evidently, free and voluntary "communism out of love" (to quote Ernst Troeltsch). But Luke used the individual instances he knew of in order to compose a picture of an ideal, an ideal such as constantly appears in Greek literature since Plato. Hans von Schubert has sketched the history of this ideal in his studies on the communism of the Anabaptists. In assessing the circumstances of early Christianity, we must keep to the principle that individual elements of tradition, such as the story of Ananias and the note about Barnabas, are older tradition and therefore more reliable than what the author added, namely the narrative-summary. We come to realize something which is almost a paradox, and which is repeatedly confirmed in Acts, that just where Luke wants to work as an historian and just where we admire what he has achieved on completely new ground, he very often begins to diverge from the old tradition. When contradictions arise, he must therefore—if judged by the standards of historical criticism—be considered a reporter of only secondary rank. Even in this capacity, he has much to say to us as a well-informed critic. But it is not so much his knowledge that deserves our admiration as his ability, we might say, to trace on a vacant space a clear and typical image of the earliest communities or of Paul's mission, and the way in which he supplies connecting links and introduces connecting passages—in short, how he turns stories into a history.

History and Meaning

In addition to producing a consecutive narrative, an author must also endeavor to interpret events if he is to be an historian. He must work out the meaning of what has taken place. And this Luke has done.

One example may make this clear. As Paul starts out for the second time from Antioch in Syria upon a missionary journey, he first visits the towns in the south of Asia Minor that had already been evangelized. Then we are told that he has been prevented by the Holy Spirit from going to the west coast of Asia Minor (that is, along the great road through the valley of the Lyke into the Greek towns of Ephesus, Smyrna, and Pergamum in Asia Minor). He goes therefore with his companions through Phrygia and the province of Galatia and wishes to reach the north coast of Asia Minor, Bithynia. Again we read: "the Spirit of Jesus did not allow them" (16:7). Thus the only way remaining open to them was to go in a northwesterly direction through Mysia to Troas. And here follows a third divine intervention: in a vision in the night, Paul sees a man from Macedonia, who says: "Come over to Macedonia and help us" (16:9).

This is a strange way to write history. We are not told how the interventions by the Spirit were manifested, or whether Paul evangelized in Galatia on the way. We read no names of stations or of persons. The type of information that, in other parts of the book, Luke has taken from the itinerary is missing here. Was it the source that failed? Did Luke have no records at all for this part of the journey?

It is very improbable that the author's silence is due to a failure of the source, for Luke is not really silent at all. He still reports on the strange coming and going of the missionaries in the provinces of Asia Minor. If he knew the names of the provinces, he must have known the names of the places as well. In describing the zigzag course of the missionaries, his object is not to narrate the changing fortunes of the mission to the towns of Asia Minor. In this section (16:6-10), the sole aim of his narrative is to show how three times divine intervention caused the mission to make a wide detour through Macedonia and Greece. It does not matter, regarding these instructions, whether it was a case of visions, persecutions, floods, damage to roads, or other hindrances to travel; the important thing is simply that divine power guides the steps of the apostle. If we recognize this as the meaning which Luke sees in the events and wishes to express here, we shall be left in no doubt that he intentionally omitted in this passage the names and notes contained in the itinerary of stations.

He attaches great importance to the fact that Paul reaches Greece, for it is the winning of Greece rather than the missionary journey into Asia Minor that is the beginning of the mission to the world. To him, the most important station is Athens. And the picture of Paul speaking to Greek philosophers on the Areopagus is one on which he lingers with special devotion. He is deeply conscious of the significance of the occasion when the man who, to the Greeks, was simply an uneducated Oriental proclaims to Epicureans and Stoics the Lord Jesus Christ and the impending judgment of the world. The occasion marks the first momentous encounter of Christian belief with classical culture.

But there are also one or two critical observations to be made with regard to this magnificent composition. In the first place, the sermon in Athens has only symbolic significance. According to the accounts given by Luke (7:34, evidently from the itinerary), this sermon had little success; it probably did not result even in the founding of a community. Corinth was, to a far greater extent, the real center of Paul's mission in Greece. Secondly, the speech itself, the famous Areopagus speech, does not conform at all to the theology of Paul.[5] In connection with the altar to the unknown god, it attributes to the Gentiles a far greater knowledge of God than Paul allowed to himself. It speaks also of God's relationship with humanity in its natural state (in connection with a quotation from Aratus) far more positively than Paul, who held a very realistic view of human nature, would ever have spoken. Quite obviously, Luke composed this Areopagus speech himself, a conclusion which will not be surprising to anyone who is familiar with the custom of Greek historians of illuminating events by means of speeches.[6] But Luke also wrote the major part of the introductory scene. At least, the expressive calls from the circle of hearers, "What would this babbler say?" and "He seems to be a preacher of foreign divinities" (17:18), cannot have been taken from an itinerary. Similarly, the cultural-historical observation about the Athenians, that they are continually looking for something new, is attributable to the author, who here, in Eduard Norden's opinion, has composed the most Attic passage of the New Testament. Once more we experience that paradox which is found in the work of Luke as historian: that although criticism may lead us to question the reliability of the speech, it confirms how surely Luke has portrayed the meaningfulness of the occasion in this very speech.

Another example illustrating the author's literary method of working out the significance, for the life of the community, of an individual incident is the case of the centurion Cornelius in Caesarea. His conversion by the apostle Peter and the confirmation of it by a manifestation of the Holy Spirit was already familiar to Luke from the tradition of the community. In reproducing it he elaborated the story in the most striking manner, at the beginning adding a vision seen by Peter, in the middle inserting a speech made by the apostle, and at the end adding the story of how Peter gave account of himself to the authorities in Jerusalem. And even this is not enough, for when the apostles meet later in Jerusalem for that discussion, to which the name "Apostolic Council" has been given, both the speakers, Peter and James alike, do not speak on the real subject under discussion—keeping to Jewish circumcision—but refer to the conversion of Cornelius and God's willingness to accept the Gentiles, as it was manifested in this conversion.

Why does Luke attribute so much significance to this story? In tradition, and indeed in fact also, it was simply the story of the conversion of a so-called "God-fearing Gentile," the conversion of an uninitiated visitor to the synagogue, who was thus, in any case, not far from the religion of the Bible. There are much more striking conversions in the history of Christianity, but what makes this conversion of Cornelius so important in the eyes of the author of Acts is the fact of its being the means by which Peter, the first of the apostles, is reconciled to the evangelizing of the Gentiles. The fact that, in the Apostolic Council, Peter also becomes an advocate of the policy of carrying the gospel to the Gentiles is of very great importance for the structure of the whole book. We are not to be allowed to think, as we might if the events were given only a superficial treatment, that it was Paul who had the idea of evangelizing the Gentiles. Peter arrived at the same conviction quite independently; Luke wants to show this in the story of Cornelius. In fact, it was not humans at all who conceived the idea of evangelizing the nations of the world; the reader sees in Paul's strange zigzag course that it is God himself, or, as Luke says, the Spirit, who sends the missionaries to Macedonia and Greece.

Here again, modern historical criticisms cannot concede this equivalence of Peter and Paul. We must note what Paul himself wrote in his Epistle to the Galatians about Peter's timid reserve when confronted with fellow-Christians from the Gentile world; or about the allocation to the apostles of various areas, in which a mission to the Jews only is assigned to Peter, but to Paul a mission to the Gentiles. This all suggests a considerable disparity between the apostles. But Luke wants to show that the course of the Christian mission was not, in the last resort, determined by any one apostle, such as Paul, or by humans at all, but by a supra-human power. He can do this the more easily by following the practice of historians of antiquity, who did not aim at all at portraying the personal characteristics and special activities of their heroes, but who were more commonly concerned with what was *typical* and *general* and *ideal.* Thus in both the apostles, Paul and Peter, we are intended to recognize the type of the Christian missionary.

Since the so-called Tübingen School of Ferdinand Christian Baur, which was also represented with distinction in my professorial chair by Carl Holsten (1876-97), we have been accustomed to see in these resemblances in the depicting of Peter and Paul in Acts attempts to smooth out the differences between rival parties: for example, each of the two apostles is exalted by means of his awakening someone from the dead, by his overcoming a false prophet, and by his being released from prison in a miraculous manner. Actually, however, we can see from an analysis of these "pairs" of stories that each has a completely different point. In the story about Peter's imprisonment, the miracle of his release is the main point; in the corresponding story about Paul, the point is the winning over of the prison guard. The false prophets, Simon Magus and Elymas, possess no points of contact at all. Similarity between Peter and Paul appears just as clearly when Paul makes a speech in a synagogue in Asia Minor which is identical in construction with the speeches of Peter in the first part of Acts. Here there can be no question of attempting to standardize the characters involved, for in that case, Paul would have to make several such speeches in order to be the equivalent of Peter. The author's sole concern is to introduce a typical sermon, to show how the gospel was preached in the Christian community or how, in his opinion, it ought to be preached.

LUKE'S INTENTION

In this way we can clearly see a concern of this author that extends beyond that of the literary historian. We have already observed that the technique of this historian enables him to dispense with the details of the sequence of events; that he leaves out some stations in order that it may the more clearly be seen that God is the real controller of the missionary journey; that he adds the narrative summaries in order to describe the development of the community, or rather, of an ideal community; and that he exalts the conversion of Cornelius to such significance that he can use it to prove the divine, rather than human, origin of the mission to the Gentiles. Now we can understand why the speeches of Peter in chaps. 2, 3, and 10 sound so similar to that of Paul in chap. 13. These, like most of the speeches in Acts, drawn up by the author either on the basis of accounts he possessed or independently without such accounts, are intended not for the audience who actually heard them but for the readers. The readers are to hear what is preached, and what is believed, and it is therefore not surprising that Luke obviously uses ancient Christological formulas such as "servant of God" and, to a certain extent, a classical Christology. The whole work aims not so much at letting the readers know what really happened as at helping them to understand what all this means, this invasion of the world of Hellenistic culture by the Christian Church, but particularly they are to recognize and cherish the gospel itself and the success it achieves among mankind. We can see that this point of view has also played a part in the selecting and stylizing of individual stories. Gentiles in Lystra regard the apostles as gods; the apostles reject this and thereby endanger their lives. When the doors of the prison in Philippi open as the result of an earthquake, the Gentile guard thinks the prisoners have escaped and is confounded when he finds that the apostles have remained in prison praising God.

While every reader here feels that the specific powers of the Christian faith are stirringly expressed in these stories, this particular type of portrayal seems to be entirely absent from the final chapters of Acts (22–28). Here quite a number of hearings and defenses of the apostle are reported, and finally the adventures of his voyage to Rome. But Luke is evidently not concerned with introducing the reader to the legal situation and the trial of Paul. Indeed, he has not portrayed the full course of these proceedings and, in particular, has not reported the outcome. What he is concerned with is to express, clearly and repeatedly, the themes of Christian preaching. The mission to the Gentiles is a divine, rather than human, activity; and it is in the Christian message that Jewish hopes find fulfillment. This is shown in these speeches and trials particularly by the belief in the resurrection. These are ideas that enjoyed a special hearing in Luke's day, in the decades when the Church was visibly detaching herself from Judaism. In these chapters, then, Luke wishes to present first of all not what has taken place but what is taking place.

From the same point of view, we must now look at a section of Acts that, at first sight, appears to be completely secular and purely literary: the great description of the voyage to Rome in chap. 27. This portrays Paul, in an almost romantic manner, as the companion who utters timely warnings, as a valiant comforter and a discerning helper; but the essential part of this account is that which affords a detailed description of the voyage and the shipwreck. In this section the notes on Paul are added with some awkwardness and difficulty. The nautical correctness of this part shows clearly that Luke (never more a literary man than he is here) did not work without models. But why the nautical details which so little concern the apostle? Why the vast scale of the narrative of the voyage which all these details produce? Luke did not embellish this chapter so richly in order to attain literary distinction. We are reminded of another passage in his work that had an obviously literary quality—his characterization of the Athenians prior to the Areopagus speech; this served to emphasize a symbolically important scene, the encounter of the gospel with the Greek spirit. As he now undertakes this journey, Paul, the real apostle to the nations, is on his way to the metropolis of the Empire. But Luke cannot allow him now, as he did in the scene on the Areopagus, to enter the forum as a speaker, for Paul is making the journey as a prisoner; he does, however, emphasize the significance of the story of the voyage by adding nautical details and so giving prominence to the story as such. Thus he shows at the end of his book that the promise by Jesus in the first chapter has been fulfilled: "You shall be my witnesses in Jerusalem and in the whole of Judaea and Samaria, to the ends of the earth." So we see Luke once more as an historian who expounds the meaning of an event by striking description; we see him also in his capacity as *herald* and *evangelist,* a role which he fulfills completely in his first book and wishes ultimately to fulfill also in Acts; in his capacity as an historian he finds abundant opportunities of doing so.

Who then was this author? It is well known in the tradition of the Church that the author of the Gospel and of Acts was called Luke and was identical with that "beloved" physician who is mentioned several times in Paul's epistles; ever since the addition of the ancient prologues to the Gospels in the second century there has been available also the information that he came originally from Antioch in Syria. But this tradition of the Church concerning the Gospels probably first arose at a time when the larger communities were beginning to possess several gospel-books side by side. Originally each community possessed only one, and that was the "Gospel of Jesus Christ"—and no author's name was mentioned in connection with it. Then, when the different gospel-books had to be named in order to distinguish them from one another, it may be that authors' names were derived from the places from which, according to the tradition of the Church, the books concerned had originally come, without any critical investigation being made as to whether the man who was known and named as the author had really written the book. Thus there is some justification, based on critical research, for doubts about the authorship of Matthew and Mark.

If, in contrast to many, I devote no space to such doubts in Luke's case, I feel justified in so doing, since I have taken into account the quite different literary circumstances out of which both these books, the Gospel and the Acts, came into existence. Both are dedicated to Theophilus, and indeed in a quite usual way; in the Gospel especially, we might even call it a secular style of dedication. We can conclude with complete certainty, therefore, that both these writings were intended, not only for the Christian communities, but also for the book market. The fact and nature of the dedications meant scarcely anything to the Christian communities of about 90 C.E. They were intended for people who knew and respected literary customs. Had the author written the dedications for Christians, he would have said something about the importance for salvation of the "things which have happened amongst us" (Luke 1:1) or of "what Jesus has done and taught us from the beginning." As this is not the case, the books evidently also had other readers. Perhaps the Theophilus who is addressed was himself one of them and, as addressee of the dedication, had to attend to the distribution of the two writings. They probably also had parallel titles (perhaps "Acts of Jesus" and "Acts of the Apostles"), for the designation "gospel" meant nothing on the book market. It goes almost without saying that the author's name was included. It would have been strange indeed if the person to whom the book was dedicated had been named, but not the dedicator. The title would then perhaps have been "Luke the Antiochan's Acts of the Apostles." As the Church now began to describe its writings by the name of their authors, there was no need to search for long in the case of the books concerned here, for the name had already been given to the other "edition." This was the name of Luke, the Antiochan doctor who had sometimes accompanied the apostle Paul.

Now it is quite in accordance with this that, in the accounts in Acts of the short journey from Troas to Philippi and, years later, again from Philippi to Jerusalem, the third person plural, the "they" of the narrative, becomes a "we." The narrator indicates in this way that he himself took part. The old view was that a special source becomes evident in these passages, the so-called "we-account," the work of an eyewitness. This view is discredited by the very fact that even the story of the voyage in chap. 27, that is to say, that passage which, more than any other, is "literature" rather than mere recording, is written from beginning to end in the "we-style." Besides, we can see quite clearly from the accounts about Paul's missionary journeys that the "they-passages" and the "we-passages" are very similar in vocabulary and style, so similar in fact that we have no justification for attributing them to different authors. We may rather suppose, as is most probably the case with the sea-voyage, that, from the first, the author introduced his "we" into an account that he had, in order to indicate when he was present. The "we" would then be, not as was once thought, an original element, but an addition. The resulting inconsistency in the account, sometimes "they," sometimes "we," appears also in other ancient narratives.

This whole view is completely opposed to the one that was known to the generation of our teachers (with the exception of Harnack) as the "critical" view. They did not tire of telling us that the Acts of the Apostles could not have been written by Luke, Paul's companion, because it contained more errors than could have been made by one who was so close to Paul. This theory somewhat exaggerates both the proximity to Paul and the number of errors. But especially, however, the ancient historian does not wish to present life with photographic accuracy, but rather to portray and illuminate what is typical, and this practice of aiming at what is typical and important allows the author of Acts partly to omit, change, or generalize what really occurred. So it is that, where he sometimes appears to us today to be idealizing, and describing what was typical, he was really trying to discharge his obligation as an historian. Thus, through the literary methods of the historian, he was able to discharge his other obligations of being a preacher of faith in Christ.

3

The Book of Acts
as an Historical Source

T he oldest Christian writing that aspires to give an historical presentation
is the Acts of the Apostles. The Gospels repeat a succession of traditions
concerning historical events; but it was the Acts of the Apostles that first tried
to form from traditional material the continuous account of an actual period
in history. Many details, however, especially the speeches, will make it clear to
the reader that this is not the ultimate object of the book, which aims to
preach and to show what the Christian belief is and what effects it has. This
dual aspect of the book has, from the beginning, ever since there has been any
critical knowledge of the Bible, compelled those who investigate the book of
Acts to ask what value it has as an historical source. In doing so, scholars have
often reached an impasse because they have considered the question subjectively; they have referred, for instance, to the improbability of certain scenes,
as, for example, to the fact that both Stephen and Paul make long speeches
before raging crowds, or that Paul assumes toward the Jewish Christians in
Jerusalem a yielding attitude which we cannot possibly believe he would have
adopted.[1] In doing this, however, each critic really forms his own personal
conception of the times and the characters in order to measure events, which
is a dangerous procedure. The form-critical method uses the form and style of
the tradition in order to draw conclusions about it as to its origin and the conditions out of which it arose,[2] and in this way seeks observations which are
universally valid in order to establish less subjective criteria of the tradition's
historicity, criteria which can be verified at any time.

Before each particular analysis we must acquire a certain amount of general information about the author's method. Nothing in this book indicates
that the author had already had models for the preparation of his version. In
his Gospel he speaks of "many" who had undertaken the same thing (Luke
1:1), but he does not similarly mention any in Acts. A consideration of the contemporary circumstances makes it seem likely that he was a pioneer in this

work. To collect the traditions of the words and deeds of Jesus in one volume was a task that would have seemed obvious to the early Christian community. But to write down the history of the earliest community, to give an account of its difficulties and conflicts, to describe its spread to Rome, to tell how the way was prepared for the reception of Gentiles and of the obdurate refusal on the part of the Jews—all this could not possibly have seemed an obviously necessary undertaking to those Christians who were waiting for the end of the world and who had neither inclination nor ability for literary work. Whoever fulfilled this task must have been capable of combining current stories about the apostles with accounts he himself had discovered and of transforming this diverse material into a unified whole possessing dignity and inspiration.

Thus the writer's literary ability has a far greater part in the Acts of the Apostles than it had in his Gospel. This fact throws further light on the book. This book was not written only for the Christian communities, which consisted primarily of the poor and uneducated, but also for cultured readers, whether *Gentile* or Christian. Only they were able to appreciate the full scope of his work. The fact that the book was destined for a "higher" circle of readers comes out in a number of details. The stylized description of Athens, with its carefully weighed words, which introduces Paul's Areopagus speech; the speech and trial scenes interwoven with uniform, apologetic ideas (Acts 22–26); or the placing of the Pentecost story, by means of the "catalogue of peoples," in its setting of world evangelism—who but the cultured reader could understand the full significance of all this? Finally, the dedication to Theophilus (Acts 1:1-2), stylized from the literary point of view, was relatively unimportant for the Christian community—the Gospels of Mark and Matthew have no such introduction—and was obviously meant for those who would in any case have been accustomed to reading books with such dedications. If we keep in mind this difference between the Gospels of Mark and Matthew on the one hand and the two writings of Luke—his Gospel and Acts—on the other, it is extremely probable that these two writings were provided with an author's name from the beginning. Two books cannot very well both have been dedicated to Theophilus while the author himself remained unknown. On the book market—which, unlike other early Christian writings, these obviously reached—they were probably known as "Luke's Acts of Jesus" and "Luke's Acts of the Apostles." So we must assume that Luke, who, according to Col 4:14 and Phlmn 24 (see also 2 Tim 4:11), accompanied Paul for a time, was really the author of the Acts of the Apostles.

This does not go as far toward settling the question of historicity as people today are accustomed to assume. The writer of ancient times may present an account even of events which he has experienced in a different way from his actual experience of them, if by so doing he can make it clear how the event happened and what it means.

We must first consider what material the author used. In the case of Acts, some critics think an important consideration is the fact that Paul's journeys are narrated at times in the "we-style."[3] In a writer who assimilated his material so well, it is not very probable that a source (identified word by word, as in the Old Testament), should be discernible within the text; moreover, the "we-passages" resemble the "they-passages" both in vocabulary[4] and in style. It must certainly be assumed that Luke had available as a source for Paul's journeys an itinerary of the stations on the journey, for he mentioned even unimportant stations. It appears that this itinerary also contained comments upon the apostles' reception, their hosts, their activities and the results; these comments cannot always, however, be distinguished from Luke's original work. Within the framework of Acts 13; 14; and 15:36—21:18 we have before us a source of the first order, whether the story is told in the first or third person. The frequently used "we"—which, under the influence of modern historical ideas, used to be taken at one time as the earliest element of the whole account of the journey—was, perhaps, only introduced by Luke into his version in order to make it clear that he himself took part in Paul's journeys.

How did Luke use this itinerary? First, he filled it out with stories, stories of very varied styles and, as we must conclude, of varying value historically. The fact that they are additions by the author is proved with considerable certainty from time to time by the way in which they are introduced.[5] Of course, we cannot believe that every detail of popular tradition of this kind is authentic, but neither should we discredit it as a matter of course. Secondly, Luke added speeches—and here we touch a great theme that can only be dealt with in the context of ancient historical writings.[6] Let it suffice to say here that both criticism of content and comparison with speeches of ancient historians show that these lay no claim to historicity. This does not exclude the possibility that they contain, in elaborated form, the original intention of the speaker. This assessment will include the speeches Paul makes in his defense in Acts 22–26, which together give a very effective apology of the new religion, only—as the Pauline epistles show—not in the manner in which the real Paul would have made it. Peter's speeches in the first part come under the same critical judgment; they consist of variations on a kind of original community-theology. The fact that Acts 13 ascribes a similar sermon to Paul shows that in these speeches Luke did not aim at being true to the speaker's personal characteristics. Finally, Luke provided the itinerary with short accounts that we owe to his own search for information, sometimes, however, to his own reflections. In this case, what we have is not old traditions, but the communications of a well-informed man upon what he was able to ascertain.

Such collected accounts cannot, however, make up for the lack of good tradition. This can be seen in the first part of Acts (chaps. 1–12), which is not based on anything we might call a source; there is no thread, such as the itinerary provides for chaps. 13–21. At least there is no philological criterion that would permit us to establish a unified source in this part of the book. So we are left with traditional, separate stories of very unequal value, reproducing certain events with the community at Jerusalem and with Peter's preaching activities. They are mainly in the style of legend, that is, the emphasis lies on the miraculous element and on the pious character of the people involved in the stories. By inserting speeches, and by composing connecting-links both as introductions and conclusions, Luke has extended two of these stories to great compositions. The story of Pentecost (2:1-41), which is really the account of the first ecstatic "speaking in tongues" in the community, becomes, by means of the enumeration of the countries from which the hearers come, a prototype of the mission to the world. The way has been prepared by a prophecy of the Risen One. The story ends with a rudimentary description of the life of the community. The conversion of Cornelius (10:1-48) is, for the author, the fundamental case of a Gentile conversion that is validated by a vision from God and therefore, later, in 15:7, regarded as a test case. The martyrdom of Stephen (6:8—8:2) has been extended by a long speech—an example of the eloquence of the first martyr. The connecting-link with what went before is furnished by the conflict in the community; the link with what follows is found in the description of the persecution the gospel brings to the community. Moreover, there is an opportunity here to introduce Paul, the story of whose conversion is presently to be told. With great artistry Luke has composed a wealth of connecting-links, and so out of a small fragment of community tradition—the first martyrdom—has brought a real story into being.

Admittedly he cannot make good the absence of a "thread" in this part. As a result, the chronology of this period is lacking. And the interval between the crucifixion of Christ and the conversion of Paul cannot be determined even approximately from the Acts of the Apostles. Nor can Luke give a continuous account of the development of the community based upon an older source. Instead of this, he has joined together individual stories and accounts which have been handed down, such as the story of the conflict or of the first conversions of the Gentiles in Antioch, and, by means of his interpolations, he reminds us that everything he reports stands within the general stream of development. At the same time, important factors in this development may escape him. Thus, for example, he has not described how the "elders" and James, the brother of Jesus, came to hold positions of authority in Jerusalem. It is also possible that he has inserted correct accounts in the wrong places; that might well apply to the collection journey (11:30) and the so-called

"Apostolic Decree" (15:23-29)—neither of which, according to the evidence supplied by the Epistle to the Galatians, belongs in the place given to it by Luke.

While we have dealt to some extent with the author's possibilities and methods as far as Acts 26, we shall have to be very cautious in our assessment of the account of the sea-voyage to Rome at the end of the book. Using the "we-style," the author describes the voyage and the shipwreck with an abundance of nautical details, and, for this reason, the older school of criticism, which thinks only of the event and not of the account, has ascribed particular authenticity to this description.[7] But Paul is mentioned only in brief episodes, and these seem to have been added later to the account of the voyage.[8] Literary criticism will certainly lead us to suppose that the nautical description is taken from the numerous accounts of sea-voyages in literature and not from experience.[9]

Once more we see here the difference between the old and the new methods of criticism. The important point in the source criticism of Acts is that we do not at first approach the text with criticism of the subject matter and with questions as to whether an event was possible or impossible; we ask first of all what the author intends and what means are available. In Acts, as in the Gospel, Luke wishes to be an evangelist; he wishes to portray God's leadership of the Christian community within the framework of its history. He certainly had only Paul's itinerary at his disposal as a unified, written source; for the rest, he had to use current stories and accounts that he had discovered. His own special contribution lay in arranging them, linking them together and illuminating them, particularly by means of speeches; it also includes the theological point of the book, which is the acknowledgment that the way the gospel progressed was the way God desired. But the historical reliability of Acts must be measured in each individual case, according to the material that Luke worked on. We are perhaps better able to recognize and assess this material by means of the more recent method of literary criticism than we are by the old method, which was concerned only with the story and not with how it was told.[10]

4

Style Criticism of the Book of Acts

LITERARY GENRE

When examining literature such as Jewish and early Christian literatures, one must first raise the question of the literary genres. Hermann Gunkel has constantly impressed this principle upon us. In examining forms in the Old Testament, we learned to proceed from the collections and larger complexes of narrative to the small units: the song, the single story. In the same way, corresponding works on the Gospel literature have also endeavored, from the viewpoint of the form-critical (*Formgeschichte*) theory, to establish small units as the elements of the tradition.[1] This examination is still in its early stages, but even now one may express the hope that this method of analyzing style according to forms will achieve what analytical source criticism could not, profitable and indispensable as it is in making intelligible the evolution of the pre-literary tradition. Obviously we should apply the same method to the book of Acts in the New Testament, and begin by considering, according to this principle, what can be discovered about the tradition underlying the book by an analysis of its style. The particular difficulty of the examination lies in the nature of the book of Acts, the literary form of which is not immediately clear.

When considering a book that undertakes to present pragmatically—and evidently according to a plan—a portion of contemporary history, and that begins with a "literary" prologue and puts speeches into the mouths of its heroes, one might certainly feel inclined to place it, as far as form is concerned, beside the work of contemporary historians. But this placing would not be entirely appropriate, since the book is not really uniform in style. The writer, whom I call Luke (without prejudice to the question of authorship), indeed takes pains to elevate his subject to the plane of world history; but the words "this was not done in a corner" (Acts 26:26) are really more significant for him than for the things of which he tells. For, despite their future immensely important effect and despite the universal importance that Luke ascribes to them, they are, nevertheless, minor events that take place among unimportant people and are, at first, relatively unnoticed. In many parts of the book the style of the narrative accords with this fact; consider the raising of Tabitha (Acts 9) or Peter's release from prison (Acts 12).

On the other hand, the literary genre of the book is unique in the New Testament. This opinion is valid even though the text forms the continuation of Luke's Gospel. We must not over-emphasize the importance of this homogeneity with the Gospel, which was so strongly stressed by Eduard Meyer.[2] Certainly the language and choice of material of the one book can be well-illustrated by examples out of the other. Moreover the remarkable *destiny* of the book of Acts in the history of the canon—that is, its apparently unforeseen but unquestioned acceptability in the circle of New Testament writings—is explained not only by its suitability for use in the struggle against heresy but more particularly by its connection with Luke's Gospel. For, although the book of Acts was separated by the formation of the canon of the four Gospels from its kindred work, nevertheless it was by this work that it was drawn over the threshold of the canon. As far as genre goes, however, both these works by the same author do not belong to the same category.

First, in Acts, Luke has employed a much higher standard of writing than in the Gospel. There it was a case of framing and piecing together fragments of tradition. There the writer could, and wished to, restrict himself to minor interpolations, chiefly of an editorial nature. If, however, we read in Acts the scenes of the Apostolic Council or of the trial (Acts 24–26), we become easily convinced that here Luke has not only fitted together, joined, and framed fragments of tradition, as in a mosaic, but that in Acts there is a greater depth of original composition. It is worth establishing what proportion of the whole work is taken up by these literary endeavors; until this is done, we must consider as hopeless every attempt to divide entirely into different sources the text of Acts as a whole, apart from editorial interpolations. In this way, the author's own work is not accorded its proper place.[3] The safest way is to regard the speeches in Acts as Luke's work: since, for reasons concerning the history of tradition, they can hardly have been handed down and, considered from the literary angle, they have their parallels in the historians and, as regards content, they often enough express a later standpoint (15:10-11, 19-20; 20:25, 29-30). Certainly I have no doubt that older formulae of a kerygmatic or liturgical nature are occasionally used.[4] The actual conception, however, is the work of the author. Even where it was thought necessary to decide upon different sources because of supposed contradictions between one speech and another, as in the portrayal of Paul's conversion in Acts 22 and 26, this is simply a case of literary variation, the intention of which becomes clear from the actual situation. The speeches, then, give us an idea of how Luke wrote when he was not bound to any source.

The fact that the author employed a different technique in the writing of the Acts of the Apostles from that which he had used earlier in the writing of the Gospel proceeds from the nature of the task which he had here set himself. In writing the Gospel he had predecessors, whose work he used and whose technique of piecing together the tradition provided a model also for his more reflective and pragmatic style; indeed, one of them, Mark, had even, to a fair extent, authoritatively determined the sequence of the Lukan narrative. Of predecessors of the Acts of the Apostles we know nothing. Moreover its special plan is not evident in itself, and its main theme—somewhat in the sense of 1:8—one could imagine treated quite differently.

From all this we may conclude that Luke was the first to set himself the task of describing the progress of the gospel from Jerusalem to Rome, and that we thus have before us in Acts a work of more individual stamp than the Gospel of Luke. In Acts we are not at all entitled to presuppose the same state of affairs that prompted the examination of the Gospels from the form-critical point of view—the fact that authors preserve the forms created by tradition. For we have yet to consider whether the author of Acts had any such tradition at his disposal. So we cannot, in the first place, consider this work from the perspective of form criticism, but only from that of its style.

I tried to show in *From Tradition to Gospel* that practical interests were decisive in forming the oldest tradition about Jesus: namely, the sermon—the word taken in its broadest sense and applied to an activity which took place for purposes of propaganda as well as of edification—and the paranesis, or moral teaching, both for those under instruction and for mature Christians. In the antecedents of Acts such interests are not under consideration. Paranesis is not to be found at all in Acts, and purposes of evangelism or edification are directly fulfilled only in the speeches, that is, in paragraphs that, as a form, have no antecedents in the sense that we are considering.

The formation of a later, broader type of narrative in the gospel tradition—I call them *Novellen* or tales—I have traced back to the story-telling impulse in association with christological-cultic interests. This impulse sought to make known the details of the miraculous life of the Son of God and so to serve the Christian faith. Though it is certain that much in the anecdotes concerning the apostles has arisen from the impulse to tell stories, the cultic-christological interest is, for the most part, absent. As a rule, a pious interest in the lives of holy men predominates. From the "gospel" point of view, these men are certainly subsidiary figures, but in the stories they take a prominent place. Here we enter the world of legends.[5] It is only a question of where the old tradition of legend has been preserved in its original form and how much of his own the author has contributed.

Tradition and Composition

It will now be clear that Luke could not proceed by the same method in working on the Acts of the Apostles as he had in writing the Gospel. The material was of a much more complicated kind; it was more comprehensive, less homogeneous, less clearly defined, more difficult to arrange. The writer could therefore employ no uniform principle of arrangement.

It is in the central portion of Acts, Paul's journeys, that we see most clearly how Luke has arranged the different pieces of tradition and combined them with his own compositions. The examination of this section (13:1-14, 28; 15:35—21:16) has for a long time been determined by the attempt to exclude the so-called "we-source."[6] Taken as a whole, these attempts seem to me to make it quite clear that the appearance of the word "we" is not in itself sufficient to determine a source or tradition, for it is just as possible that the significance attached to the word "we" has been increased as that is has been diminished.[7] And both the linguistic[8] and the literary[9] styles of the "we-passages" are not essentially different from other passages that deal with similar events. Everywhere it seems that an itinerary of stations where Paul stopped underlies the account of the journeys, an itinerary which we may suppose to have been provided with notes of his journeys, of the founding of communities, and of the results of evangelization. Where this itinerary seems to fail (i.e., in 16:6-8; 18:22-23; 20:1-3), either notes on the stations were not available—thus, perhaps, the journey through Greece has not been recorded at all—or, for reasons of composition, Luke has abbreviated. I consider the latter possibility as particularly likely for 16:6-8 because here the author is concerned with presenting the Spirit's influence when all human factors are eliminated.[10] Such an itinerary seems to have formed the framework for the central part of Acts.[11] That appears from the uniformity with which the stations are introduced and explained by short notes.

Had the writer worked without such a source and used only local traditions of the communities, he would probably have considered certain stations more fully, but excluded others. And if he had been anxious to invent something for the edification or entertainment of his readers, we should certainly not read in his book the reports from Derbe (14:21), Thessalonica (17:1-9), and Beroea (17:10-15), which serve neither to edify nor to entertain. A series of notes had been supplied to him for this central part of his work. He now made his own additions to this itinerary, as well as inserting other traditions. Among the former we may especially include the speeches, but also many editorial observations, such as 14:22-23; 19:20, and other elements which we cannot eliminate with certainty, since it is impossible to determine the exact scope of the itinerary. To the passages from another tradition belong the few stories which are complete in themselves and which, therefore, would have been handed down individually. We must bear in mind that the writer had to work things out. He had to weave together elements from different origins. Nevertheless it can occasionally be seen in the stories, as well as in the speeches composed by the author, that, because these additions were made, the original basis (i.e., the itinerary) was abandoned. The Lystra-story is told in 14:8-18 although, according to the itinerary, the missionaries' stay in Lystra (and also in Derbe, the next station) had been reported earlier (14:6-7). Thus at the end of the Lystra-episode (14:20) Paul and Barnabas must once more head for Derbe. A similar doublet can be seen at the end of the speech in Antioch,[12] and the context of the Areopagus speech also suggests that through the introduction of the speech the proper sequence has been interrupted.[13] Throughout, the itinerary functions as the structure of the composition.[14]

In the latter part of the book there is little trace of a corresponding basis. These chapters are characterized by speeches and by scenes involving speeches: namely, the great speech to the crowd before the castle of Antonia (22:1-22); the conflict-scene in the Sanhedrin (22:30—23:11); the argument between Tertullus and Paul (24:1-21); and the speech before Agrippa (26:1-23), which is reported in great detail. All this suggests that, here, the writer has mastery over the tradition. This supposition is confirmed when we note that several of these speeches quite obviously exercise no influence upon the progress of the action but are solely of an epideictic character. The raging crowd is silent as soon as Paul wants to speak, but renews its shouting immediately when the writer's stage-managing can use it to emphasize the conclusion (21:40; 22:22). Before the procurator, Felix, Tertullus, and Paul strive apparently quite in vain to present their points of view (24:1-23). The scene concludes in the same way as the similar argument in Josephus between Antipater and Nicholas before the emperor (*War* 2.2.5-7 [§§26-38]; *Ant.* 17.9.5-7 [§§230-49])—the matter is adjourned. The speeches are thus really intended for the reader. We cannot know what accounts Luke had and applied in this part of his book, for, as they lie before us, the chapters in question are marked by his own literary treatment.

This judgment also applies to the account of the sea voyage (Acts 27–28). Although here again the first person plural is used, there is more literature than observation in the description of the shipwreck, with all its technical details. Norden has shown that these descriptions belong to literary convention.[15] We may thus assume here that, whether through Luke's being an eyewitness, or whether by means of someone else's tradition in his possession,[16] the recollection of Paul's stormy journey to Italy was elaborated by him according to literary models into the great composition that we now read. The analysis of individual paragraphs supports this theory: both the abundance of nautical material and the secular, dispassionate mood in the story of what took place among the "barbarians" on the island of Malta (28:1-10) betray a literary purpose, while the preceding episodes concerning Paul have the effect of being intrinsically improbable interruptions of the conventional description of a journey; and the Jewish scene which concludes the book represents more the fundamental anti-Jewish thesis of the book than inner probability and Paul's disposition toward his people.[17] Besides, the problematical conclusion of the whole book is best explained if the author did not possess a continuous account of Paul's fortunes as a prisoner which he could have employed as he had previously used the itinerary; that is to say, the conclusion is best explained if from 21:17 onwards he no longer had a guiding "thread."

It is not difficult to show that such a thread was not available in Acts 1–5 also. For there is no continuous narrative at all of the fortunes of the community at Jerusalem; on the contrary, narratives, speeches, and trial scenes succeed one another, and it is not clear, for example, whether or how the conflict in 5:17 is connected with that reported in Acts 3 and 4. For the present we shall not discuss whether it was tradition or composition that was responsible for producing the individual passages; at any rate, a continuous account, to link them together, was neither handed down to the writer nor formed by him. If we consider how little the thoughts of these earliest Christians were set upon preserving the course of history, we shall not be surprised at the lack of a tradition. But the author himself had too small a grasp of the course of this inner development, which was very difficult to perceive, to venture upon a free presentation of it.

His pragmatic endeavors are seen only in the various general summaries that, interposed between the various scenes and narratives, provide links and elaborations. In this way individual events reported in those stories are made to appear as particular instances in those parts of the text that give generalized descriptions of typical circumstances. The technique employed in such general summaries is familiar to us from Mark's Gospel. In 3:10-12, for instance, Jesus' deeds are described in a generalizing way in order to show that they were typical. In Acts this technique seems to have been applied more consciously in introducing the sections of narrative. The first collective account (Acts 1:13-14) goes very uneasily at first from narrative to generalized description, but by means of the list of apostles makes the best introduction to the story of the calling of Matthias which follows; in the same way in 2:43-47 the mention of the signs leads on to the miracle which follows; 4:32-35 (the sale of possessions) leads on to the story of Ananias; in the last general summary (5:12-16) the contradiction of the sentences (5:13, 14) is explained by the attempt to show a motive for the imprisonment which comes next.[18] This technique of giving a generalized description of the circumstances is seen also in the sentences 2:42; 4:4; 5:42. They are also pragmatic interpolations by the writer, who by this means indicates how the community developed. Tradition provided him with no connected description of the process, and in the nature of the case could not do so.

Finally in the course of this analytical survey let us look at that section of Acts which in content runs from 6:1—12:25, but which, according to its literary form, extends to the beginning of the itinerary and thus includes 13:1-3. The whole section is dominated by long, connected narratives that are characterized by the names Stephen, Paul, and Cornelius. Traditional material is undoubtedly included in these accounts (6:8—8:3; 9:1-30; 10:1—11:18), and this will be discussed further later. But it is equally certain that these sections would not have reached the great extent which we now have if the author had not added something of his own. Since two of the most comprehensive accounts contain speeches, a certain part of what the author himself contributed can be determined with certainty. At the end of these narrative pages, to which might be added a number of smaller narratives (see below), we find short, independent sentences, quite different in style and compass, which in the generalizing manner already described indicate the circumstances of Christianity in its early days and thus, like the corresponding sentences in 1–5, can be ascribed to the author; these sentences are: 6:7; 9:31; 12:24. The author's own hand is also to be seen wherever he links together complexes of material; he introduces Saul into the narrative about Stephen (7:58; 8:1; 8:3), and with this same event, the stoning of Stephen, he skillfully connects the conversion both of the Samaritans and the Antiochans (8:1, 4, 25; 11:19). The editorial nature of the appropriate verses has long been recognized.[19] Besides, in the way in which they form bridges between material that is separated in the text, they are identical with what we have seen in corresponding parts of Luke's Gospel.[20]

Although in some sections of this part tradition and literary composition can be clearly separated, in other sections a critical analysis is difficult. Smaller texts are involved: they contain too little formed narrative to present traditions such as we should expect to find solely among the Christian communities whose interest was edifying or personal. On the other hand, the substance of these smaller texts is most important and cannot be inserted straight away into the context; therefore they cannot be editorial observations or literary compositions. It is the same with the two lists of names (6:5; 13:1),[21] with the account of the mission to the heathen Antiochans (11:20),[22] and with the much-discussed notice of the collection (11:28-29).[23] These little passages, too impartial and brief to be legends, short stories, or anecdotes, too independent and laden with facts to be mere inventions of the author, can only be explained as Luke's assimilation of certain accounts he had collected together from the communities. Since they were not available to him as formed traditions, he had to insert them to fit in with the context. But, as he had no other accounts and reconstructed events which took place within the earliest communities after the analogy of the more highly developed condition of the Church, he was quite liable to misinterpret. The complicated nature of this section of Acts illustrates the fact that the whole book cannot be traced entirely to a few sources; nor can the author's own contribution be worked out evenly and according to a uniform principle in all parts of the work. The question as to what is tradition and what is the author's own composition has to be repeated with reference to each section, often indeed to the individual accounts.

Fragments of Tradition

I do not claim in this sketchy analysis to have answered the question of tradition and composition for every verse in the book of Acts. But I have tried, without being influenced by the subject matter, to determine by an analysis of style what contribution the author himself has made in several passages; and I should like to attempt further at least to pave the way to an understanding of the small units which, as traditional fragments which were originally handed down independently, provided an important part of the tradition used by the writer. For beside the itinerary, which covers only the chapters concerning the journeys, they are the main items of tradition, and it is from them that any more detailed analysis will have to proceed.

I shall begin by investigating one or two stories of miracles because, by virtue of the affinity of their subject matter, they can most easily be compared with stories in the Gospels.[24] The *raising of Tabitha* (9:36-42) is an independent story and therefore to be judged differently from the preceding one of the healing of Aeneas in Lydda (9:32-35). This, told with no description of the details of the story and with no proper conclusion, appears to be only an echo of the story of a miracle and not a faithful reproduction. The story of Tabitha is a faithful reproduction, however; it starts as an independent story, and its conclusion in 9:42 is entirely calculated to edify.[25] Nor does it belong to an account of a journey, for Peter's whole "journey" is introduced only in order to bring him to the stations at Lydda and Joppa: there is no mention of a mission here; in both places Peter finds Christian communities in existence. The story of Tabitha is told in edifying style like that of the Gospel narratives, which I call paradigms. No emphasis is laid upon the technique employed in performing the miracle; the way in which the miracle is worked is given prominence only in order that the people present may be asked to leave and the words that achieve the working of the miracle given explicitly.[26] But even that extends beyond the limits of the "paradigms" of the Gospels. And there is a complete divergence from them in the abundance of personal details: Tabitha's name is given, her character is described, the garments she made for widows are mentioned as evidence of her beneficence,[27] and perhaps some reference to her appearance is implied by the particular mention of the care of the corpse. This all gives a sort of portrait that is not found at all in paradigms. We are dealing with a "legend" which has a personal interest in Peter and Tabitha. It is difficult to ascertain how much historical fact underlies each isolated individual case, nor is this subject to enter into the present examination.

The story of *Cornelius* (10:1—11:18) is also a legend in the sense of an edifying narrative concerning devout people. Luke, however, has extended it to a great composition, intended to show that it is right that the Gentiles should be converted. Thus the story has a purpose beyond the legend itself. The conversion of one "Godfearer" (that is to say Gentile who had become relatively unobjectionable in the eyes of the Jews) does not in itself provide a basis for the discussion of the more serious issue. Moreover, this story of the conversion does not say that the Jewish Christian apostle and the "Godfearer" who had become a Christian partook of any meal together; yet it is for such eating together that the vision in 10:9-16 is to prepare Peter. We can see, therefore, that this vision has no place in the original story, neither has the allusion to the experience that is made in 10:27-29, which also comes as an interruption of the narrative.[28]

The story begins impressively with the vision of Cornelius, which is recounted in the genuine, broad style of legend; in accord with this vision are the Holy Spirit's instructions to Peter (10:17b-28 without the beginning of 10:19), which attain their full significance only when Peter's vision is ended. Again, the witnessing by other Christians of the gift of the Spirit to the Gentiles and their amazement at it (10:23, 45) accord with and arise out of Luke's elaboration of the theme. Since the speech (10:34-43) rests ultimately upon literary elaboration, the event was probably presented originally in the way that 11:15 presupposes: scarcely had Peter begun to speak when the Spirit came upon his hearers and they spoke in tongues. This was a proof, not that the mission to the Gentiles was justified, but of the power of the apostle's words, which, as soon as they were heard, caused the Spirit to be poured out on the hearers. Peter's words are in accord with this genuine motif of legend: "Can any one forbid water for baptizing these people?" (since no one can prevent the Spirit from coming upon them). We may suppose that originally this also was not a justification of the conversion of the Gentiles but a reference to the independent, effective power of God. Baptism was now to follow. But more important to the author were Peter's stay with Cornelius (which involved eating together) and the justification of the event offered by him in Jerusalem. Thus the conclusion of the legend about Cornelius has been lost to us.

In the story of the *lame man at the gate of the temple* (3:1-10), we are struck by the fullness of the description: the visit to the temple is made because it is the hour of prayer. The gate (the Nicanor Gate) is mentioned by the popular name not preserved for us anywhere else; the circumstance of the miracle is given in detail, including the long illness, the fastening of the eyes, the formula (in the "name"), the gestures which together achieve the miracle, and the description of the recovery. As a result, the one who is healed walks and can even jump—and this is confirmed by the people's recognition of the one who has been healed (compare John 9:8-9). There is no attempt to edify,[29] but neither is there any special interest in the people involved: the lame man's name is not given, Peter withdraws and John plays the part of the mute to such an extent that, for reasons connected with the technique of the miracle, he has to be removed from the story.[30] This is not a legend about apostles in the narrower sense, nor is it a "paradigm," but the genre of narrative which, when found in the Gospels, I have described as a tale (*Novelle*). It is consistent with this genre that the conclusion (3:10) contains no religious motif, but merely emphasizes the extent of the miracle. Verse 11 provides a link with the literary composition of the scenes containing the speech and the trial, and, because the author does not know the exact locality, a contradiction is found in his account. According to v. 8, the heroes of the story are in the temple, that is, in the inner forecourt; but, according to v. 11, they are in Solomon's porch, that is, on the east side of the outer forecourt.[31]

As far as I can see, we cannot discern traditional material in the immediately preceding story of Pentecost, for the part contributed by the author is considerable, and is seen not only in the sermon but probably also in the well-known catalogue of the nations (2:9-11). On the other hand, there is a particular danger here that critical consideration of the subject matter may prejudice the analysis of style, so that the method of style-criticism certainly cannot be illustrated from this story.[32]

The *conversion of the eunuch* (8:26-39) is similarly told in the genuine style of legend and on the whole without literary embellishment. The angel of the Lord directs Philip to the lonely road;[33] the Spirit leads him to the eunuch's chariot; the Spirit snatches him away again. There is an element of secrecy in the whole event. The writer of Acts has certainly made an adjustment in the case of one character: in order to link up with 21:8, he has added a postscript (8:40), based on inference, which conceals the place where Philip stayed from the reader.[34] The eunuch is thought of as a "God-fearing" Gentile, and is prepared for the sermon not by a vision but by a reading from the Bible. The sermon is not developed in a literary manner: only the theme is given. Baptism takes place without canonical or dogmatic formalities such as are contained in 8:37, which was inserted later. The quotation of the passage from the Bible serves a devotional interest, the account of the eunuch's position a personal one. A genuinely legendary style arises out of the combination of devotional, personal, and miraculous elements.

A "devotional" interest in subsidiary characters is seen in the story of *Ananias and Sapphira* (5:1-11). Luke has used this story as a case to illustrate what he has summarized in 4:32-35 and has linked it with this by the story about Barnabas. It begins, however, quite independently, and it ends by giving the result of God's judgment. We notice what effect the death of them both is to have upon us: we are to beware of committing the same sin; God sees everything and gives his apostle keen perception! The threatening attitude of the shrewd apostle corresponds with the threatening conclusion. Moreover, the biblical sound of the phrase "the feet of those that have buried your husband" (compare Isa 52:7) is intended to increase the devotional sense of horror. Devotional interest also reveals for us the names of the sinners and one or two details of the burial. There is no trace of the technique of miracle stories or of the use of one of the usual formulas of cursing. In this, too, we see characteristics of legend.

The other stories involving curses are more problematic. In the story of *Elymas* (13:8-12), the conclusion is preserved in traditional style. The technique of the miracle is emphasized: the look given by the apostle, who is filled with the Spirit, the words of reproach and the curse, all bring about the sudden blindness, which is vividly described together with the groping of the man who has been thus punished. The miracle has its effect: the proconsul confesses belief in Christ.[35] But the beginning of the story is not preserved in the form in which we must presume it would have existed in tradition. There is no clear account at all of the setting. The colorless statement "he opposed them" cannot be the beginning of such a detailed miracle story. In addition, Barnabas obviously does not belong to the story, since he does not feature in it any further. Moreover, vv. 6 and 8 can hardly be taken as affording a reconciliation of two different names for one sorcerer; obviously, several traditions clash here. Lastly, this is also true of the beginning of the account: the one story "they came upon a certain magician" clashes with the other, which reads "He was with the proconsul, Sergius Paulus . . . who summoned Barnabas and Saul" (v. 7). Here the author has intervened, and therefore we cannot say to what extent the religious, and to what extent the personal and the "tale" elements dominated the original account.

It is even more difficult to determine the nature of the tradition in the story of *Simon the sorcerer* (8:9-24). In our text the sorcerer is introduced into the story of Philip with an observation that is undoubtedly the author's own.[36] Thus, since it is assumed that we know of Philip already, we do not know how he originally came into the story. His first appearance in it is concealed by vv. 11 and 12, which particularly strike the reader because they repeat something that has been said before. Moreover, it has long been recognized that the middle of the story has been omitted by the writer, who wanted to assert the apostolic right of confirmation and therefore introduced Peter and John.[37] Originally, Simon probably asked Philip himself if he could buy the gift of performing miracles and was refused by him. But our text misses the point of this refusal as it takes place in an atmosphere half of cursing and half of regret and with no result.[38] It is possible that the author already knew other legends of Simon and, with them in mind, reduced the judgment of Simon (somewhat in the nature of that described in connection with Elymas) to a mere threat.

The story of the *reviving of Eutychus* (20:7-12) occupies a special place among the stories of miracles in Acts, and can be paralleled with the legend of Tabitha only if style is completely disregarded. Luke has interwoven it with the itinerary. Most of v. 7 and perhaps the whole of v. 11 can be taken as his own contribution.[39] Otherwise, the mood of the story is as secular as possible; this is seen particularly in the rationalized description of the miracle. We should expect Eutychus to be dead after his fall from the window, then everything that follows would be a great miracle. But the storyteller leaves open the question as to whether it is a miracle: he "was taken up dead" (v. 9). Paul throws himself on him and embraces him. It is not made clear whether this happens in order to exorcise the spirit or to examine the unconscious boy; we are left equally uncertain as to whether Paul is seen as a worker of miracles or a physician: "his life is in him" (v. 10). When Jesus says of Jairus's daughter "The child is not dead but sleeping," there is a conscious ambiguity in his words, and the believing listener suspects what the unbelieving witnesses ridicule (Mark 5:39-40). Here, on the other hand, it is the story that is intended to be ambiguous and not the words; and the skeptical reader is intended to be interested by the very fact that the matter remains unexplained: "they took the lad away alive" (v. 12).

The storyteller could have concluded as Philostratus concluded his account of the raising of the Roman maiden by Apollonius of Tyana: "whether he found in her a spark of life which had escaped the notice of the doctors . . . or whether he rekindled and recalled the extinguished life, it is impossible for me as for the eyewitnesses to discover" (*Vita Apollonii* 4.45). The secular manner of telling the story, to which, in some sense, even the lamps in the room belong,[40] is in accordance with the secular conclusion. Only the occasion of the accident and the height of the fall are described: there is no edifying motif, neither is there any mention of prayer before the boy is restored to life, nor of praise to God afterwards. The whole account concludes: "they . . . were not a little comforted." Dismay now gives way to peace of mind.

This nondevotional style can certainly not be attributed to the author; indeed, he has introduced a certain Christian interest into the framing of the story and has taken the incident as a miracle (and not as a good diagnosis) by Paul. Thus we are dealing with what was originally a secular anecdote, probably containing a humorous undertone. Although the room was brightly lit, the boy fell asleep: the length of the speech was the reason! But the speaker made good the harm he had caused. How he did it we do not know. It is improbable that Christians with a literary education would have told of one of Paul's deeds in this style. Rather, I would assume that a current anecdote had come to be applied to Paul, that Luke found it in this form and introduced it into his narrative.

This is not the only "secular" passage in Acts, for the anecdote about the *sons of Sceva* (19:14-16) is a story that serves to entertain and fosters no religious or personal interest whatever. The evil spirit will not be driven out by unauthorized exorcists, who have simply borrowed a formula which they have heard used by genuine exorcists—this is the sense of the story, told in a strain which is not without its comic element. It is not clear whether the misused formula was ever a Christian one, for the anecdote is embedded in a summary passage (19:11-13, 17-19) so that we no longer have the beginning of it. We have no description of the details of the incident and it is only at the end, and rather surprisingly, that we hear anything of the house in which the story takes place. Even if the incantation had been Christian in the first place, the story was certainly not fashioned by Christian interests.

The story of the *death of Herod* (12:20-23) is also of non-Christian origin. Admittedly the point of the story is contained in a conception that could be Christian: he who makes himself as God calls forth God's judgment. But we know from Josephus that an anecdote with a similar point was current in Jewish circles (*Ant.* 19.8.2 [§§343-352]). It is worth comparing the two forms— Acts and Josephus.[41] In Josephus the idolatry has a more picturesque reason, and one that is very interesting when considered with reference to the history of religion: the beams of the rising sun make the king's silver robe gleam, an incident that is obviously interpreted by the flatterers of the court as the brightness of an epiphany. In Acts the idolatry arises out of an historical episode, namely the conflict between Herod and the inhabitants of Tyre and Sidon. But this motivation is abbreviated by Luke and becomes obscured. The not quite successful and obvious transition from generalized description to an account of individual events (12:20) makes it quite clear to the reader where tradition begins.[42] We noticed the same thing in connection with the story of Elymas, and the story of the sons of Sceva. Originally, of course, the reason for the dispute was recounted, and moreover, it was recounted how Herod dealt with the matter in a speech that then occasioned the idolatrous acclamation. In Acts the judgment is described, quite naively, in biblical terms, as a direct result: "Immediately an angel of the Lord smote him, because he did not give God the glory" (12:23). In Josephus the instantaneous effect is in terms of a miracle: Herod sees an owl sitting opposite him and immediately feels death coming upon him. Josephus is more miraculous, but also more secular. Acts has its starting-point in history, but is told in a more naïve manner and as if by one who believes in miracles. Since the whole story is concerned with the ethos of belief in retribution and pious abhorrence of the deification of men, we may take the form found in Acts as older than the one in Josephus and regard the whole story as a Jewish legend.[43]

The apotheosis motif is reminiscent of the anecdote relating to Malta (28:1-6). This experience of Paul, together with the miracle of healing which follows, is preserved in a literary version,[44] which does not directly allow any style-critical conclusions. The first anecdote also has a strange ending. No early Christian story about Paul would have presented the motif of the apo-theosis of Paul as though it were to the apostle's credit, without at the same time correcting the impression. This can be clearly seen in the story from *Lystra* (14:8-18), which, as I have shown above, was inserted into the account of the journey.[45] Luke obviously added a speech at the end and thus weakened the point of the story, for this cannot conclude with the statement that the apostles "scarcely restrained" the people from sacrificing to them.[46] Originally the crowd was probably not persuaded, but became angry and attacked the apostles. Luke would then have weakened the ending in view of what followed.

Apart from this pointless ending, the style of legend prevails. The technique of the miracle is disclosed unobtrusively in the course of the story of the sick man—the gaze which could work miracles, the formula of healing and the approval of the crowd. The devotional element is seen in the mention of faith,[47] and also the point of the story, which is the condemnation of Gentile apotheosis. The description of Paul and Barnabas as Zeus and Hermes represents the personal interest.[48] Everything is made to fit in with the main theme, which is the refusal to accept glory belonging to God; this theme must therefore be taken as older than the sermon that has served as a vehicle for Luke's presentation of it.

The style of legend is seen even more clearly in the story of *Peter's release from prison* (12:5-17). It seems that Luke preserved this tradition—almost ungarnished—in the form in which, as an isolated story, it was current among Christians. In particular, the words "he . . . went to another place" (v. 17) would be obscure if they had not originally come at the end of an independent story that was not concerned with further journeys made by Peter.[49] Moreover, the mention of John Mark in v. 12 does not give the impression that a pragmatizing writer was anxious to introduce his readers for the first time to a subsidiary character who was, after all, of some importance. How differently Barnabas is introduced in 4:36! Obviously the traditional story postulated an acquaintance with Mark, as it did later with James the Just, who also had not yet appeared in Acts. The mention, at the beginning, of the praying community must have originated with Luke himself, for in 12:17 we see that the whole community was not assembled. Verse 5a provides the beginning of the story, however.

Luke has put the event in its context in history, not only by adding a footnote about Herod (12:18-19), but especially by prefixing an account of the persecution of Christians; and, by means of a note in v. 4 about the military guard, he has prepared the way for the story of the sentries and soldiers. This arrangement has resulted in some doublets. Our text twice mentions the imprisonment and twice the intention of bringing Peter forth before the people. The story itself, however, is a special gem among the legends of Acts; for purity of style it is comparable only with the stories of Tabitha and of the eunuch, and it is superior to them in the beautiful way in which it is presented. The miracle is related in a spirit of absolute faith that makes the outcome seem certain. But, because the outcome remains as yet a divine secret, it is treated with pious and reverential reserve: the angel enters, clothed in brilliance, the chains fall off, the door opens by itself, but Peter still believes that he is being carried away by a vision. He first becomes aware of the reality of the situation when the angel leaves him standing alone in the street. The reader is impressed still more deeply with the awe that surrounds what is happening; consider the maid's excitement, the incredulity of the Christians,[50] and the silent command to hold their peace given by one who has only just been touched by the angel and who, as though he were not yet completely theirs, again departs from them. Consider, too, the interest in every detail, in the way out of the prison,[51] in the house into which Peter went, even the maid's name. It is a genuine, satisfactory legend, reflecting devotional feeling and satisfying devotional curiosity![52]

The story of the *release of Paul and Silas in Philippi* (16:25-34) shows itself to be an independent legend which can be removed straight out of its context, for, as it must astonish the reader of our text to observe, in the account of the release of the apostles (16:35-40), which is told in abundant detail, the terrible earthquake is not mentioned. Apparently the itinerary dealt only with the imprisonment and the release (without giving further reason), and also with Paul's desire for complete restitution. The story of the earthquake is therefore an insertion into the itinerary, without in fact being connected with it.[53]

The story about the miracle begins with the song of praise at midnight (v. 25). We cannot reconstruct an introduction to it, for the description given in the preceding verse of how Paul and Silas were imprisoned could have been contributed by the author just as well as the description in 12:4, while the itinerary has certainly played its part in v. 23. At the end of the story, however, the author has obviously intervened in the reference to preaching in v. 32 and to the baptism in v. 33, thus completely confusing both sequence and subject-matter.[54] In view of this, we begin to have doubts about the conversion itself, but without justification, for the dialogue in 16:30-31 is too essential a part of the whole to be detached from it. And if the story were to have ended with the guard and his entire household becoming believers, this could still have given Luke cause for adding the preaching and baptism as stages in the process of conversion.[55]

What we now recognize as tradition shows the characteristics of legend: a miracle related in naïve style; a concern solely for the chief characters; no pondering on the fact that other prisoners can escape, or upon the question as to how Paul knows in the dark what the guard is planning to do, or upon how the guard knows that the earthquake is connected with the apostles. Those who for devotional purposes are the heroes of the story are evidently in the center of what is happening; therefore, the prison-guard turns immediately to them, now calling them "Sirs." The devotional interest, too, is preserved: even in prison the Christians praise God, and the miracle not only breaks the apostle's chains but also changes the heart of the Gentile. His pious zeal is described in detail: he takes the apostles with him, washes their stripes, leads them to his house, and invites them to his table. The reader is intended to feel with satisfaction that all injustice has been made good by the respect shown by the convert.

As far as I can see, we have now come to an end of the smaller units that, simply by taking style as our criterion, and without detailed examination, we can detach from the text of the Acts of the Apostles. The martyrdom of Stephen, which we might still consider, requires special consideration that would lead to more detailed treatment than is possible here. This first Christian martyrdom cannot be investigated without reference to 2 Maccabees and 4 Maccabees, to the early Christian martyrs James the Just and Polycarp and, especially, to the passion of Jesus. Only then can we fully assess the literary style of this account.

In the present chapter my intention was to use only the simplest examples in order to examine the tradition used by the author's work, as literature; and then to analyze the style of the most important and most appropriate of the stories which he tells and, from their inner rhythm, their pathos and their ethos, to discover what is their individual quality. I hope I have shown that such a work is in the interests not only of the history of literature but also of interpreting the oldest stories about the apostles.

I have intentionally not considered whether all these stories are authentic or not; for, in placing the stories according to the different types, namely "legend," "tale," or "anecdote," we are assessing only the storyteller's method of writing and not the authenticity of what he relates. This, at least, we may record as the outcome of this attempt at analysis, that in the Acts of the Apostles historical reliability varies in the different sections. It is to be judged differently where the author has used the itinerary from where he has merely linked different traditions by means of summary passages; differently when dealing with legends from when dealing with literary speeches; and differently again when dealing with individual legends in comparison with one another. All these questions can be resolved only after the style-criticism has been carried out; any premature solution of the problems will do more than endanger the integrity of the style-critical method; it will obscure our understanding of the stories themselves. Intrinsically these stories are far removed from the problems of historiography, and it is only when we begin to look away from the questions that have been raised in connection with them that we learn to listen to what the storytellers have to say to us.

5

The Speeches in Acts
and Ancient Historiography

Purposes of the Speeches

The historian's art begins where he no longer contents himself with collecting and framing traditional events, but endeavors to illuminate, and somehow to interpret, the meaning of the events. Delight in knowledge and desire to understand must unite in his soul, otherwise history remains a heap of facts or dissolves into pseudo-prophecy. The questions of sequence of events, development, and meaning need not necessarily be unequivocally answered, but the possibilities offered in reply to the questions must help to make the subject clearer to the reader. It may be that the deeper meaning of things will be inherent in the portrayal itself, or that the historian will give his own judgment, concurrently with the story, upon the events that take place. Finally, it may be that the persons involved speak and indicate the meaning of the events either in a speech or in argument.[1]

This last method has become foreign to us. When considering historical characters, we expect the account not only of their actions but also of their speeches to conform to the standards of reliable tradition, and we wish to hear reported in an historical account only words genuinely spoken by the persons involved. Since authentic words are usually spoken on the spur of the moment and do not often penetrate to the deeper significance of the occasion, it is relatively seldom that an authentic speech can serve to make the situation clear, in any fundamental way, for the historian.

Historical writing in ancient times began from a different point of view. There, speech was regarded as "the natural complement of the deed";[2] to the Greek and the Roman historian, speeches served as a means for their purpose, however differently this purpose might be conceived. The ancient historian was not aware of any obligation to reproduce only, or even preferably, the text of a speech which was actually made; perhaps he did not know whether a speech was in fact made at the time; sometimes he did know, but he did not know the text of it; perhaps he could not have known it if the speech was made, for example, in the enemy's camp to a limited audience. Even if the text was known, the historian did not incorporate it into his work. We have an oft-quoted example of this in the speech by Claudius about the conferring of the *ius honorum* upon the people of Gaul. The text of it is preserved in CIL 13.1668, but Tacitus did not use this text in the *Annals* 11.24; instead, he adopted one that had been revised in the interests of style. In doing so, he "intentionally and completely obliterated the personal note in the original speech."[3] As further proof we might quote the fact that Josephus, in the first and second books of *Antiquities*, when reproducing the content of the Old Testament book of Genesis, does not abide by the text of the speeches in the Bible at all, although he probably considers it as reliable, but invents speeches that put quite different points of view.[4] Or we can give as an instance of the indifference of that same Josephus toward the genuine text of speeches the fact that twice he reproduces the same speech—by Herod in the war against the Arabs (*War* 1.19.4 [§§373-379]; *Ant.* 15.5.3 [§§127-146])—but in such a way as not to correspond with one another at all: this shows how little he feels bound by respect for the text.

The historian of antiquity usually has quite other aims in view when he records speeches, but these aims vary. The question is what the speech is intended to impart to the reader:

1. An insight into the total situation—for this, several speeches are frequently required in order to illuminate the situation from different angles.
2. An insight into the meaning of the historical moment concerned, but one which goes beyond the facts of history. Even though this insight may not have been revealed to the historical character at the moment when he is making the speech, the writer nevertheless lets him supply it.
3. An insight into the character of the speaker.
4. An insight into general ideas that are introduced to explain the situation, even if they are only loosely connected with it.

Of course, there are also speeches that merely serve to further the action. They reproduce what was to be imparted at this stage of the development by one person to a host of people. Such a speech is not then a special technical device; it is obvious even to the naïve narrator that, in such a case, he will do better to let the historical characters speak directly, rather than supplying a summary of the words spoken, or giving the words in indirect speech. Even the naïve narrator knows, however, that he is not bound in such a case to abide by the words as preserved by tradition.[5] A stylizing of the direct speech may often enough be ascribed to him. At any rate, whether the speech is an artistic device or not, the historian of antiquity felt differently from ourselves about the relationship of speeches to historical reality.

It was Thucydides who treated the whole problem in the most energetic manner, and it was also he who raised the speech to an artistic device of the highest order. In his exposition of the famous and much-discussed scientific[6] method employed in his work (1.22) he gave his views on the principles involved in his composition of the speeches. He said it had certainly been difficult to retain the exactness (*akribeia*);[7] he had, therefore, allowed the speakers to express themselves in the way he thought individuals would have found it necessary to speak on the subject to be discussed. If, after these words, the speeches seem to be freely composed, the following observation will claim a certain objective basis for them: Thucydides added the words "In doing so, I kept as much as possible to the general sense (*xumpasa gnōmē*) of what had actually been said" (1.22.1). The ambiguity of this remark presents a real problem. As a result, no agreement has yet been reached among the interpreters of Thucydides concerning the relationship of subjective judgment and objective reproduction in the speeches. If we refer the *xumpasa gnōmē* to the general content of the authentic speeches, the question arises in quite a number of cases how Thucydides found this content. It was therefore attempted formerly to refer the whole scientific method only to that part of the historical work that was written first; according to this view, Thucydides was supposed to have later adopted a subjective interpretation that allowed him to draw up the speeches quite freely.[8] In view of the fact that this is improbable, and that it is much more likely that the scientific method should be applied to the whole work, the expression *xumpasa gnōmē* must be understood differently. It is a question not of the content, but of the intention of the speech (Grosskinsky), or even only of the speaker (Egermann). In support of this, Grosskinsky has very rightly pointed to the fact that this observation implies the considering of the whole drift, not as a general principle, but as a principle to be used in asking subjectively what the speakers could have said. In answering the question, the author is in point of fact helped by envisaging the meaning that the speech had at the time when it was made. Either he knew this, from his own recollection or from the reports given to him by those he regarded as his authorities, or he drew it from the situation presupposed by the speech. That is the objective basis of the speeches, "the general sense of what was said" (*xumpasa gnōmē tōn lechthentōn*). It distinguishes those of Thucydides from those of Herodotus, who is compelled to invent, because he tells of things that happened a long time ago. But Thucydides writes of contemporary history and is therefore in a position to know the speaker's purport, or, to some extent, to make an appropriate reconstruction. And on this foundation he can now build up and elaborate the speeches as he considers necessary. This foundation is not "historical" in our sense, however, for who knows whether the speeches that were actually made expressed the purport as clearly, precisely, and fundamentally as Thucydides has done? His chief concern is what is characteristic of the situation, rather than what is characteristic of the persons. An exact reproduction of the actual historical speeches would undoubtedly reveal certain differences among the speakers in their styles of speaking, but Thucydides has not attempted to characterize the speakers at all. As a result, Dionysius of Halicarnassus later reproved him for being too monotonous (*homoeidēs*).[9]

Although Dionysius may exaggerate, this criticism which he makes of Thucydides at the beginning of our era shows us what it was that alienated from Thucydides some of those who came after him, and what it was that caused them to work along other lines when using speeches in historical works.[10] It is Thucydides' crudeness and obscurity of style particularly that repels representatives of a new, dramatic method of presentation, and of rhetorical arts.[11] And orators find that the great classic of historical writing has not provided in his speeches any serviceable model for speeches in court.[12] Even Sallust himself deviates from him where characterization is concerned. He does not employ the impersonal method of presentation that allows the author to retire completely behind the subject and to illuminate the events only by the story and by the speeches that are inserted; he follows Polybius's example in introducing direct characterization and reflections. Moreover, the speeches in Sallust are styled differently; sometimes they are diffuse, sometimes brief; they vary also in the measure of rhetorical art which the speaker applies—at the same time, however, regard for the personality of the speaker is maintained.[13]

It is Xenophon who, as an historian, rises in status during the Empire and becomes increasingly worthy of imitation as a model. Atticism goes so far in its estimation of him as to place him along the greatest—as a philosopher beside Plato, as an historian beside Herodotus and Thucydides.[14] The ground for this attitude of respect toward Xenophon was indicated by Dio of Prusa[15] when he said that Xenophon was an example for politicians (just what Thucydides in his speeches was alleged not to be); his style was clear and simple, both convincing and pleasing. To quote an example of the simplicity (*apheleia*), Xenophon's speeches become the classic model for the so-called second Sophism.[16] In actual fact, the *Hellenica* in particular shows a large number of examples of short speeches not intended to be reports, but really speeches, each introduced by an apostrophe, admittedly without prelude and conclusion, but containing all that is necessary in simple, yet convincing, language, only on a miniature scale, so to speak. We might perhaps think of a miniature photograph in comparison. We shall have occasion to deal further with this type of speech.[17]

Besides the long and weighty discourse, and this type of simple speech (*apheles logos*), there are of course other varieties to be found in the writings of the ancient historians. Especially we may mention here the epideictic speech, in which rhetorical art is demonstrated, without there being any deeper meaning in the work as a whole.[18] We include in this connection speeches containing maxims from which are developed philosophical doctrines expounded not in the interests of the historical situation but in order to inform or instruct the reader.[19]

This survey was merely intended to show concerning historical writing in ancient times that, where it contains speeches, it follows certain conventions. What seems to the author his most important obligation is not what seems to us the most important one: establishing what speech was actually made. To him, it is rather that of introducing speeches into the structure in a way that will be relevant to his purpose. Even if he can remember, discover, or read somewhere the text of the speech that was made, the author will not feel obliged to make use of it. At most he will use it in composing the great or small pattern of the speech with which he provides his account. This pattern will, however, either enliven the whole, if direct speech takes the place of a prosaic report, or it will serve as an artistic device to help to achieve the author's aims. In any case, the tradition of ancient historical writing teaches us that even the interpreter of historical speeches of such a kind must first ask what is the function of the speeches in the whole work.

Acts and Historiography

I now wish to place the Acts of the Apostles of the New Testament into the context of this historiographical tradition. Commentators on this book have already referred from time to time to the speeches found in the works of ancient historians,[20] but up till now they have not been aware of the task which should therefore have fallen to them, the task of discovering what place the speeches in the Acts of the Apostles take among the quite varied types of speeches recorded by historians, and thus, at the same time, of determining the meaning to be attributed to the speeches in the work as a whole.

First of all, however, we must ask whether the author, whom, after careful consideration, I can with a clear conscience call Luke,[21] really belongs among those writers to whom we may attribute the use of speeches as an artistic device? New Testament writing as a whole, particularly, seems against this view. The early Christian writers have not yet become *literati*. They seldom coax a pun from the language, and, when they do so, they are usually quoting a popular turn of phrase. The speeches of Jesus in the Synoptic Gospels are compilations of sayings, and not "speeches" in the sense of rhetoric. The speeches in John, however, belong to an Oriental setting and have nothing in the way of style or construction in common with the speeches in the Acts of the Apostles. Even if the Epistle to the Hebrews is considered to be in some sense literary prose,[22] it is still not on the same plane as the artistic devices of the historian. Paul's own rhetoric,[23] moreover, is the rhetoric of the spoken word, not of great literature. The Acts of the Apostles would therefore, if its speeches were found to be an artistic device in the sense we mean here, assume a unique position in the New Testament.

The earlier work of the same author, Luke's Gospel, seems, however, to be evidence against this, for despite its literary prologue, this first work is no different in kind from a Gospel such as Mark or Matthew. Luke has revised the texts of his sources from a linguistic point of view; in the interests of probability and clarity he has also re-arranged their presentation; he has added observations and supplementary passages that provide connecting-links and continuity, but all this has not essentially changed the character of the Gospel. It remains a book that contains collected material, stories, and sayings, in addition to the story of the Passion and traditions of the community, revised certainly, but not newly formed. It is a book that, on the whole, represents the people among whom the tradition had been collected and into whose hands it was once more delivered in book form. Is it conceivable that the second volume of Luke's work was of a totally different kind, that the author of the Gospel, in this continuation of his work, made use of literary devices of the sort that were used in the realm of "great" literature? Can we believe this, especially in view of the fact that even this second part is concerned not with stories about states and wars, not with the lives of politicians, generals, or philosophers, but with the fates of the poor, Christian communities, and their mission?

The answer to this question must be that in fact all this is perfectly conceivable. For, of the presuppositions I have just mentioned as reasons against this view, one at least is not conclusive—and this has often been overlooked—namely that this second work by Luke is of a totally different kind, for it was not intended only for the communities of people in humble circumstances, but *also* for another circle of higher social standing. This is true not only of the Acts of the Apostles but also of Luke's Gospel—despite all that seems to contradict this view. The prologue to the Gospel serves as evidence of the author's more far-reaching intention. This completely literary text that, in vocabulary and construction, resembles the proem of works of cultivated literature, has but little to say to the Christian communities of its own time. The dedication to a person of rank—here the "most excellent Theophilus" (*kratistos Theophilos*)—honors the addressee, but also puts him under an obligation to distribute the book, whether he is a believing Christian or an interested Pagan. The communities would not have been interested in these literary customs. The mention of the "events which have taken place among us" says nothing of the meaning of salvation, and the wish that the reader may be convinced of the "reliability of the information" which he has heard is expressed with a certain impartiality toward the subject-matter.[24] The same words could have introduced a work that had as its subject a much-discussed event of secular contemporary history.

This prologue shows that the author wants to have not only simple Christians as his readers, but also people of literary education, whether of the Christian or some other faith, who are accustomed to such prefaces in the books of their choice. The succeeding text of Luke's Gospel does not correspond at all with this prelude; the subject compels the author to adopt another style, for the subject is the tradition, available in abundance, which Luke wishes only to recast and edit, but certainly does not wish to transcribe into the style of a literary work.

We must thus reckon that Luke's Gospel had from the beginning (speaking in a modern idiom) two market outlets: it was intended as a book to be read by the Christian community, in the same way as Mark, Matthew, and other books now lost to us (the "many" [*polloi*] of the prologue to Luke), but also, at the same time, it was intended for the private reading of people of literary education. The first group could understand from the prologue only the assurance that the book was reliable, but then, for them, this went without saying. This group was concerned with the content of the book, with the tradition concerning the Lord. Right from the beginning, they would have called it "the gospel of Jesus Christ (*euangelion Iēsou Christou*)—and only where there were several books of this kind would the name of the author have been added: "according to Luke" (*kata Loukan*), that is, "in the form Luke has given to the 'Gospel.'" It was, however, by this very prologue that the other readers of the book were to be introduced to a correct understanding of the content which was unfamiliar to them, of the fact that this, too, was history; that it rested upon carefully collected evidence of the eyewitnesses, and was thus reliable, as an historical presentation must be. It would certainly not have been offered to these readers under the title "gospel" (*euangelion*)—in that case, the prologue would not have been written in such an impartial manner, with such reserve on the subject of the meaning of salvation as contained in the material. If this prologue gave the name of the person to whom the dedication was addressed, the name of the author could hardly be omitted from the title, and, if we may be permitted to draw a conclusion in reverse from the title of the second book, then the title of the first was (*Louka* [*Antiocheōs*] *praxeis Iēsou*).

What was said about the prologue to Luke's Gospel applies also to that of the Acts of the Apostles. It is aimed at readers who are accustomed to such things, but this time the continuation brings no basic change in style, for this books is not, in the first place, one to be read by the community;[25] obviously there were no models for it, so that, unlike Luke's Gospel, it is not arranged according to an already existing type of Christian writings. Here, then, the author can fashion the material he has collected as far as it permits; he can select, abbreviate or elaborate; he determines the sequence of events; he creates connecting-links and independent passages in between. All these practices of the historian's technique can be appreciated by those who are accustomed to reading historical books, but not by the simple Christian. We need not overrate this technique, for the countless stories (legends, tales, anecdotes)[26] that the author adopts may have been revised from the point of view of language, but they have not been remodeled as regards style, in fact they have kept their old form. Nevertheless, we can feel the author's hand fashioning them also when, for example, the broad development of the story of Cornelius clearly betrays the fact that Luke wants this story to illuminate the crucial turning toward the conversion of the Gentiles at God's command. Breadth of style indicates here, and abbreviation elsewhere points to the fact that, in Acts 16:6-10, Luke has omitted all the stations on Paul's journey into Asia Minor with the exception of Troas. It would be strange if he had not had details of them in the itinerary (the account of the stations on Paul's journeys) that he undoubtedly used. This abbreviation obviously implies that Luke wants to show that it was divine dispensation and not the will of man that brought Paul to Macedonia and Greece. Three times, therefore, he mentions the intervention of a higher power. The Holy Spirit, the "Spirit of Jesus," and a nocturnal vision determine the direction of the journey (16:6, 7, 9); the objectives are Troas and Macedonia. No stations in between are mentioned. Luke does not wish it to appear as if Paul were undertaking a missionary journey of the usual kind through these provinces of Asia Minor; he has no objectives in any of these provinces and does not stop in any of them for long; it is only when he reaches Macedonia that he halts.

Toward the end of Acts we see the author's own hand at work in the way in which Paul's defense is presented: no less than six times the apostle has to submit to questioning, before the people, before the Sanhedrin, twice before the procurator Felix, twice before Festus. The intention in these paragraphs cannot be to pursue Paul's trial further, for, apart from the appeal to the emperor in 25:11-12, these trials never lead to even a preliminary decision. Besides, Luke cannot be greatly interested in the trial of Paul, for it is one of

the mysteries contained in his book that no account is given of the final outcome in Rome; the narrative breaks off before the verdict is given. The meaning of these many hearings must therefore lie in their aim, rather than in their
outcome. Indeed, arguments are given here which speak not for or against
Paul, but for or against Christianity, and they did so especially in the author's
own day. The intention is to edify the reader through these arguments—not
only as one observes their effectiveness in this particular trial, but in order
that one might be so strengthened by them that he or she too will be able to
withstand such accusations.

One last sign of the active part taken by the author is that three times in the
course of Paul's missionary journeys we hear formal renunciations of the
Jews: in Pisidian Antioch (13:46), in Corinth (18:6), and in Rome (28:25). The
attitude of the Jews in Antioch and Corinth to the Christian mission is only
hinted at; about the situation in Rome we are told only that there was a division of opinion within the Jewish community. The author thus does not consider it important to give reasons for the apostle's harsh judgment of the Jews.
What he wants to emphasize, and what he therefore repeats three times, the
last time even rather abruptly, is the fact that it was the Jews themselves who
cause Paul to turn to the Gentiles. Paul may often have experienced something of this kind. The accusation in 1 Thess 2:15-16 suggests that he had had
such experiences, but the way in which the renunciation of the Jews is introduced without being substantiated,[27] and its careful spacing through chaps.
13, 18, and 28, that is, through references to all the provinces in question (Asia
Minor, Greece, Italy), can only be considered as the work of an author who
was consciously creating, rather than renouncing, literary devices.

SPEECHES ILLUMINATE THE SIGNIFICANCE OF EVENTS

This author thinks it important to intersperse his work with speeches. If we
count up the large and small compositions that are really intended to be
speeches (because they are addressed to, or are known to have claimed the
attention of a large number of people in some other way), they amount to
about twenty-four.[28] They are distributed in all sections of the book; eight
belong to Peter [29] and nine to Paul,[30] one each to Stephen (7:2-53) and to James
the brother of the Lord (15:13-21), and only five are made by non-Christians.[31]
It is therefore only extremely rarely that an exchange of speeches (*hamilla
logōn*) can arise. A contest of this kind takes place only once, before the procurator Felix (24:2-21). Here, the orator Tertullus speaks as prosecutor for the
Jews, and Paul speaks in his own defense. In the Apostolic Council (15:7-21)
Peter and James speak in agreement with one another, and along the same
lines, so that this is not a debate. At most we might mention the gathering in

the Sanhedrin in Acts 5, in which Peter first summarizes the Christian preaching in a few words and then Gamaliel, in the absence of the apostles, gives that advice which has since become famous, of leaving the issue to God; even this, however, is not a real debate, but simply one speech being made after another.

Even such a survey as this makes it possible for us to draw one negative conclusion, namely, that it was obviously not Luke's intention to prepare the way for a final decision by first quoting the two sides of a controversy, or to encourage the reader himself to make an independent judgment of the case. Sallust did both these things when he allowed Caesar and Cato to speak one after another, Caesar for the milder but lawful punishment, and Cato for the harsher punishment for Catiline's conspiracy (*Bell. Cat.* 51, 52); or Xenophon, when he lets Procles and Cephisodotus express their opinions upon confederacy and supreme command (*Hellenica* 7.1.2-14). Appian has also placed in juxtaposition a lenient and a harsh judgment of Carthage (*Lybica* 57-61, 62-64). This, however, cannot be the author's aim, even in the one duel of words, the one between Paul and Tertullus, for there Paul's opponent simply puts forward the charges against Paul, without applying any arts of persuasion, and refers us to the next speaker, the defendant Paul, or the tribune Lysias.[32] Thus the more detailed speech by Paul is destined to prevail. The author does not wish to be impartial, indeed he wants to plead his cause; we shall see that this attitude differs fundamentally from that seen in ancient historical writings; Luke tells a story, but, while doing so, he is also preaching.

The meaning of the speeches in Acts cannot, therefore, be derived from that one debate. We shall come closest to the meaning if we consider the place of the main speeches within the structure of the whole book. In so doing we shall have to examine particularly those speeches that do not seem to have arisen directly out of the situation in which they have been placed. At the feast of Pentecost it is necessary for Peter to speak in order to explain the miracle of Pentecost; similarly, when Paul goes into the synagogue in Antioch, we may expect that he will make a speech there; but why should a speech be reported from Athens, one of the stations on the journey, and none from Philippi or Corinth? The missionary Paul must have spoken at each of these three places; the author could therefore choose freely from which city he would report a speech. Certainly he did not choose Athens for historical or biographical reasons, for he is himself compelled to record that the apostle's success in Athens was quite small. The city where he was successful was Corinth and, according to the evidence of the Epistle to the Philippians, a lively community was successfully established in Philippi that had a large place in Paul's affections. If, even so, Luke makes Athens the scene of the single example of a sermon to the Gentiles preached by Paul, the missionary to the Gentiles, this is done because he ascribes a particular importance to the city of Athens.[33] He has prepared the way for the speech by a description of the spiritual condition of Athens that, in style and color, stands out above all similar descriptions in the New Testament.[34] The Athenians, with their interest in anything new, their piety, the Epicurean and Stoic Schools—all these details are intended to give the reader the impression that Paul is standing here in the heart of the spiritual life of Greece. The Christian apostle has penetrated into that center of the ancient world that epitomizes the spirit; at the end of the book he will penetrate to that other center which epitomizes power. It is in accordance with the best tradition of Greek historical writing, as established by Thucydides, that Luke lets the apostle make here, in a famous place, a speech which is mostly closely connected with the ideas of hellenistic philosophy and only very slightly with Paul's theology.[35]

The speech is finely conceived. In contrast to Gentile worship it is established first of all that the deity does not need anything; next comes the idea that God created men that they might inhabit the earth,[36] that he appointed the seasons and the zones of habitation for them in order that they should seek after him.[37] Finally, the speaker refers to the relationship of God with man in his natural state; those who belong to the family of God may not honor him with images. The speech is concluded with a reference to the coming judgment.[38] These motifs would have been worth developing further. Each idea could have been subdivided into between five and eight further sentences, but that was not what the author intended; he was content to express each motif only once. In this way the speech became strikingly concise, but it is neither an extract from a greater work nor a summary of contents. The style and tone are that of an actual speech, but on a very small scale; the analogy of the miniature photograph is appropriate here too. Thus a compact whole was formed.[39] The fact that it really is packed full of ideas is proved by the way in which the reader is given the impression of an actual speech, although it would take scarcely three minutes to deliver orally.

Apart from the few sentences spoken in Lystra (14:15-17), this is the only sermon to the Gentiles by the great apostle to the Gentiles that is given in Acts. It does not come from any of the cities involved in Paul's missionary work, but from Athens, and the author of Acts thinks it important that the speech should begin with a motif which is typical of Athens[40] and be introduced by a description characteristic of Athenian life. It is because Athens, which is not intrinsically important in the history of Paul's mission, is the center of Hellenistic piety and Greek wisdom that this city is chosen by Luke as the setting for a speech in which the Christian apostle employs Greek ideas. All questions as to whether Paul really made such a speech, and whether he made it in Athens, must be waived if we are to understand Luke. He is not concerned with portraying an event which happened once in history, and which had no particular success;

he is concerned with a typical exposition, which is in that sense historical, and perhaps was more real in his own day than in the apostle's time. He follows the great tradition of historical writing in antiquity in that he freely fixes the occasion of the speech and fashions its content himself. Even the way in which the ideas are compressed into a narrow space, however much it may contrast with famous examples of great history, is still not altogether unprecedented in historiography.[41]

The speech made by Paul in Miletus to the elders of the community of Ephesus (20:18-35) is of broader compass. It is not important to the sequence of events but it is important for the story in Acts, for it is not only the one speech made to a Christian community by Paul, the founder, but it is also the last time that Paul speaks publicly before his imprisonment. As a result, part of the speech is something like a will: it provides for the future. Other parts contain a retrospect on Paul's work:

> You know how, from the day when I first came to Asia, I remained with you the whole time, how I served the Lord in all humility, with tears, and with the opposition which fell to my lot because of the persecution of the Jews, how I did not neglect to proclaim to you and teach you anything profitable, in public, and house by house, and in so doing have borne witness, both to Jews and to Gentiles, about repentance toward God and faith in our Lord Jesus Christ.

This is the picture of Paul as sketched by Luke; this is how Luke wishes him to be regarded, and in this retrospect we are told many things which have not been said in the story: we are told, for instance, how, in Ephesus, Paul supported himself and his companions by the work of his hands (20:34); how in every city the Spirit told him of his impending imprisonment (20:23), and that the stay in Ephesus lasted three years (20:31). And, if Paul must himself proclaim to his hearers that his communities in the east will not see him again, we can see that Luke would also like to provide the apostle with an encomium of the kind that biographies often give to their heroes.[42]

At first sight, the style of this retrospect appears artificial; that is especially true of the apologetic phrase "that I have neglected nothing that is profitable to you" (20:20; *ouden hypesteilamēn*). But the rejection of a reproach, which we should not consider worth mentioning in this circle, obviously belongs to the style of this speech. Acts 20:26-27 and 20:33-34 offer the same sort of self-defense: "I am pure from the blood of all men," that is, according to what follows, "It will not be my responsibility if you do not accept salvation" and "I have not required silver or gold or apparel from anyone" but (this is the sense of what follows) have supported myself and my fellow-workers with the work of my hands. We know that this last point was very important to the historical Paul (1 Corinthians 9; 2 Cor 11:7-11), and that, when he recollects his first visit to those communities which were very dear to him, he reminds them of this fact (1 Thess 2:5-12). We must realize that the public might easily have confused Paul's mission with the activities of wandering speakers, mendicant philosophers, pseudo-prophets, and sorcerers. Therefore, the missionary's first concern had to be to dissociate himself from them by emphasizing that his aims were not self-seeking.[43] In the company of the elders of Ephesus, however, this constantly recurring apology would still have seemed strange if all this was really aimed only at that audience. Obviously, that is not the case; it is, on the contrary, in these sentences that at first seem so curious that the style of the speech is shown. The self-justification forms the motif, which constantly recurs between other ideas in the course of the speech, in rather the same way as, in a rondo in music, the first theme constantly recurs interwoven with others. We must simply observe that 20:31 also belongs to this retrospective self-defense: "Remember that for three years I did not cease to warn every one of you with tears (!)." Thus we see that this speech, which at first sight does not seem to be particularly well arranged,[44] has nevertheless been constructed according to a plan, for every paragraph ends with a reference to the apostle's example.

1. Vv. 18-21—Retrospect, concluding with self-defense.
2. Vv. 22-27—Anticipation of death, concluding with self-defense (vv. 20 and 27—the same apologetic expression "withhold nothing" (*ou[den] hypesteilamēn*) although with different construction).
3. Vv. 28-31—The apostle's testament (anticipation of the heresy which will arise after his death), concluding with the reference to his example.
4. Vv. 32-34—Blessing, concluding with self-defense and reference to his example.

The references to his own work leads on in v. 35 to the obligation of caring for the needy, which is confirmed by the words of Jesus: "It is more blessed to give than to receive."

Even the section I have described as the apostle's testament is not only and not essentially directed at the elders of Ephesus. They are exhorted to be watchful and are warned against the wild wolves that will break into their flock. Luke obviously means particularly agitators who come from without, but also men from within the community itself who speak pervertedly "in order to bring the disciples to apostasy and to cause them to follow false leaders." If Paul had had a particular doctrine in mind here, something in the nature of the gnosis which is opposed in the Epistle to the Colossians, whose appearance in Ephesus might be expected soon, he would have spoken in more definite terms. Actually the words apply to the whole Church and describe the dangers of heretical teaching as it first appeared among the Gnostics, but without emphasizing particular characteristics of Gnostic doctrine. But we know from the Pastoral Epistles that gnosis was often fought with the same weapons which philosophy used against sophistry.[45] Paul's testament deals only with this formal aspect of the struggle.

Once we have learned not to assess the speech by its authenticity, the speaker's anticipation of his death (20:23-25) will become intelligible as regards its literary significance. Apart from the oracle of Agabus (21:10-14), this is the only time that Luke makes any reference to Paul's death. Since the book of Acts does not tell of the end of the apostle's life, this prophecy is all the more important. Paul now disappears from the east; the elders of Ephesus did not see him again[46]—whether he regained his freedom in Rome and actually undertook the journey to Spain or not. He has reached the end of his public work in the chief theatres of activity and, since the author does not intend to tell about his martyrdom, Luke does to some extent press the crown of martyrdom upon his head, giving a retrospect of his life and making him direct a warning to the whole Church. We can see that this speech could scarcely have been placed anywhere else; in all its parts it achieves a certain spiritual object that Luke intended to achieve, just at the point where Paul laid down his missionary work in the east. This judgment is quite independent of our answer to the question, which can never be answered for certain, as to whether Paul spoke in Miletus at all and, if so, in what words. We do, at any rate, hear the author in this speech, and through the speech understand some of his intentions. As in classical historiographical tradition, his intentions are to illuminate historical events by means of speeches and, by embellishing his narrative with them, to emphasize definite places and occasions.

Of the speeches that Paul made as a prisoner, the one he makes to the people on the steps of the fortress of Antonia (22:1-21) is the most comprehensive and important. It contains the story of his conversion and links with it the story of a vision that Paul claims to have seen in the temple at Jerusalem. Both sections are of importance for our enquiry; the first, because in Acts we read, apart from this description, two more accounts of Paul's conversion, so that we can conclude from the divergences in these account the meaning of the relevant sections of each speech.[47] The last, shorter section of the speech refers to that vision in the temple that is not mentioned elsewhere in the whole book. Here too we shall have to investigate first not the historicity of the event itself but the value that Luke ascribes to the story.

Paul stands before the excited Jewish crowd that accuses him of a capital crime, that of bringing a Gentile into the temple court, thereby defiling the holy place. We should expect that, to prove his innocence, he would give an account to show that he had not done such a thing; Paul, however, seems to ignore the dangerous situation from which Roman protection has saved him. In the introduction to his speech he simply reminds the hearers of his earlier life according to the law, of his instruction by the Rabbi Gamaliel, of his, the speaker's, part in the persecution of the Christians in Jerusalem, and in organizing, with the high priest's sanction, a similar persecution in Damascus. The speech then proceeds straight away to a description of his conversion when on his way to Damascus. It is obviously important to the author to let the apostle testify before this forum to his departure from orthodox Judaism. Luke does not investigate the situation—and that also is not without analogy in historical writing in ancient times;[48] he neither says how it is that the Jews come to listen quietly to this man whom they have only just been wanting to lynch, nor does he give any reason why Paul speaks in terms so irrelevant to the situation. In fact, Luke transports his readers out of the situation and lets them hear what they do not yet know of Paul's biography for, up till now, he has included only a brief note on the subject of Paul's part in the stoning of Stephen,[49] and the story of his conversion has been given in concise form (9:1-19), without any connecting link or introduction. Evidently, in so doing, Luke is reproducing the story of conversion that was already existent, without submitting it to an extensive revision. Whatever was lacking in the original version is now made good in the introduction to the speech (22:2-5).

The conversion itself is related in a shortened form in the speech, since the reader is familiar with it already. Ananias's commission is left out, so that Paul's particular mission is not mentioned at this point; instead, the author has it in his mind when writing of the vision in the temple; the declaration of it thus comes very effectively as the real point at the end of the whole story, with what right, historically, we still do not know. In Gal 1:16 Paul makes a closer connection between his conversion and his mission, but that would provide no argument against the historicity of the vision, at most against Luke's interpretation of it. For him it is the literary, not the historical, interest which is decisive; Paul's reply to God's command that he should leave Jerusalem is not in the nature of an excuse but simply a recollection of his own earlier deeds, of his participation in the persecution of the Christians and in the killing of Stephen, that is, in the very events upon which the author of this book has laid particular stress. The Lord replies with the command: "Depart; for I will send you far away to the Gentiles." The reference is thus a literary one within the book itself, leading on to a missionary command; but the author had aimed at this from the start. The speech was not intended to be a justification of Paul in the one instance of desecration of the temple, but a justification of the mission to the Gentiles generally. In order to let the speech end at this important point and so to emphasize the meaning of the final words, the author again employs a literary device, that of an intentional interruption of the speaker by the hearers. We can see from the frequency with which Luke uses it that this really is a literary device. The speeches of Stephen and Demetrius and Paul's speeches on the Areopagus and before Agrippa are concluded in a similar way. The fact that these interruptions each occur at a significant point suggests literary technique; the speech is always allowed to reach just that point which is important to the author. We should certainly miss the author's intention were we to suppose that each of these speeches did in fact lack a concluding section. Are we, for example, to justify the real poverty of Christian content in the Areopagus speech by asserting that the Christian ideas that are lacking were just about to be introduced? We shall be less inclined to do that if we remember that, on other occasions, Luke supplies the significant conclusion to a speech with external events.[50] This device is one that is rarely to be observed elsewhere in the work of the ancient historians,[51] and it seems therefore to be a technique peculiar to our author.

Thus, at the end of his labors, Paul once more gives a fundamental defense of his work, which has been the mission to the Gentiles. This was not a task of his own undertaking. It was the will of God, of that same God whom Paul served as a Jew, that God who revealed himself in the temple. That is the particular meaning of the vision in the temple: it is intended to show that no contradiction exists between the God of the temple and the God of the Gentiles. From within the Jews' holy place itself God has commanded that there should be a mission to the Gentiles! It is understandable that this assertion by the great renegade was felt by the Jews to be highly provocative.

Although this systematic evangelizing of the Gentiles was Paul's work, according to Acts it was not Paul but Peter who was responsible for the first, decisive conversion of a Gentile, for it was through Peter that the centurion Cornelius was converted. There are various opinions regarding the meaning of this conversion.[52] Luke has it that the Ethiopian eunuch was converted first (chap. 8), and then later (Acts 11:19-26) records the important fact of how in Syrian Antioch, also, the mission crossed the boundaries of Judaism. But from the literary point of view Peter's action was the decisive one for the book of Acts, and Luke has made that clear in many ways. First of all, he has made a great composition out of the story of Cornelius, which, as an elaborated narrative, has no equal in the whole book. Cornelius is directed by an angel to send messengers to Peter. It is revealed to Peter in a vision that he is to have no hesitation in entering the Gentile's house and partaking of a meal with him there.[53] So Peter comes to Caesarea to the centurion's house and proclaims his message to him (10:34-43); we recognize the same scheme that formed the basis for Peter's sermons elsewhere in Acts. The Gentiles receive the Holy Spirit and then baptism. But the story does not end here. The authorities in Jerusalem require a reckoning with Peter on account of his activities. This is given in Acts 11:5-17 in a speech which is a shortened repetition of the content of chap. 10, and which very quickly satisfies his accusers, so that the conclusion to the whole composition can be made with the words: "Thus has God given to the Gentiles also atonement unto life."

The repetition of an already well-known event in the form of a report is an old device of epic writing. It is quite in accordance with this style that slight changes are made in the story and that it is filled out in places. It is worth noticing as we make this investigation how Peter's sermon (10:34-43) is glossed over, and is indeed omitted in the repetition in 11:15. For while, according to 10:44, the Spirit, in some form of ecstasy, comes over the listeners only at the end of Peter's sermon, according to 11:15 this happens "As I began to speak" (*en de tō arxasthai me lalein*). We see how the speech before Cornelius is intended simply to be a typical example of a sermon for Gentiles; it has nothing to do with the course of events in the house, and therefore can be passed over lightly in the repetition of the account. Luke probably inserted it into a legend about Cornelius that was already in existence.

A further section to be mentioned here is the Lukan account of the deliberations by the apostles given in Acts 15. This so-called Apostolic Council was occasioned by the complaint of the Jewish Christians concerning Paul. To justify themselves, Barnabas and Paul tell about their successes, but, instead of this account forming the central point in the Lukan narrative, the only speeches actually recorded are not those made by Paul and Barnabas, but by Peter and James. These latter do not deal, however, as we would expect, with Paul's mission, but with the conversion of Cornelius. "You know," says Peter, "that in the early days God made choice among you, that by my mouth the Gentiles should hear the word of the gospel and believe" (15:7). After the assembly has listened to the account by Paul and Barnabas, James begins to speak in such a way as if they had not spoken at all. He says: "Simeon has related how God first visited the Gentiles, to take out of them a people for his name" (15:14). All this again refers to the conversion of Cornelius. The recognition of the mission to the Gentiles by the authorities in Jerusalem is therefore not in Acts based on the successes of Paul and Barnabas, as we might have imagined from the previous episode, and as Paul himself has represented in Galatians 2; it is based on the conversion of the centurion Cornelius, that is, upon the event to which Luke ascribes supreme significance, regarding it as God's means of making known at that time and in an unmistakable way his will that the Gentiles should be received into the community.

The question arises as to whether Luke has perhaps exaggerated the meaning of an individual event, for the inconsistent attitude which Peter himself later adopted toward the question of Jewish and Gentile Christians eating together (Gal 2:11-21) would be scarcely intelligible if Peter had experienced the conversion of Cornelius as a declaration of the will of God, indicating the principle he was to follow, in the same way that this was done in the vision (10:9-16). It may well be that the conversion of Cornelius took place more or less as reported in Acts; Luke, however, has given it special emphasis in three ways:

1. By Peter's preliminary vision, in which he is commanded by a voice from heaven to eat unclean animals (10:9-16);[54]
2. By the subsequent justification before the Jewish Christians in Jerusalem (11:1-18);
3. By the reference to the story of Cornelius made in the Apostolic Council (15:7, 14).

It is clear here, if anywhere, that in this rendering of a story which was already traditional the author of Acts is not content with mere reproduction, but wishes to use his own methods to express the significance of what has happened, as he perceives it. He sees Paul as the man who, by his evangelizing, has succeeded in carrying the gospel from the Jews to the Gentiles. The progress in the way from Jerusalem to Rome has been described by Luke in the second part of his book (chaps. 13–28). The principles involved in this act of bearing the gospel to Rome he deals with, however, within the setting of the story of Cornelius. He does this, no doubt, because Peter, the chief of the apostles, here becomes the witness and agent of the great change. An individual story passed down by tradition could not illuminate the meaning of the event in the same way as Luke has done here by making his own version.

One small observation will be sufficient to show that it is literary intention which has consciously fashioned this whole composition. Normally, in Acts, Peter is called *Petros*, even in this story about Cornelius, so long as only he is the subject of the narrative; but where the name is used from Cornelius's side, that is, where the angel first speaks of him to the Gentile (10:5), where the messengers enquire after Peter (10:18), where Cornelius tells Peter of his visit by the angel (10:32) and even where Peter, in Jerusalem, gives his account of the story about Cornelius (11:13), there he is referred to as "Simon called Peter" (*Simōn ho epikaloumenos Petros* or *hos epikaleitai Petros*). And when James, who speaks Aramaic, uses the name in Jerusalem, the Greek transcription of the Aramaic name, *Symeōn*, is found (15:14). This gives some small indication of how conscious intention has governed the whole narrative.

We have seen that, at four important turning-points in the events described by him, Luke adds speeches to his account to illuminate the significance of the occasion; that is, at the first and fundamentally important conversion of a Gentile; at the apostle's penetration into the heart of Greek spiritual life; at his departure from the mission field; and at the time of his dispute with those Jews who were most closely concerned with the temple. We notice repeatedly that the speeches are not really related to the historical occasion but reach out beyond it. We wonder why the successes of Paul and Barnabas are not mentioned in the Apostolic Council, why Paul says so little that is Christian in Athens, why he defends himself before the elders of Ephesus with whom he was on intimate terms and why, before the Jews in Jerusalem, he makes no mention at all of the real point at issue with which the conflict began. All this explains itself if we ignore completely the question of historicity and see here the author's hand fashioning the material.[55] By employing much that is his own individual style, though still really complying with the great tradition established by Thucydides, the author wishes to use these speeches to give heightened meaning to the moment and to reveal the powers which are active behind the events.

RECURRING THEMES AND OUTLINES

In other speeches the author has employed quite a different device, namely repetition, in order to lay stress upon the significance of what is said. Elsewhere, in analyzing the apostles' missionary speeches (Acts 2; 3; [5]; 10; 13), I have pointed out the stereotyped repetition of the same outline.[56] Regularly an introduction showing the situation at the time[57] is followed by the kerygma of Jesus' life, passion, and resurrection (2:22-24; 3:13-15; 5:30, 31; 10:36-42; 13:23-25), mostly with emphasis upon the fact that the disciples were witnesses (2:32; 3:15; 5:32; 10:39, 41; 13:31); to this is added evidence from the scriptures (2:25-31; 3:22-26; 10:43; 13:32-37) and an exhortation to repentance (2:38-39; 3:17-20; 5:31; 10:42-43; 13:38-41). The harmony not only of outline but also of content is so striking as to require explanation. In the first place, this type of Christian sermon certainly seems to have been customary in the author's day (about 90 C.E.). This is how the gospel is preached and ought to be preached! And if no distinction is made in Acts between Jewish and Gentile listeners and between Peter and Paul as speakers, we can assume that the scheme of preaching indicated was not calculated simply for specific audiences. Luke would not ascribe this type of sermon to Peter and to Paul indiscriminately and let it be made both in the centurion's house and in the synagogue if he had not considered it as a type common to all Christians. Finally, however, the agreement, even in little matters such as the mention of witnesses, is so great that the question arises as to whether the author possessed something of this constantly recurring outline in written form. The use of old-fashioned phrases in the kerygma—such as "servant/child of God" (*pais theou*) in 3:13; "a man attested to you by God" (*anēr apodedeigmenos apo tou theou eis humas*) in 2:22—speaks for, rather than against, a dependence upon older texts. But, as far as I can see, the question can only be raised, not answered.

At any rate, we are faced here with a tradition which has nothing to do with historiography in ancient times, for here the chief concern is not what the historian wants to convey to his readers about the historical moment, not a "possession for all time" (*ktēma es aei*) in the sense of the famous words of Thucydides (1.22.4), or political wisdom for future instances; here, the author is concerned with the gospel. Its content is to be given in compressed form in these speeches, it is to be supported by proofs from the Old Testament and the readers are to be exhorted to repent for the sake of their souls. This gospel is to be proclaimed to the readers in the same way as the apostles once preached to their listeners. The repetition is intended to offer the same material in constantly new variation, to summarize what is essential in the message and to produce the impression which Paul, also speaking of the kerygma, formulated in 1 Cor 15:11: "Whether then it was I or they, so we preach and so you believed." The political aim of ancient history is supplanted here by the desire to preach and to teach.

Moreover, the speech made by Peter in Cornelius's house (10:34-43) indicates that the historical and the didactic traditions may also meet. The very fact that a speech is made here at all means that the moment is heightened in the historiographical sense. The content of this speech classes it, however, as a missionary sermon, intended to instruct the reader and to proclaim the message of salvation to him anew. A particular variation of this type of missionary sermon is given by Paul in the synagogue at Antioch (13:16-41); in outline it is very similar to the other examples of the same type, but we are immediately struck by the fact that the first section (13:16-22) has no connection with the missionary—and there is certainly none with the content of the missionary sermon. All that is given is a survey of the history of Israel. Any Jewish speaker might have spoken along the same lines. If we now compare this with the other examples of this type of speech, we shall see that the first verses regularly contain a link with the situation, and this is how, in fact, the section in question is to be understood: it provides the beginning of a sermon preached in a synagogue. Paul has been commanded by the ruler of the synagogue to give the community a "word of encouragement" (*logos paraklēseōs;* 13:15); this he does, and indeed exactly as any other Jew would have done in the same place. This opening, which apparently has no underlying meaning, is not without a certain charm, for such a quiet introduction will emphasize all the more the effect of the new proclamation which Paul immediately joins to the reference to King David: "Of this man's posterity God has brought to Israel a Savior, Jesus, as he promised" (13:23). Thus the apparently irrelevant start is connected with the situation after all, and the mere presentation of the history of Israel is intended to awaken the memory of instructive dissertations in the synagogue.

This paves the way for the understanding of another speech in Acts, the longest of all, namely, Stephen's speech directly before he is stoned (7:2-53). The irrelevance of most of this speech has for long been the real problem of exegesis. It is, indeed, impossible to find a connection between the account of the history of Israel to the time of Moses (7:2-19) and the accusation against Stephen: nor is any accusation against the Jews, which would furnish the historical foundation for the attack at the end of the speech, found at all in this section. Even in that section of the speech which deals with Moses, the speaker does not defend himself; nor does he make any positive counter-charge against his enemies, for the words "but they did not understand" (*oi de ou synēkon*) in 7:25 do not constitute such an attack any more than does the report of the gainsaying of Moses by a Jew in 7:27. It is not until 7:35 that we sense any polemic interest. From 7:2-34 the point of the speech is not obvious at all; we are simply given an account of the history of Israel. It is not until 7:35 that the purpose becomes evident, and then we read: this Moses whom the Israelites rejected (7:35), whom they did not obey (7:39), was sent to them by God as a leader, a deliverer out of Egypt, as a prophet, as bearer of the "living words" (*logia zōnta*; 7:35-43). This change from historical review to controversy becomes quite clear from 7:35 onwards (compare "this" [*touton*] twice; "this" [*outos*] three times). A further tendency is seen in the section 7:44-50: God's house among the Israelites at first took the form of a tent, then the temple of Solomon, but God does not dwell in what men have made. After this, and only in the concluding words (7:51-53), are we told the real accusation against the people: You have always opposed the revelation of God, both through the prophets and through the Law! We might say that the two sections already dealt with (7:35-43 and 44-50) paved the way for this accusation. We should then have to reckon the significance of these two sections to consist, respectively, in the themes of resistance to the lawgiver Moses, and a mistaken conception of the house of God, although the latter of these two themes is only hinted at. Then we could connect them with the two-fold charge against Stephen (concerning the holy place, and the customs delivered by Moses). With reference to the temple, however, the speech is extremely reticent and seems to be very loosely connected with the charge—indeed, we ourselves shall probably be reading into it any significance that we may find.[58] All this cannot alter the fact that the major part of the speech (7:2-34) shows no purpose whatever, but contains a unique, compressed reproduction of the story of the patriarchs and Moses. There are two suggestions as to what the speech is intended to mean:

1. Luke has obviously inserted it into the story of the martyrdom of Stephen, which he already had at his disposal. This story is told from 6:8 onwards: the trial by witnesses takes place but, to the members of the Sanhedrin, the face of the accused appears like the face of an angel (6:15). The continuation of this verse is found in the heavenly vision (7:55-56): the martyr, who has already been transfigured by heavenly light, now looks up to the open heavens and sees the Son of Man on the right hand of God. In our text, however, the description of the transfigured face of Stephen is followed by the question of the high priest, which gives rise to the long speech (7:1-53). The speech breaks the sequence between the transfiguration and the looking upward to heaven; obviously Luke contributed it himself when he took the story of the martyrdom into his narrative.[59]

2. The most striking feature of this speech is the irrelevance of its main section. If there are long sections of it that are simply reproductions of the history of Israel, the explanation for this is certainly not to be found in the occasion of the speech, but rather in the speaker himself. Stephen, as he is described in the prelude to the martyrdom, belongs to the world of Hellenistic Judaism. Thus, as a Christian preacher, he becomes involved in an altercation with others of this same group. Blessing, power, wisdom, and the ability to work miracles are ascribed to him. When a speech by this man is recorded, it is because the author intends to make it clear what is involved when such a personality aligns himself with the Christian cause. In this case, a Christian is able to speak in the style characteristic of the synagogue, giving a recital of facts, and can in a unique way challenge the spirit of the synagogue.

It is, of course, the spirit of the Hellenistic synagogue, just as Stephen's opponents are Hellenistic Jews (6:9). It is in accordance with this that quotations from the Bible are taken from the Greek Bible. There cannot and need not be any question of an Aramaic original of the speech, but we may well ask whether this recital of facts was composed by Luke. As in the case of the missionary speeches, so here also we should not wish to exclude the possibility of dependence upon an older text, at least for that section which consists solely of a recital of facts: this would be the best explanation of its impartial tone. The polemic passages may be ascribed to Luke, who would of course have worked over the whole.[60]

Thus in Stephen's speech, as in the missionary speeches, the didactic element prevails; but the other tradition, that of historical writing, is also to some extent a determining factor here, for the content of the speech paves the way for the separating of the Christian from the Jewish community. It is not a typical speech by a martyr, for neither the danger nor the gain in martyrdom is discussed. It needs to be appreciated, not within the setting of the martyrdom but of the book as a whole. It inaugurates that section of Acts (6–12) that portrays the progress of the gospel to the Gentile world. It shows how far, inwardly, the speaker is from Judaism, but does so by means of devices which are themselves borrowed from Judaism. That too is typical of the conflict between Christianity and Judaism that is introduced by this speech. It is not only Paul who has taken from the arsenal of Hellenistic Judaism the weapons that he directs against Judaism. The author of Acts does the same thing, and so introduces the conflict between Christianity and Judaism by means of Stephen's speech in a characteristic manner appropriate to the circumstances.

We can understand also, in the light of this kind of repetition of similar material, how it is that Paul's words to the inhabitants of Lystra (Acts 14:15-17) have already provided a unique prelude to his Areopagus speech. That God has revealed himself by sending the rains and the seasons, by giving man food and gladness, is introduced in the chief sentence of this little "sermon" as proof of God's existence. The Areopagus speech proceeds along similar lines and introduces these things in the same way as the speech in Lystra, by means of an affirmation of God's nature that is reminiscent of the Old Testament.

Finally, the Jewish-Christian idea of the resurrection is to be counted among the ideas that Luke wishes to impress upon his readers by use of repetition. Three times it receives emphasis, at a vital point, as the core of a Christian sermon (23:6; 24:15, 21; 26:6-8). In particular, the scene in the Sanhedrin (22:30—23:10) culminates in Paul's assertion that it is because of his hope of the resurrection that he stands before the court (23:6). This account suffers from several improbabilities: for instance, the chief captain hands over again to the Jews the man who is in protective custody; Paul, instead of speaking of the accusation against his own person, makes belief in the resurrection the central point in this discussion; the Pharisees take up this theme and declare Paul innocent: all this is very dubious. But Luke suggests no other motivation for the scene; obviously he simply wishes to emphasize the fact that the Pharisees had to make what was really a conditional acknowledgement of Christianity, with its belief in the resurrection.

And this is the ultimate object of the speech made by Paul before the procurator Felix in reply to the orator Tertullus (Acts 24:10-21; compare especially vv. 15 and 21), a speech which is much better adapted to the situation than that in chap. 22. It has here been elicited by the speech of Tertullus (24:2-8), already mentioned on p. 57, and which we shall characterize briefly. The matter with which it deals, the alleged desecration of the temple by Paul, is at least mentioned here, but without adequate treatment from the legal, moral, or religious points of view (24:6-8; on the subject of the text compare p. 178, n. 32). There is a somewhat firmer tone in the general description of the accused:

he is regarded as a "dangerous character" (*loimos*) who arouses unrest every-where among the Jews and is a ringleader of the sect of the "Nazarenes." But as regards extent and style by far the greatest weight in the speech is given to the introductory *captatio benevolentiae*, which speaks of the peace and improve-ments the Jews owe to the providence (*pronoia*) of the governor. The intention is not, however, to contrast the flattery of the Jews[61] with the apostle's reason-able manner, for Paul also begins, in 24:10, with a *captatio benevolentiae*, although the sentiment is more moderate. The orator's words are simply intended to place Paul's hearing in its proper setting, which is described in a remarkably clear style. Latin or Greek parallels taken from official language[62] can be found for each of the orator's courtly phrases in vv. 2 and 3, which are of no importance as far as the subject-matter is concerned. If Luke's aims had been to show the art, and thus the dangerous nature of the oratory of Paul's opponents, or if an historical recollection of the orator and his ability were being given here, this art would have been best demonstrated in the presenta-tion of the dispute itself. It is not in the subject of the dispute, however, but in the introduction (which, in itself, is unimportant) that we find this deliberate stylization. This leads us to conclude that the author was concerned more here with giving a literary presentation than with portraying history. He wishes to describe the setting of the action with the same accuracy, and as impressively, as he has already portrayed the setting in which the Areopagus speech was made. Thus a "masterpiece of . . . well-chosen rhetorical miniature-drawing" has been produced.[63] In this setting the characterization of Paul in Tertullus's speech becomes all the more impressive, and also what Paul him-self now has to say, for his speech leads on from the short *captatio benevolen-tiae* to an assertion of his innocence and his own self-characterization. Here again, however, one thing is striking: the principal subject of the speech is not the alleged desecration of the temple (this receives but a brief mention in v. 13) but the apostle's general activities (24:12, 14-17). It is exactly the same type of general assurance of innocence as when Paul summarizes once more before the procurator Festus (25:8): "Neither against the law of the Jews, nor against the temple, nor against Caesar have I offended at all." Here, too, repe-tition shows what Luke considers important, and, because of the use he is making of this device of repetition, resurrection is mentioned twice now in this context. Paul shares his belief in resurrection with his accusers (24:15), and he has already professed this belief before them in the Sanhedrin (24:21).

One small detail will show, perhaps, that this speech also, despite its prox-imity to the situation, means more to readers of Acts than to the hearers in Caesarea: the collection of money which Paul had arranged for the assistance of poor Christians in Jerusalem, and which we know of from his epistles, is referred to here, but nowhere else in Acts. It seems that the reader is to hear about it once, at any rate. The reference to this would have meant more to the Jews if it had come in the speech to the people in chap. 22, but "historical" considerations of this kind seem not to have mattered greatly to Luke. Even the way in which he twice emphasizes the resurrection is not in the interests of historical narrative but belongs to some extent to apologetic preaching. The reader is intended to know what agreement there is on this particular subject and what inferences are to be drawn from this in connection with the dispute between Christians and Jews.

The same thing is true of the last of the speeches made by Paul as a prisoner in Caesarea, the one before Festus and Herod Agrippa. It has as its main theme the description of Paul's youth as a Jew and his conversion to the Christian faith. But the whole speech is drawn up in such a way as to show Christianity as the natural outcome of Judaism, and the account of Paul's persecution of the Christians (given in far greater detail than in chap. 22) served this end. He is portrayed as a member of the[64] "strictest party of our religion" (26:5); there is a similar emphasis upon his corrections as a Jew and upon his belief in the resurrection: "For this hope I am accused by Jews, O king!" (26:7). The scene of his conversion is compressed, so that the command to evangelize the Gentiles is actually given here in the setting of the heavenly vision; his fulfillment of it thus becomes an act of obedience that even the Jew would have to acknowledge. The end of the scene is to be understood in the same way: the Jewish king confesses, though perhaps only to show that he appreciates what Paul has said, rather than in complete earnest, that next Paul will convert even him. When Agrippa says this, Paul has just, as a final appeal, referred to the way in which his doctrine is supported by the scriptures and has shown how teaching concerning the Suffering Servant and his resurrection, and concerning salvation for both Jew and Gentile, is not inconsistent with Moses and the prophets.

This speech also, of course, is intended to mean more to the readers than to the Jewish king. This fact emerges in small points: for instance, when the Christians are called saints (26:10); readers would expect this Christian usage, whereas Agrippa would not. When, according to this speech, the voice from heaven says not only: "Saul, Saul, why do you persecute me?" but adds the well-known saying from Euripides: "It hurts you to kick against the goads," this is a comment, a cultural addition,[65] which is not actually out of place in a speech made before a distinguished audience, but yet is intended more for educated readers than for the king and procurator. Finally, we should stress the renewed, third, and particularly striking emphasis upon the resurrection, upon believers (26:6-8) and upon the Christ (26:23). This emphasis is given in order to convince readers that they can have a clear conscience as far as

Judaism is concerned, a point which Luke obviously held to be of special, theological importance.

The Acts of the Apostles was written at a time when it was abundantly clear to all that Christianity was moving away from Judaism. The whole book of Acts furnishes apposite evidence in support of the contention that the carrying of the gospel to the Gentiles did not depend upon an idea of Paul's or of any other man but upon the dispensation of God. It was God who led Philip to the Ethiopian eunuch's chariot, who brought Peter and Cornelius together, who chose Paul, the apostle to the Gentiles; it is the fault of the Jews themselves if they fail to find salvation. For this reason their sin is pointed out to them three times, in Antioch, in Corinth, and in Rome (compare p. 57). Their sin becomes all the greater since the Christian message represents the fulfillment of Jewish hopes—a point upon which the greatest stress is laid in the final chapters of the book (23, 24, and 26) and which is made plain by belief in the resurrection. Behind this proof is the conviction that it is the same God whom the Jews desire, and ought to serve, whom the Christians now proclaim; that very conviction, also, which separates the Church from heretical gnosis, namely that the God of the Old Testament has revealed himself in Jesus Christ.

It has again and again been remarked how the figure of Paul as revealed in Acts gives little indication either of that breach with Judaism which comes out in his epistles, or of his vehemence, or of the radical nature of his understanding. This led Ferdinand Christian Baur and his Tübingen School in the middle of the nineteenth century to conclude that there was a conciliatory tendency in Acts, a compromise Paulinism, which preserved an Hegelian synthesis between Judaism and true Paulinism. This conciliatory tendency, they declared, forced the real historical struggles of the Apostolic Age into the background. But Luke is more interested in theology than in the politics of the Church. To him it is more important that the way from Jerusalem to Rome should be represented as the way pointed out by God, that Christianity should be portrayed as the completion of Judaism, and Paul as the messenger of Christ who, from his youth up, was developing under the special providence of God. Thus in Acts Paul becomes the bearer and expounder of a theology that grows directly out of the Judaism of the Dispersion. By this theology (and not from any deliberate policy of compromise) is explained the conciliatory attitude in Acts which is to some extent silent about the great contrasts in the Apostolic Age and which to some extent bridges them. The last words spoken by Paul in public resemble a proclamation: whoever believes in the prophets must believe in Christ also. The historical Paul had seen the tragedy of his people in the fact that, in their efforts to serve God, they failed to find salvation; the Paul of Acts shows that true service of God leads on to Christ.

THE SPEECHES IN CONTEXT

It has been shown in these pages that most of the longer speeches in Acts are to be understood less from the historical situation than from the context of the book as a whole, in which their function becomes evident; for the book has a theme and the speeches play their part in developing it. The words of the Risen One to the disciples (Acts 1:4-5, 7-8) are also to be reckoned among the speeches but, as they are really only two sentences separated by a question,[66] they are not included in the total given on p. 57. This speech ends with the words: "Ye shall be my witness both in Jerusalem, and in all Judaea and Samaria, and unto the uttermost parts of the earth." After considering the other speeches it becomes clear that this sentence also, although it is ascribed to the Risen One, has a literary significance,[67] for it outlines the plan of the book: Jerusalem (chaps. 1–5); Judea and Samaria (6–12); and expansion of the mission to become the universal Church, delineated by means of Paul's journeys as far as Rome (13–28).

I shall disregard the few speeches which remain for, as far as I can see, their texts do not reveal any particular literary intention; they simply contain words which have to be spoken in order to introduce an event. In this way Peter introduces the co-optation to the band of the apostles (1:16-22) and Festus opens Paul's trial (25:24-27). Or it may be that certain words are necessary in the course of an event, as, for example, when Peter speaks in the Sanhedrin after healing of the lame man (4:8-12, 19-20), when Paul speaks on the ship (27:21-26), or Demetrius and the town clerk of Ephesus at the beginning and end of the disturbances (19:25-27, 35-40).

We ought, however, once more to summarize the relationship of the speeches in Acts to those in ancient historiography.

There is here one striking parallel: at vital points in the history of the community Luke has inserted speeches which do not necessarily fit the occasion but which have an obvious function in the book as a whole: they help to make intelligible the rejection of Christianity by the Jews (Stephen), and to defend the rightness of the mission to the Gentiles (Paul's speech before the people); they show how God himself ordains the conversion of the Gentiles (Cornelius); how the Christian sermon takes up Greek ideas (Areopagus speech); they indicate both the past and the future destiny of the community (Miletus). All these speeches, which appear at significant points and bear the impress of the author's mind, he has inserted into his narrative, or rather into the narrative provided by his sources.[68] In doing so he has followed the tradition of ancient historical writing.

Once we have become convinced that the relevance of each of these speeches arises only partly from the specific situation, we are in a position to understand what has long been observed as a feature peculiar to these speeches. This is that they do not agree in all respects with the narrative part of the text, but supplement the narrative, sometimes to some extent correcting it. The Areopagus speech contains a well-known example of this sort of inconsistency.[69] According to the narrative, Paul is perturbed to find the city has so many idols, but when later he speaks to the Athenians, who are so well known for their piety, he praises them, in the introductory *captatio benevolentiae,* on account of this pious attitude toward the gods. This cannot mean either that Paul has suddenly changed his mind, or that he is speaking hypocritically; certainly not the latter, for Luke would never have ascribed such a thing to his apostle. The explanation lies rather in the comparative independence of the speech; it is for this reason that it is opportune to express praise although perturbation had so recently preceded it. This sort of inconsistency frequently appears in Acts. For example, the reader learns from the speech in Miletus that already, in other cities, affliction in the future had been prophesied to Paul, and also that he had been three years in Ephesus and had earned his bread by the work of his hands; none of this has been mentioned previously. One of the most remarkable instances of the completion of an account by means of a speech concerns the matter of the collection made by Paul. This is not mentioned at all in the place appropriate to it, nor in 20:4, where the representatives of the communities who accompany Paul, and who presumably owe their function entirely to the collection, are mentioned; it is in the speech before Felix that Paul speaks of gifts for his people (24:17); there the reference to the collection is intended as evidence of the apostle's loyalty. Nor was Paul's vision in the temple discussed in the story of his conversion in chap. 9, but later he tells the people about it.

After this has been accepted, the oft-discussed contradictions between the three portrayals of the conversion in Acts 9, 22, 26 cannot possibly be taken as isolated features and made the point of departure for the argument that there were different sources. As we have already shown, they are in accordance with the special development of the two speeches, Acts 22 and 26.[70] There are, in historical literature also, parallels for such incongruities,[71] and they indicate the measure of independence which each speech possesses; the speeches are not, in fact, bound to the historical events in the setting in which we find them; they exist in their own right and can therefore speak of things other than those dealt with in the accompanying narrative. Thus, in the Areopagus speech, the style used in the opening of a speech evidently requires that the assiduous idol-worship of the Athenians shall be judged as piety, although, in fact, Paul is shocked by it. Similarly, the command to evangelize is connected with the voice from heaven in 26:17; whereas the vision in the temple in 22:17-21, which was perhaps traditional, is also elaborated so as to include a missionary charge.

Both are determined by the aim and the situation of the speech, and are to be understood as a conscious divergence from the original report in Acts 9. Accordingly, Ananias appears in one speech, but not in the other. The accounts of Paul's youth and of his part in the persecution of the Christians are, in 22:4-5 and 26:9-11, interwoven into the speeches by the author in order to supplement his report in Acts 9, which is less informative on these subjects. The same may be said of the afflictions that, he says in the departing speech (20:23), are prophesied for him "in every city," and also of the belated note about the collections (24:17). In this way the author consciously fills gaps, which he had previously left for reasons connected with style or with the source.

Beside those speeches, whose character can be understood by comparison with ancient historiography, there are others whose meaning lies in the repetition and emphasis of certain themes. By these I mean the missionary speeches of Paul and Peter. (As far as content is concerned we may also include Stephen's speech here, the meaning of which, in the context of the whole book, places it, of course, in the first group.) Here the analogy of historical writing fails, and the kerygmatic aim of the book, i.e., not only to narrate, but also to proclaim, comes into evidence.

Nevertheless we can observe the use of certain artistic devices in both groups, particularly that of sudden interruption. Another technical device, widely used in "great" literature, is found only in one missionary speech, which is in one of the second group (Acts 2:40).[72] I refer to the indication that the speaker said more than has actually been imparted. This is a literary device that gives the author freedom to record those words of the speaker which fit in with the author's plan, but at the same time to indicate to the reader that these words do not exhaust what the speaker said.

Luke's neglect of the differences of language[73] is proof of this independence of historical considerations, an independence, however, which corresponds entirely with the customs of ancient writes. The fact that language differences were not felt to be a problem requiring specific mention reflects the increasing cultural unification which was brought about by the spread of the *koiné*. In Acts we might expect that the author who allows James in Acts 15:14 to use the Aramaic form of *Symeōn* instead of *Simeōn*, when recording elsewhere the speeches of Aramaic-speaking people (e.g. of Peter and of James in the Apostolic Council), would there also have added corresponding local color; but that is not the case; in fact, in this speech, James quotes a text from the Bible in the Septuagint form, which is essentially different from the original. In the Hebraic text of Amos 9:12 we read of the remnant of Edom, in the LXX (as the result of the misreading: *'adam* for *'edom*) of the remnant of men; in Acts 15:17 James says "the rest of people" (*kataloipoi tōn anthrōpōn*), as if he were a Jew of the Dispersion, who knew only the Greek Bible. A characteristic example of the disregard of linguistic differences is found in the missionary speeches in chaps. 3 and 13; they show the same style, although Peter had to speak Aramaic in Jerusalem, and Paul Greek in the synagogue in Asia Minor. The speech before the people, in Acts 22, which the author tells us expressly was made in the Aramaic language, also shows no trace of Aramaic color, but where the voice from heaven at the conversion is described as Aramaic (26:14), and only there, there is added to the question: "Why do you persecute me?" the words "It hurts you to kick against the goads" (*sklēron soi pros kentra laktizein*)— which is a quotation from Greek literature (see pp. 84–86).

One reason for the disregard of the language question by ancient historians is perhaps to be sought in that striving after unity of style, which determines the form the author gives to the speeches. Linguistic nuances could well have been renounced for a reason such as this, but such considerations cannot possibly be decisive in the case of Acts, for Luke's concern is not preeminently for unity of style. Admittedly the speeches do, on the whole, reflect his style as regards vocabulary and phraseology; and it is this very fact that must constantly lead us to doubt their authenticity. In the case of the speeches to the Jews, however, we find that they contain appreciably more quotations from the Septuagint than the others and more closely resemble its style. Again, there is a special stylistic quality in the narrative about Athens, and there should be no need to explain why the speeches before Tertullus and Agrippa show a somewhat more "polished" type of Greek.

In the interests of unity of style many ancient historians prefer indirect speech; this seems gradually to have become regarded as superior to direct speech. Trogus Pompeius rejected direct speech altogether and reproached Livy and Sallust for having used it.[74] Caesar used direct speech in his *Bellum Civile* in at least a quarter of the speeches; in *De Bello Gallico* he restricted its use to scarcely one-seventh of all speeches.[75] Appian leans toward a mixture of indirect speech (*oratio oblique*) and direct speech (*oratio recta*).[76] In view of this it is highly significant for the literary character of the Acts of the Apostles that direct speech only is seen in the real "speeches" and that a mixed style is used in only a few instances that should not really be counted as "speeches" at all.[77] It is significant because we can see from this that Luke is evidently not conscious of that feeling of distance between the narrator and the event which results in indirect speech, and which has the further result of preventing the author from passing on the words of the persons engaged in the action to the reader direct, as if they were spoken to him as he reads, but allows him only to take them into account, and so, in minor measure, to pass them on to the reader as part of the story.

There is nothing of this in Acts. The cause does not lie, however, in the author's pleasure, shall we say, in direct description, but in the preaching task which he has set himself. What indirect speech is intended to avoid is exactly what Luke wishes to achieve. The speaker's words are to reach the reader as directly as if they had been spoken contemporaneously, for the content of the speeches in the Christian message itself, the defense of the community against Judaism and against the danger of gnosticism in the future, the presentation of individual Christian ideas—of God or of the resurrection of the dead—and finally, the justification of the conversion of the Gentiles on the grounds that it was a task ordained by God. If I have stressed frequently the fact that in many instances the speeches by-pass the situation of the time, this is because such license has in the first place been suggested to the author by the example of the great historians; but it is from his sermonizing attitude that we understand why and how he availed himself of this liberty. What in fact do the accusation against Stephen and the charge against Paul mean to the reader of Acts, one or two generations after these events? They are unimportant in comparison with the ideas that are constantly emphasized by the speakers. They are not, however, intended to be conveyed to the reader simply as part of the story, but as a living proclamation and as an exhortation.

It is here that we can see between these speeches and those of ancient historiography a difference that is characteristic of the whole book. The writer knows the art of enhancing the significance to the moment by the insertion of a speech but, while it is certain that the author has adopted this art from the ancient historians and that he has availed himself of their independence of historical reality, it is equally certain that his fundamental assessment of the meaning of these speeches is different. He writes a history that he believes has happened according to the will of God. He never says this outright, but shows it, for example, by deriving the evangelizing of Syria from the persecution of Stephen, by making Paul travel to Greece at God's command and by showing, finally, how imprisonment procures for the apostle the journey to Rome which has been planned. Luke does not venture to make a personal judgment; he portrays the works of God and exercises no criticism of events, nor does he offer alternative opinions, from which to choose, as do the historians.[78] For him, such methods would not have seemed in accord with a right attitude to the story. His praise of Paul is contained in the speech at Miletus; his approval of the mission to the Gentiles in the composition of the story of Cornelius. He does not need to deal in detail with conflicts within the community, for such descriptions would have no kerygmatic value for the reader. Accordingly, in the deliberation of the apostles in chap. 15, he records only the two speeches, those by Peter and James, which finally substantiate one another, but gives no record of the opposing voices. He mentions the dispute about the provisions for the widows in chap. 6 not in order to record for posterity a dispute among the community at Jerusalem, but in order to use the choice of the seven as an introduction to the martyrdom of Stephen.

We must now turn once more to a peculiarity of the speeches in Acts which makes them essentially different from the majority of those written by historians, namely the fact that the Christian speeches are much *shorter*. Admittedly we have seen that speeches consisting of only a few sentences are not without analogy in the works of the historians, but even the longer speeches in Acts are still much shorter than their secular counterparts, for they lack at least two elements very prominent in the speeches of the historians: the deliberative element, the debating of the "for" and "against," and the epideictic element, the rhetorical elaboration of the ideas concerned. These considerations of "for" or "against" do not belong in a book that is aimed at showing ultimately how the development described goes back to the counsel, not of men, but of God. The author avoids rhetorical elaboration, moreover, because it would demonstrate his own ability rather than what he has to affirm and proclaim. Thus a comparison of the external appearance of the speeches in Acts with those of the historians helps us to recognize the depth of the essential difference between them.

In recognizing this we must, however, be clear that the speeches in Acts do bear a certain relation to those of the historians. It is only when this is established that the interpretation of the speeches in Acts ceases to be prejudiced by the question of authenticity, which has always been given such importance. On the other hand, there is the leading consideration that the author, like the historians, had no intention whatsoever of reproducing the exact text of the speech as it was actually made, even if he was to some extent familiar with it.

At first it seems that Luke, like the historians, composes speeches for crucial situations and in order to illuminate important moments, but we find that, in the course of the speech, he often pays no further regard to the situation and the actual problems of the moment. Any doubt regarding Luke's literary contribution will be dispelled by consideration of his description of the so-called "Apostolic Council" in Acts 15. The speeches say nothing of the historically decisive report of Paul and Barnabas, but refer only to the story of Cornelius, which Luke had dealt with in detail and had elevated to the position of a prototype.

Finally, we have seen that Luke aims at no ideal of unity of style, but displays a variety of styles in his speeches. This variety, which is far removed from the laws of style that govern historical writing, is due mainly to a desire to be appropriate to the occasion, sometimes as a concession to traditions that have been adopted, but never to any wish to characterize individual persons. The use of speeches in order to portray character, which to us today appears such an obvious function, no doubt appeared to the author as too secular a consideration in comparison with his aim of proclaiming the gospel. He intends that the apostles are to appear as living characters by virtue of the cause they stand for, not through their own personal qualities.

If we now contemplate the many similarities, and also the many divergences between the Acts and the other ancient historiography, we shall be somewhat embarrassed in our attempt to explain historically the fact that we have established. On the one hand Luke follows the tradition of historical writing so closely that we must assume that he has read the historians. On the other hand the speeches in Acts are, as we have shown, both in detail and taken as a whole, so different from the speeches we know in the work of ancient historians that we cannot name any historian whom we might say Luke had taken as his model.[79] He has obviously followed the historians in introducing speeches at all, in the evaluation of these for the whole presentation, and in their relative independence of the actual event. Certainly he is indebted to them also for many artistic devices, and even uses some of them for which we can find no parallel in the writings of the historians—such as the intentional interruption of the speaker by the listeners, which is mentioned on pp. 63–64. But even if we concede that historical writings known to us provided models for Luke, there is still enough that is really original left in the elements of the speeches as characterized in pp. 75–81 to permit us to speak of a considerable contribution by Luke himself. He has found a new method of presenting material which has not yet been dealt with in literature; in doing so he has made new use of the traditional art of composing speeches, an art which had already been employed in many different ways. He used this device not only to illuminate the situation but also to make clear the ways of God; he did not desire to testify to the capabilities either of the speaker or of the author, but to proclaim the gospel.

Thus by comparing the speeches in Acts with those of the historians we observe an important ambiguity. Luke indeed uses the historical technique and does set himself certain historical aims; this becomes clear enough when we give up trying to measure him by our ideas of historiography and historians. In the last analysis, however, he is not an historian but a preacher; we must not allow our attempts to prove the authenticity of the speeches to cloud our perception of their kerygmatic nature.

All the preaching, however, whether it serves the interests of history or of proclamation, has Luke as its author. Even those speeches by Paul, which Luke himself heard, could not possibly have been reproduced by Luke word for word; to do this was, as we have seen, no part of the author's task. If he did employ individual "authentic" motifs,[80] this would have happened only because he was able to use them for the task he had set for the speech concerned in the whole of the book. The author did not feel himself obliged to be loyal to what he had heard or to the text that had come into his possession. There can be no question of deceiving the readers, for even the reader who asked "historical" questions did not expect an authentic reproduction of the speeches. The very admission that the author worked historically prevents the speeches in Acts from being used as sources for the ideas and words of the speakers themselves.

In the speeches made by Paul in his own defense we have a good source of information as to the extent of the author's knowledge of the apostle's life, youth, and conversion, but they must take second place to Paul's own testimony in the epistles. The missionary speeches, with their repetitions, have their value as sources, because they are undoubtedly derived from sermons remembered by the community from a long time before, but we cannot draw any conclusions from them about the particular way in which Peter, Paul, and Stephen preached.

Here also we must not allow ourselves to be led astray by the analogy of Luke's Gospel. Luke has not ascribed one single speech to Jesus. The shorter counterpart to the Sermon on the Mount in Matthew, which he gives in 6:20-49, is a composition formed from traditional sayings, as is the Sermon on the Mount itself; the same is true of all other speeches in the Gospel, even those included only by Luke; it is always sayings which are recorded, never a speech of the kind we have in Acts. Only in the sermon in the synagogue at Nazareth can we recognize something created by Luke (4:17-27). Even here, however, a detailed analysis shows that at the heart of the sermon stands the word about the despised prophet that is traditional. The end duplicates the saying about the selection made by God; this doublet is self-contained and does not fit into the context, and evidently represents a fragment of tradition. Thus the one thing that Luke could have contributed is the words from Isaiah, which are set at the beginning of the sermon. So it would not be a case of the creating of a speech by the evangelist, but only of collating traditional material by means of a quotation from the Bible; that is to say, here too Luke would be simply elaborating.

The difference from the method followed in Acts is clear. When he wrote the Gospel, Luke had to fit in with a tradition that already had its own stamp upon it, so that he had not the same literary freedom as when he composed the Acts of the Apostles. On the other hand, unless we are completely deceived, he was the first to employ the material available for the Acts of the Apostles, and so was able to develop the book according to the point of view of an historian writing literature. How he did that is shown by a comparison with ancient historiography; it shows also, however, that Luke did not completely become an historian; for though it is certain that, as the author of Acts, he adopted different methods from those he used as author of the Gospel, in the second work, though in a higher sense, he remained an evangelist.

LITERARY ALLUSIONS IN THE SPEECHES

When the question of Luke's education is raised, we must consider whether certain passages in Acts suggest that the author introduced allusions to works of "great" literature in order to strengthen the literary character of his book. There are three passages to consider in this connection.

Josephus

The famous speech by Gamaliel (Acts 5:35-39) includes two historical incidents, and thus links up with a custom prevailing in the speeches of the historians.[81] Here, two revolutionary movements are mentioned, the uprisings of Theudas and of Judas of Galilee. Their example is intended to show that in some circumstances, when the leader is dead, the adherents cease to be dangerous. Gamaliel cannot have spoken in this way for, at the time of this speech, Theudas had not yet appeared on the scene. Besides, the historical sequence is reversed here; it was not Theudas who appeared first, and then (*meta touton*) Judas, but first Judas "at the time of the census" and then Theudas under the procurator Cuspius Fadus, who assumed office in 44 C.E. This is reported in Josephus, *Ant.* 20.5.1-2 (§§97-98).

In one of the following sections (§102), the name of Judas of Galilee is also mentioned, and, according to an opinion that is widely held, this circumstance led to Luke's placing of Judas after Theudas in Gamaliel's speech. It is said that he glanced very quickly through the text of Josephus and thus confused the chronological order. This is extremely improbable for the following reasons: (1) It is not Judas himself who was concerned, but his sons, who were put to death by Fadus's successor, Tiberius Alexander. The supposed reading of Josephus by Luke must therefore have been hasty in the extreme. (2) The name Judas is not mentioned in connection with the episode regarding Theudas in such a way that a source of Josephus could be responsible for the chronological error. On the contrary, the section about Theudas (§§97-98) is followed by a sentence (in §99) that concludes the reign of Fadus (in §100) with the introduction of the new procurator Tiberius Alexander and with information about his father. Then the famine in Judea and the help given by Queen Helena of Adiabene are mentioned as the first event under the rule of Tiberius Alexander (in §101). And it is not until §102, as the second event under the new governor, that the crucifixion of the sons of Judas of Galilee—Judas and Simon—is recorded.[82]

Whatever connection there may have been between Luke and Josephus, we cannot conclude from Acts 5:36-37 that the Acts of the Apostles was dependent upon the *Antiquities*. On the contrary, Luke has obviously recorded these incidents as freely as he composed the whole speech; we can ascribe to the author both the desire of the educated man to employ such elements, and also the error of one who was not fully informed on the subject of the insurrection of Theudas and on the period when Theudas lived.

Aratus

The Areopagus speech contains the well-known quotation from Aratus's *Phaenomena*: "for we too are his offspring" (*tou gar kai genos esmen*; Acts 17:28). I can be brief on this point, since I previously dealt with this speech,[83] and shall therefore simply make the following observations. (1) The words are introduced as a quotation from the poets. The plural form of the quotation— "as even some of your own poets have said" (*hōs kai tines tōn kath' humas poiētōn eirēkasin*)—is in accordance with literary convention. (2) Luke seems to know the whole poem by Aratus and not only this verse. This is suggested by the fact that both the speech and the poem contain some of the same ideas, and is confirmed by the way in which the quotation is introduced. (3) In view of Pohlenz's findings,[84] I should prefer no longer to take the preceding words: "In him we live, move and have our being" as a direct quotation from the poets. It should not be overlooked that the idea expressed in these words, and in support of which is added the quotation from Aratus, is one that would be familiar to people of culture.

In 1 Cor 15:33, the historical Paul uses a verse from Menander; but he has used it like a popular saying, without showing that he knew its origin.[85] Here, on the other hand, in the Areopagus speech, it is clear from the way the quotation is introduced and used that an educated man is making allusion to contemporary literature.

Euripides

The third passage which furnishes evidence of the author's education is Acts 26:14, where the saying "It hurts you to kick against the goads" (*sklēron soi pros kentra laktizoimi*) is quoted. This is introduced simply because the author was an educated man, for only a familiarity with such phrases can explain the use of the saying here, where it is not really appropriate. The exalted, heavenly Christ speaks to Saul, or Paul, as is expressly observed here, in the Aramaic language. A voice from heaven does not speak in proverbs, and, if the voice speaks in Aramaic, it will certainly not be to utter Greek proverbs. The proverb is not found in a Semitic form; nor is it recorded in the other accounts of the same voice from heaven in Acts 9:4 and 22:7.[86] It must therefore have been added by the author, in accordance with the style of what is the most literary of the three accounts of the conversion. It is intended to show that Paul is among those who have struggled against God in vain. It is also intended to provide for the educated reader the pleasure he will find in this kind of literary embellishment.

We are concerned then with a saying, perhaps a quotation from the poets. Evidence of this was provided some time ago.[87] Examples of the saying are found both in the singular, as in Pindar's *Pythian Odes* 2.94ff. (173ff.), *poti kentron de toi laktizemen telethei olisthēros oimos*; and in the plural, compare Aeschylus, *Agamemnon* (1624), *pros kentra mē laktize, mē ptaisas mogēs*; and especially the *Bacchae* of Euripides (794-95).

> Better to slay victims to him than kick
> against the goads—a mortal raging against God.

> *thyoim' an autō mallon ē thymoumenos*
> *pros kentra laktizoimi thnētos ōn theōi.*

Reference must also be made here to quotations from Euripides, *Iphigenia in Tauris* 1396: *pros kyma laktizontes* ("kicked against the waves");[88] and Euripides, *frag.* 604 (Nauck), *pros kentra mē laktize tois kratousi sou.* Thus it is clear that Luke has ascribed a Greek saying to the voice from heaven. He wished to show by this that in his persecution of the Christians Paul was dashing himself against the driver's goad; it was a useless effort; ultimately he would have to submit. Luke, however, did not wish to say that it was because Paul had been already wounded by the goad, that he was now aggravating the wound by thus dashing himself against it; that is to say (if we may dispense with the imagery), that his persecution of the Christians was simply the reaction from his own encounter with the Christian faith. It might have been possible to have advocated this interpretation had the image been newly coined by Luke; but since it is obviously a saying which was frequently used to describe vain struggling (often against God or fate), its use in Acts cannot have any greater significance than it generally had. The question arises, however, as to whether Luke took the words perhaps not from everyday usage but directly from the *Bacchae* of Euripides. Two reasons have been suggested in favor of this possibility: firstly, reference has been made to the plural "goads" (*kentra*), which is not appropriate in this context, its appearance in Acts being explained only if the quotation has been taken from some poetic work, such as the *Bacchae,* where the plural would be inevitable on account of the verse. The plural is found not only in the *Bacchae,* however, but also elsewhere in poetry.[89] Moreover, it is found not only in this phrase, "kick against the goads" (*pros kentra laktizein*), but in other contexts as well.[90] There is thus the possibility that, because of its being employed in verse, the plural—especially when used in conjunction with "kick" (*laktizein*)—has become stable. There is the other possibility that the existence of goads with two points may have given rise to the frequent use of the plural.[91] In any case, the use of the plural "goads" (*kentra*) in Acts furnishes no absolutely certain conclusion that the saying was borrowed from the *Bacchae*.

Some commentators have claimed evidence elsewhere in Acts that Luke had read the *Bacchae*. They have done this by emphasizing the parallel provided by the disputed words concerning the goad; it is a god, the new god Dionysus, who warns his persecutors not to kick against the goad; it is the newly preached Son of God, Jesus Christ, who warns his persecutors by means of the same image, used with the same meaning. In the *Bacchae*, this persecution of the new god is constantly characterized as a struggle against God, as *theomachein*.[92] Now, *theomachoi* ("fighting against God")—coming from the same, less common, stem—is used by Gamaliel in his speech in Acts 5:39.[93] Here it is not only the word, but also the *ethos* that is to some extent connected. This suggests that Luke himself may possibly have used the *Bacchae*; it cannot, of course, be proved, nor can any of the other connections between the Acts and Euripides which have been supposed to exist.[94]

But whether Luke knew the proverb concerning the goad either as a direct quotation or as an everyday saying, the use he makes of it again shows most clearly where he stands in relation to contemporary culture. He desires in Acts (in quite a different sense from that in the Gospel of Luke) to be an author who has complete freedom of action, who can compose freely (as far as the speeches are concerned), arrange the material, omitting or completing as he wishes, and in the way which literary convention permitted to such an author. Scholars have constantly emphasized his participation in contemporary culture, but without vigorously drawing also the consequences; in particular, it is impossible to understand the intention behind the speeches and their significance within the book of Acts unless they are regarded as compositions of the author.

PART II

PAUL AND PETER IN THE BOOK OF ACTS

6

Paul in the Book of Acts

The literary and historical assessment of Acts in present-day scholarship is so far from unanimous that anyone who wishes to use Acts for purposes of theological study is compelled to lay his own foundations. This includes, first of all, the acquiring of a literary judgment, and it is only when we have understood why the author of Acts tells us so much and yet not more than he does about Paul, and when we have seen what sources and information were at his disposal, and what was his literary intention, that we can decide what parts of the book may safely be considered as historical.

This book, though called "The Acts of the Apostles," does not contain as much about the apostles as we should expect. It tells about Peter, and in a quite shadowy manner about John, and about the preachers Stephen and Philip; over half the book is dedicated to the apostle Paul, yet this by no means turns it into a biography of Paul. A remarkable selection of episodes out of the apostle's life has been portrayed in Acts. He appears in 7:58; 8:1, 3 as an eye-witness at the stoning of Stephen, with whom the "witnesses" left their clothes. It can be shown that Luke is using an older account here, a "martyr-dom" of the first Christian martyr as it was current in the Christian community before the composition of Acts.[1] Even without literary evidence we could assume the existence of such a martyrdom,[2] and that mention might have been made in it of those witnesses who had been particularly concerned in the stoning,[3] but certainly not of a young man at whose feet the witnesses laid their clothes. This assumption is confirmed by observations made from the literary point of view.[4] Thus Luke has inserted three notes, on the presence of Saul, on his agreement with the killing of Stephen, and on his active part in the persecution. The third is significant as the transition to the story of the conversion (9:1-19). Luke has a habit of making his connecting links in this way, even in the Gospel, now much more so in Acts.[5]

This is no proof, however, that his information was not authentic. In fact, Luke seems to have had a good deal of detailed knowledge, since, according to the prologue to the Gospel (1:3), he has "followed all things closely for some time past." Paul's associates would have possessed such knowledge, for Paul spoke freely about the measures he took against the Christians (1 Cor 15:9; Gal 1:13-14)—why not, therefore, of this detail also? And, the scantiness of the reference prevents our assuming finally that the three observations were meant as an edifying legend; in that case they would have been more richly stylized, and, instead of the colorless remark "Saul was consenting to his death," there would have been reported perhaps a cheer or some other expression of feeling from the man who was such a passionate enemy of the Christians. We may therefore assume that Luke inserted these three observations because he knew that Paul was present at the stoning of Stephen.

What Luke tells us concerning Paul's life and work, after this introduction to the apostle, appears, from a preliminary glance, to consist essentially of four complexes of stories, accounts, and speeches. Before making any analysis of courses, and certainly before considering whether the work is historical or not, we must investigate this remarkable juxtaposition of wealth and poverty of information; a duty which is all the more urgent since it is so rarely undertaken by the critics.

Luke first of all tells the story of Paul's conversion and outlines what happened to Paul, the newly converted Christian, in Damascus and in Jerusalem. Finally, he travels to Tarsus and disappears from our sight. A short note (11:25-26, 30; 12:25) tells us that he was fetched from Tarsus to Antioch and on one occasion was also in Jerusalem. The second complex of accounts begins only at 13:1 with the sending forth of Paul and Barnabas from Antioch to preach the gospel. The intervening gap is worthy of note. It may span a decade[6] (and events in these years will not have been without importance),[7] but Luke says nothing about this period. We cannot assume that he had no information about it or that he could not have obtained any. With whatever preaching and evangelizing Paul may have done at that time Luke is apparently not concerned. It seems that only those evangelizing activities were important to him which were directed toward the west and finally led to Rome; he does not wish to describe the spread of the Christian communities but the advance of the gospel into the heart of the Roman Empire.

The progress of the mission in that direction is the theme of the second complex of accounts. The activities that are reported in 13:1-14, 28; 15:36—18:23; 19:1-22; 20:1—21:14 form the central part of the Acts of the Apostles.[8] A certain scheme can be seen in the method of giving the report: after the station has been named, there follows a short account of the initial contacts that were made and the result. In some instances, another story is added, and occasionally a speech as well. The regularity of this pattern is plain, and must be taken into account in any consideration of the question of sources. It is all the more noticeable that the description twice seems to deviate from the rule

(16:6-10 and 20:1-3). The first time Paul wants to turn away from Lycaonia and Pisidia toward the coast of Asia Minor, but he is "forbidden by the Holy Spirit" and proceeds instead through the provinces of Phrygia and Galatia. No cities are mentioned by name, although it is quite possible, even probable, that Paul did preach the gospel there.[9] Then, having arrived at the boundary of Mysia, he wants to go as far as Bithynia, but once more "the Spirit of Jesus suffered them not," and instead he now "passes by" Mysia and goes on to Troas; the expression means that he does not stay to evangelize in Mysia but turns toward Troas as quickly as possible. Such summary references as these remind the reader also of 15:41, but here it is simply a case of a second visit to communities that have already been established. The silence concerning Galatia is striking, however, and "up till now, has still found no completely satisfactory explanation."[10] It may possibly be found in the several mentions of divine guidance, continuing in Troas also, since a vision calls him thence to come to Macedonia without delay. On both the former occasions, Luke gives no indication of the form of the Spirit's intervention. There is nothing to suggest that, on those occasions, also, it took the form of visions. Certain events may perhaps have been understood by the travelers, or by the narrator of the story, as signs of God's leading. From this we can clearly see the one thing that is important to the author here. He wishes to show that it is through the leading of God and not on account of his own decision that Paul has reached Macedonia and Greece, vital stages in the opening up of the way to Rome. Not until the third divine intervention in Troas is it of any importance how the command of God reached him;[11] nor does it matter where, en route in Asia Minor, Paul pursued his missionary activities; God's guidance is alone important.

The second passage in which the narrator of Acts seems to abandon his customary method is 20:1-3. Here we are told that Paul travels from Ephesus to Macedonia (but we are not told into which cities), that he spends three months in Greece (but we are not told where); we are then told of a plot by the Jews against Paul, by reason of which he alters the plan for his journey, but where that happens we are again not told. Are we really to suppose that the author's usual knowledge of the names of the stations has suddenly failed? It is far more probable that he has intentionally neglected to give these names. At that time Paul visited obviously only those cities where he had preached and founded communities some years previously; on an occasion such as this Luke has, in an earlier passage in Acts (15:41—16:5), confined himself to a short summary. In this present passage also, the brevity of the account is explained primarily by the fact that the journey is really in the nature of a pastoral visit to communities that have been established already. And there is an obvious desire on the part of the author to let everything point toward the imprisonment and the journey to Rome. This preoccupation explains what is otherwise inexplicable, namely that, in 20:4, the representatives of the communities are, admittedly, mentioned by name, but without any indication of the reason for their being sent, which, as we must assume from Paul's letters, was certainly the collection. This is first mentioned in 24:17, because there it can serve to defend Paul against the charge of desecrating the temple. Here, on the other hand, other matters are of greater moment: Jerusalem, imprisonment, journey to Rome.[12] It is in order to stress these aspects that the report becomes so sparse here, and for the same reason that it is written at times with special detail, as in 20:16, 22, 25, 38; 21:4-5, 10-13. In the last chapters this second complex points ahead to what is coming next.[13]

The third complex of accounts about Paul consists of an uninterrupted sequence; in 21:15—26:32 the apostle's reception in Jerusalem, his imprisonment, and the successions of hearings which he has to undergo are dealt with; the section closes with the reference to the appeal, which Paul had previously made, to be judged by the emperor in Rome (26:32). In chaps. 27 and 28 his journey to Rome and his reception by the Christians and Jews there are described.

It is strange that the great problem presented by the first of these two sections (21:15—26:32) is so little in evidence in commentaries and critical research. For is there not indeed a real problem in the fact that Luke allows his readers to share the experience of no less than five hearings of Paul, all of which signify nothing more than a great delay in the deciding of Paul's case? And does not the ending of Acts, which has always been felt to be problematic when seen in conjunction with these hearings, become actually mysterious? Why does the author suddenly discontinue his story, after describing these proceedings with such thoroughness? And why, in the scenes in which Paul is being examined, does Luke prelude his account of the trial with such detail, if he is not then going to describe the trial itself (and announce the verdict)?

A survey of the five hearings will reveal what was the writer's guiding interest.

1. Acts 22:30—23:10: The chief captain releases Paul from his imprisonment, commands(!) that the Sanhedrin be summoned, and places Paul before the assembled members. Paul speaks only one sentence: that he is a Pharisee and son (= pupil?) of Pharisees, and that he has been called to account because of his hope of the resurrection of the dead. This seems to be the sum total of his defense. It is followed by disorder in the assembly and further imprisonment.

2. Acts 24:1-23: Before Felix, Paul defends himself against the deputation of the Sanhedrin, saying that he has never instigated a rebellion either in the temple or in the synagogues or anywhere else in the city; he states that he is a pious Jew and advocates the doctrine of double resurrection (both of the just and the unjust); he says he was taken by

surprise at a ceremony of purification in the temple and has declared, before the Sanhedrin, his belief in the resurrection.

3. Acts 24:24-25: He speaks about justice, temperance, and the coming judgment before Felix and Drusilla.
4. Acts 25:6-12: He defends himself once more before Festus against a deputation from Jerusalem, saying that he has committed no offence, either against the law, the temple, or the emperor; he appeals to Caesar.
5. Acts 26:1-32: Before Festus and Herod Agrippa II, Paul defends himself again with the acknowledgment of the promise made to their fathers. The significance of the story of the conversion, here told for the third time, is, first, the fact that Paul's call comes from the same God whom the Jews also honor; secondly, that Paul's message, like that of Moses and the prophets, is of the suffering and resurrection of the Messiah; and thirdly, that the object of the dispute, the resurrection, corresponds to the promise which was given to "the fathers."

Even if Paul had spoken in this way on each of these occasions, the fullness of the description would still have been remarkable, in view of the similarity of the material. Acts 24 and 25 belong to the most "secular" chapters of the New Testament. Neither our knowledge of the faith nor interests of an historical nature would have suffered harm if these chapters had been condensed.

There are, in fact, other considerations that have led to the description of these trial scenes. When the same author reproduces sermons in chaps. 2, 3, 10, and 13 of almost identical construction, and attributes them to different apostles, Peter and Paul, he does so in order to show how Christian preachers should speak in similar circumstances. And when, in the five trial scenes examined here, Paul always says the same thing in his defense, it is because the author wants thereby to commend to the Christians of his day the use of such themes in their own defense. These themes are intended to emphasize the fact that Christians have not rebelled against the emperor, or against the temple, or against the law, but that the essential matter of dispute between them and the Jews is the question of the resurrection. Christians have inherited the best Jewish tradition in their belief that the hope of the fathers, the resurrection at the last day, has already been accomplished in the one case of the Messiah, and that the day of fulfillment has therefore dawned.

So, within the framework of Paul's trial, Luke presents Christian belief with an apologetic purpose, and it is only because of this purpose that his description of the trial is so elaborate.

It is quite different in the case of the two final chapters, which deal with the journey to Rome. Accounts of journeys, given in the usual style, dealing with stations as well as persons, are found only in 27:1-3 (Caesarea to Sidon) and 28:7-16 (Malta to Rome). The major part consists of the description of the voyage and of the shipwreck (27:4-44). Of these forty-one verses, only nineteen are concerned with Paul; most of the remaining verses form one of those literary descriptions of a voyage, which had already become the convention in Greek literature.[14] Into this description a few episodes about Paul have been inserted, such as the sentence, in 27:10, which, according to 27:21, is to be taken as a warning against continuing the voyage, although that thought is not explicitly expressed; some words of consolation, based on a vision of an angel (27:22-26); good advice to the centurion and encouragement to the exhausted crew to eat (27:30-35) and a brief mention of the apostle (27:43).[15] The description of the voyage, which dominates the whole narrative, is used to serve the purpose of praising Paul, the man, his farsightedness, his association with powers of the heavenly world, in this case with an angel, and his fearlessness. These are secular considerations that are not often encountered elsewhere in the Acts of the Apostles. This aspect prevails, also, in the Malta anecdote (28:1-6). The fact that Paul is bitten by a viper is seen by the Gentiles there to be a manifestation of Justice, who does not allow a guilty person to escape; that he survives the adventure seems then to them to announce the epiphany of a god in the form of the apostle. We are reminded of Lystra (Acts 14), where also the apostles are taken for gods. But there is an essential difference: there, the way in which they are mistaken for gods is regarded by the former narrator as culpable and therefore rejected; here, the sentence "they . . . said that he was a god" serves as praise of him and with it the narrative triumphantly ends. This represents not a Christian but a pagan point of view.

7

Paul on the Areopagus

The scene in the book of Acts in which Paul preaches to the people of Athens (17:19-34) denotes, and is intended to denote, a climax of the book. The whole account of the scene testifies to that: the speech on the Areopagus is the only sermon reported by the author that is preached to the Gentiles by the apostle to the Gentiles. Moreover, peculiarities of style and an abundance of motifs that here appear compressed into a few verses give the account a special importance.

Attempts to interpret this speech in the last decades have, it seems to me, suffered somewhat from the fact that those who have sought to explain it have always had either an historical or a literary thesis in mind. On the one hand they have wanted to prove that Paul actually made this speech or that he could have made it. In this case the preference is for using the letters and the environment of the historical Paul as affording the best evidence by which to interpret it; this it the view of Ernst Curtius, Adolf von Harnack, Alfred Wikenhauser, and Eduard Meyer.[1] Or the speech on the Areopagus is explained as being an insertion, the work of an editor of the book of Acts, so that we shall not be surprised to find that it contains contradictions to and passages that are not quite in harmony with other parts of the book. That is how it is regarded by, for example, Norden and Loisy.[2] My investigation proceeds by applying a reverse method; we shall look first at its meaning and then at its historicity and its importance in the book of Acts.[3]

The speech can be isolated in this way, since it is self-evident: a very clear arrangement shows its drift immediately. Groups of motifs, sometimes compressed into one or two sentences, form its content, but the choice of words and the way in which the ideas are expressed are so characteristic that, with the sole exception of v. 26, we are in no doubt as to what ideas are to be associated with it and quoted in explanation.

THE SECOND THEME (ACTS 17:26-27)

In the *introduction* (17:22-23) the Athenians are acknowledged to be religious people, "in every way you are very religious" (*kata panta hōs deisidaimones-teroi*). The altar, with its well-known inscription "to an unknown god" (*agnōstō theōi*), is mentioned as proof of their religious zeal. The real purpose of the speech is to make the unknown god known to them. The exposition, with its three main themes, serves this purpose:

1. God, the Creator and Lord of the world, needs no temples for he does not stand in need of anything (vv. 24-25).
2. God created humans so that they should seek after him (vv. 26-27).
3. The relationship of humans with God—they "are offspring of God"— should exclude all worship of graven images (vv. 28-29).

Then follows the *conclusion:* God now ordains that repentance be preached to humanity because the Day of Judgment lies ahead. Then God will judge the world by a man whom he has raised from the dead (vv. 30-31).

We see that it is a monotheistic sermon, and only the conclusion makes it a Christian one. Only at the end is God's grace mentioned—and then by implication, for the word itself does not appear; the words are simply: "The times of ignorance God overlooked" (*tous chronous tēs agnoias hyperidōn*; v. 30a). Only at the end do we find any reference to judgment, to Jesus and his resurrection. And, according to the most reliable text, the name "Jesus" is not mentioned once. In any case, the specifically Christian content of the speech is presented only in the last two verses. This is certainly strange and needs explanation.

An interpretation of the speech in the Areopagus must begin with the second theme (vv. 26-27). These are the only words in the speech whose importance and bearing on the subject are not immediately obvious. It is also, however, upon the interpretation of these words that the explanation of the speech in some measure depends. Verses 26-27 read as follows:

> And he made from one every nation of people to live on all the face of the earth, having determined allotted periods and the boundaries of their habitation, that they should seek God, in the hope that they might feel after him and find him. Yet he is not far from each one of us.

There is some doubt about the text as it has been handed down. In spite of important variations in the text, two passages may be considered as reliable.[4] In two other phrases ("from one" and "and the boundaries"), the problem of the text can only be solved as we find the explanation of the speech itself.

Paul is speaking of the *uniform descent* of humanity; all people have come from one source. But who are the "all"? "Every nation of people" (*pan ethnos anthrōpōn*) will first of all be taken to apply to "every country of people"; but the translation "the whole human race" is also possible, for in this connection[5] it is quite permissible for the article to be omitted where *pas* means "whole." An example is offered in the words immediately following, for the phrase *epi pantos prosōpou tēs gēs*, which is of ancient origin (later corrected to *pan to pr.*), naturally means "on the whole face of the earth." But of whose existence on the face of the earth is the author speaking? Does he mean the countries or the human race? Is he speaking of the world of countries or of universal humanity? Is he thinking historically in the sense of the Old Testament, in which a family—first Adam's, then, after the great flood, Noah's family—is regarded as the origin of the many and varied types of peoples? Or is he thinking hellenistically in the sense of the philosophy of the Enlightenment, in which humanity was seen in a cosmopolitan way as the sum of the inhabitants of the earth? Underlying the problem of exegesis is, as we see, the decisive question of the principles the speech presupposes.

It has not always been seen that the next difficulty in exegesis is associated with this vital question. God has ordained "allotted periods" and "the boundaries of their habitation" (v. 26). Anyone who previously had the peoples of the world in mind will think of them here also. One will immediately make "the boundaries of their habitation" refer to the boundaries of the different countries (see Deut 32:8). In this context the "periods/times" are more difficult to understand. Some see in them the "arising, blossoming and disappearing of the countries"[6] expressed as "the seasons of their prosperity,"[7] others think of the "times of the Gentiles" in Luke 21:24.[8] But this expression is an eschatological term that describes the time between the destruction of Jerusalem and the dawn of the kingdom of God. None of this is meant here; we can only refer to Daniel 8 and think of the periods of time that are granted by God to the individual empires as they superseded one another. But there is still the question of whether the author—of the book or of the speech—can expect the readers or hearers to understand this philosophy of the history of the "age of the Diadochoi." This presents a considerable difficulty with regard to the historico-political interpretation of the word "periods/times," but also, and this inference has frequently been evaded until now, with regard to the whole second theme of the speech (vv. 26-27). In view of this concentration of motifs in a few verses, it is impossible to interpret individual expressions eclectically, that is, sometimes historically and sometimes philosophically. This entire group of motifs must be understood as a whole, or it will not be understood at all.

The other explanation, which has just been described as the philosophical one, presents no difficulties for interpreting the word *kairoi*. If we consider the whole human race and the fact of its dwelling on the face of the earth, then the appointed "periods/times" are naturally the seasons. That is immediately suggested by Paul's words in Lystra, which, as we shall see, contain a train of thought related to that of the Areopagus speech: God has made himself known by his good deeds, "gave you from heaven rains and fruitful seasons" (14:17). The seasons play a part generally in the evidence of God's existence in the philosophy of the period;[9] thus the mention of them in this context presents no difficulties. But it seems that difficulties may well occur in this (philosophical) interpretation as we seek to explain the "the boundaries of their habitation." It is not a question of the unusual nature of the word "boundary" (*horothesia*), for its meaning is easily understood.[10] It is a case of whether the "boundaries of their habitation" can have meant anything other than the dominions ruled by individual kingdoms.

That is the case, however. In the teaching about zones, which was current from earliest times in Greek science, it is as always emphasized that, out of the five zones, only two are fit for human habitation. A skeptical point of view can lay stress upon that aspect of the matter: how small is the space in which all human activity takes place![11] But it is observed gratefully and to the praise of the deity that both the zones that are inhabited by human beings, ours and the corresponding one in the south, differ favorably from the tropical and the two arctic zones.[12] In this sense Cicero propounded the idea of the zones of human habitation as being evidence in the proof of God that is given in the first of the *Tusculan Disputations.* Here, no doubt, as in this book generally, he followed his Greek predecessors. He speaks of the earth which is habitable and cultivated upon only two zones (*orae*): "here, however, where we live, there do not cease in season 'Skies to shine and trees in blooming leaf, . . . Fields rich with crops, flowers out everywhere'" (*hic autem, ubi habitamus, non intermittit suo tempore "caelum nitescere, arbores, frondescere . . . segetes largiri fruges, florere omnia," Tusc.* 1.28 [§§68-69]; the final words are a quotation from Ennius). Nevertheless, there is still the possibility that "the boundaries of their habitation" (*horothesiai tēs katoikias autōn*) are also to be interpreted not historically, but philosophically. It would then be, as Cicero shows, the boundaries of the zones that are fit for cultivation which are meant, and not national boundaries.[13]

But which is the correct explanation? The answer to this question determines our understanding of the whole second theme and, to some extent, of the Areopagus speech generally. For the point at issue is whether it is the Old Testament view of history or the philosophical—particularly the Stoic—view of the world that prevails in the speech on the Areopagus. The difference of opinion that we find among the commentators seems to offer little prospect of a definite solution, and yet an answer to the question is possible. It must proceed from a consideration of the purpose of what has been done. God has made the seasons and appointed the boundaries of their habitation in order that people should *seek* him (v. 27).

The first reference to God that this expression makes is reminiscent of the Old Testament. But, as we look closer, we see that, here and there, the conditions and circumstances of the seeking are quite different. The pious man in the Old Testament seeks God in order to serve him, for example on his hill on his holy place, in Ps 24:3; he seeks God's face (also Ps 24:6; and 27:8). Whosoever puts his trust in people does not seek or inquire after God (Isa 31:1), but whoever turns to God and seeks him with his whole heart shall find him (Jer 29:13; Isa 55:6). Seeking after God is here a matter of the will, whereas the search for God in the Areopagus speech is a matter of thinking. Through the familiar and accessible manifestations of life God has revealed himself to people (not simply to his own or to his own people) to such an extent that they observe God's existence and draw the corresponding conclusions. Here, it is not a question of putting one's trust in God or submitting oneself in obedience to him; the aim here is that God should be apprehended because the world is apprehended. The most Hellenistic book of the Greek Old Testament, the Wisdom of Solomon, speaks of this seeking after God (Wis 13:6), and, understandably, Philo speaks of it also (see p. 184, n. 15). Both, influenced no doubt by the Old Testament, use the direct, personal construction "seeking God" (*zētein ton theon*); but both use the word in a completely different, Greek sense. For the Greeks used the word *zētein* for the seeking out and examining of what is true[14] and so, also, of what is divine. In Xenophon, *Memorabilia* 1.1.15, we have the words "and do those who seek after divine phenomena" (*outō kai oi ta theia zētountes nomizousin*). According to Philo "the Father and Ruler of the universe is a being whose character it is difficult to arrive at by conjecture and hard to comprehend; but still we must not on that account shrink from seeking after it" (*ei esti to theion . . . ti esti kata tēn ousian . . . zētēseis peri theou; Spec.* 1.32). And finding does not necessarily follow upon this seeking; Philo was rightly aware of that.[15] When we read in his work that seeking for its own sake, even without finding, is earnestly to be desired, we are reminded of Lessing's famous words, when he said that we should entreat God to give us the urge to truth, rather than truth itself.[16] Obviously, the speaker on the Areopagus also made allowance for this uncertainty by introducing the object of the seeking cautiously in the optative mood: "in the hope that they might feel after him and find him" (*ei ara ge psēlaphēseian auton kai euroien*). Thus there can be no doubt what kind of seeking is meant in the Areopagus speech.

People are impelled to such seeking by the "periods" (*kairoi*) appointed by God and by the "boundaries of . . . habitation" (*horothesiai tēs katoikias*). It is, however, only the philosophical and not the historical interpretation of the motif that gives rise to this understanding of the words, for the political boundaries, which would be important for the historical explanation, are no evidence of the existence of God. The intentional grouping of people upon the habitable surfaces of the earth is, however, proof of the existence of Providence. In the Apocalypse the passing away of the epochs of the kingdoms is certainly regarded as a revelation of divine power; nevertheless, the way in which kingdom follows upon kingdom provides absolutely no rational evidence of the existence of God, for it remains mysterious and obscure. Its purpose can be prophetically surmised, but not comprehended until the last days. The seasons, on the other hand, are often quoted as evidence that God rules the world. In the proof of God's existence given by Cicero (*Tusc.* 1.28 [§68]), which has already been mentioned, the seasons, among other things, are named, together with the division of the earth into habitable and uninhabitable zones.[17] That is exactly the proof which perceives the creator in the intentional arrangement of seasons and zones, and which the speaker on the Areopagus wishes to indicate.

Besides, the designation "allotted" (*prostetagmenoi*) is considerably more appropriate to the seasons than to the epochs of the nations, for the seasons are established according to an order that is always binding and universally recognizable.[18] What is described here as *prostetagmenoi*, Plato expressed: "the beautiful ordering of the seasons, marked out by years and months" (*ta tōn hōrōn diakekosmēmena kalōs outōs, eniautois te kai mēsin dieilēmmena, Laws* 10.886a), and, next to the cosmos, this division seems to him to be the best proof of the existence of gods. The epochs of nations, on the other hand, could hardly be applied in the same sense with such certainty, because the order of their passing is not evident but ordained previously by God; this explains the reading *protetagmenous* in the Areopagus speech.[19] What is expressed here by the participle is written with reference to the zones of habitation as "boundary" (*horothesia*): God has established the seasons and defined the limits of the areas where men shall live, and both seasons and boundaries are intended to induce men to seek after God.

We say "to seek after him," for it is doubtful whether God will be found completely. And this uncertainty is regarded not as a disgrace but as inevitable;[20] this is in no way altered by the strong expression "handle" (*psēlaphan*), which stands beside "find" (*euriskein*) in what follows. This idea of being able actually to "seize God with the hands" in one manifestation of nature or another is found in other proofs of the existence of God, and indeed in proofs of God based upon nature.[21]

So we are confirmed in the conclusion that the Areopagus speech refers to a seeking after God of the kind that man is brought to by the ordering of his life in time and space. The question is whether the conclusion thus reached can be applied to the beginning of the description in v. 26 as well. If so, the words "And he made from one every nation of men to live on all the face of the earth" would refer to humanity and not to the nations. In fact, that seems to me to be the case. The passage must be interpreted consistently. We cannot hold that here the speaker is referring to the nations and later to the seasons. If we accepted the historico-political interpretation, it would also be difficult to understand why the genitive "of people" (*anthrōpōn*) is put with "every country" (*pan ethnos*). If, however, the human race is meant, the genitive is then explained by the custom of speaking also of the *ethnē* of the bees or birds.[22] The reading *genos* for *ethnos* found in Clement and Irenaeus, like the reading *anthrōpou* in D, points to a philosophical understanding of the expression: *pan ethnos anthrōpōn* indicates the whole human race.

Another consideration seems to me, however, to be quite decisive. The words "he made from one every nation of men to live . . ." are intended to refer to God, who has previously been proclaimed as creator of heaven and earth, now as the creator of people as well. This is Old Testament and Christian preaching. The word "made" (*poiein*) in this context indicates creating; in the Septuagint, in connection with the creating of humans in Gen 1:27, it is used no less than three times for the Hebrew *bara'*, while *ktizein* is used in the Septuagint with this meaning and as an equivalent for *bara'* only sparingly.[23] We must translate then: "and he created out of one the whole race of humans." On this depends an infinitive of purpose, in the same way as "seek" (*zētein*) in the next verse. God has created the human race in order that it may dwell upon earth; God's intention was that many people should inhabit the earth. In view of the meaning of *poiein* in the act of creation, considerable doubts arise in connection with the translation frequently used: God has planned in such a way that all nations should dwell upon the earth. The usage of the word *poiein* is not in accordance with this; nor is the phrase which comes first, *ex henos* ("from one"), the force of which, as the translation stands, is somewhat uncertain: "that all nations of men out of one should dwell upon the earth" does not sound convincing. For *ex henos* one would expect a participle; but if we take it the other way, the translation makes good sense: "God has created out of one the whole race of humans." If taken in this way, *ex henos* had to come first in order to be taken together with *pan* ("every"); again, if it is taken in this way, no completion is necessary,[24] for "every" completes *anthrōpou* (understood) and the meaning is quite clear, since what is emphasized is that all people are descended from one. The thought obviously rests upon the stories in the Old Testament of Adam and Noah, and was not simply conceived in contrast to some autochthonous belief. But the Old Testament did not especially develop this idea,[25] and the whole conception is not worked out here according to Old Testament modes of thought; there is nothing here about the fall and the flood, the building of the Tower of Babel, and the destruction of humanity, nor anything about a chosen people and their particular destiny.[26] The distribution of people on the earth is regarded from an optimistic point of view.[27] In creating one, God created all, in order that they might inhabit the earth.

People are thought of, then, as citizens of the world; the division according to nations has no particular significance, which is not surprising, for before Paul made his speech in the Areopagus, Philo had spoken of humanity in exactly the same way. He stands between God and the rest of the human race: we are descended from the first man; God made him (*Opif.* §140); he is called "the originator of our whole race" (*ho pantos tou genous hēmōn archēgetēs*, §136); he is not only the first human but also the sole citizen of the world; he lives according to the law which is the *politeia* of the whole world, that is natural law (*ho tēs physeōs orthos logos*—§§142, 143). Such ideas, although perhaps not expressed in such strongly Stoical terms, may underlie the sentence in the Areopagus speech which refers to the one man from whom originated the whole human race which inhabits the earth. Here, then, we reach a decision between the two interpretations of this portion of the speech, the historical and the philosophical. The philosophical one prevails: it is not a case of nations, national epochs, and national boundaries, but of the cosmopolitan human race, the ordering of its life according to seasons and to its appropriate habitations and of man's search after God which this ordering of his life inspires.[28]

THE INTRODUCTION AND FIRST THEME
(ACTS 17:22-23, 24-25)

After establishing the meaning and significance of the most difficult section of the speech, we shall proceed by making our own translation.

Preamble   22 Men of Athens! I see that in everything you are anxious to honor the gods.

23 For as I went through the streets and looked at your holy places I found an altar with the inscription: "To an unknown god." Now, I am going to tell you what you honor even without recognizing it.

I   24 The God who created this world and all that is in it, he who is Lord of heaven and earth, does not dwell in temples made by men,

25 nor does he claim the service of human hands, as if he needed anything. Indeed, it is he who lends to all life and breath and everything.

II   26 And he created out of one the whole race of men, that they might live upon the face of the earth. He ordered the seasons and the boundaries of their habitations,

27 that they might seek God, if perchance they might take hold of him and find him; indeed, he is not far from each one of us.

III 28 For in him we live and move and have our being, as some of your poets have said: "for we are his offspring."

29 Now, as a divine race, we ought not to suppose that the deity resembles an image made from gold, or silver, or stone, the work of human art and imagination.

Conclusion 30 God no longer contemplates the times of ignorance; instead, he makes it known that all men everywhere should repent.

31 For God has appointed a day in which he will judge the world in righteousness by a man whom he has chosen. God accredited him before all the world when he raised him from the dead.

Eduard Norden has examined the use of the inscription on an altar as a starting-point and introductory motif in various directions.[29] In the ensuing critical discussion[30] the questions as to who was meant by this inscription and what importance is to be attached to it here were further clarified. The outcome of the discussion can be summarized in a few sentences.

1. We do not know of an altar inscription "to an unknown god" or "to the unknown god." On the other hand, there is evidence in literature,[31] and probably also in inscriptions,[32] that there were altars on the road from Phaleron to Athens, in Olympia, and perhaps also in Pergamum, which were dedicated to "unknown gods."

   We should stress that some Christian writers, who know the Acts of the Apostles,[33] also quote the inscription in the plural form, which indicates that they do not know of it only from the Areopagus speech.[34]

2. The consecration to unknown gods may have been occasioned by the fear that, through ignorance, a god might be denied the homage which was due to him; this fear, when found in places such as Athens, Olympia, and Pergamum—through which foreign traffic passed— seems not entirely unjustified[35] and may even have been kept alive by stories of gods which had become maleficent.[36] A particular event, which was understood to be the work of a god who had not previously been honored, could have led to a dedication of this or a similar kind. Thus Diogenes Laertius tells how Epimenides of Crete brought about Athens's atonement for the shedding of the blood of Kylon's followers:[37] he caused black and white sheep to run from the Areopagus into

the city and, in the places where one of these animals lay down, from time to time let them be sacrificed "to the appropriate gods" (*tō prosēkonti theōi*; 1.10.110).[38] It is less probable that by these unknown gods were meant some sort of chthonic deities, whom people were neither able nor willing to name.

3. Philostratus tells in his biography of Apollonius of Tyana that Apollonius met a youth, Timasion, in Egypt who was pursued by the love of his step-mother, as Hippolytus was by Phaedra. But Timasion, unlike Hippolytus, did not offend Aphrodite on that account, but rather respected her and therefore left his home (*Vita Apollonii* 6.3). Apollonius commended this conduct, for it was no sign of discretion (*sōphrosunē*) to offend a deity: the mark of discretion was, rather, to speak well of all gods, especially in Athens, where altars were set up even to unknown gods (*sōphronesteron gar to peri pantōn theōn eu legein kai tauta Athēnēsin ou kai agnōstōn daimonōn bōmoi hidruntai*).

The question is how we are to explain the direct mention of Athenian unknown gods. Norden's somewhat artificial construction of a literary connection has not, on the whole, been successful.[39] The mention of Theseus's son, Hippolytus, demands the mention of Athens, although the story takes place in Troezen, and the concluding sentences simply show that, whether in mockery or commendation, it was customary to quote the altars of the unknown gods as proof of the piety of Athens. This could be a reference to the altar in Phaleron, or even to those nameless altars that, according to Diogenes Laertius, originated in Epimenides' act of purification; at any rate, the pious city of Athens was known far and wide for the honor it paid to unknown gods.

4. The Areopagus speech quotes the inscription as if it were in the singular: to an unknown god. That may be due either to an intentional alteration of the plural or to a misunderstanding. If we assume the latter to be true, then we must suppose that the author had no knowledge of the place. In that case, he could make the story of the sheep (if he knew it in much the same form as we read in Diogenes Laertius, see above) refer to a consecration in the singular; for Diogenes Laertius tells how, wherever any sheep rested, the Athenians sacrificed to the "appropriate god," and for this reason there were "altars without names" in Athens. Only if he had heard that it was the custom in Athens to set up altars to unknown gods (as recorded in that phrase from Philostratus; see above) could he think that the individual altar belonged to an individual unknown god.

The singular version only of the inscription could be used by the speaker on the Areopagus, however, for he regarded the inscription as evidence of the Athenians' subconscious awareness of the true God. Now he can begin straight away to proclaim this God. This is done in Old Testament style with the declaration of that knowledge possessed by the people of Israel since the time of the prophets and Deuteronomy, the knowledge that the Creator of the world, the Lord of heaven and earth, does not dwell in temples. The affirmation of God as Creator belongs to the Old Testament; but it is a Hellenistic, rather than Old Testament usage, when the first phrase includes the word *kosmos*, whereas the Old Testament would speak of heaven and earth.[40] The idea that God does not live in temples belongs to Old Testament (though late Old Testament) thought; but the application here of the word "made by hands" (*cheiropoiētos*) to temples does not belong to the Old Testament, while the Greek Bible uses it of idols. But the implied criticism of every temple, even of the one in Jerusalem, corresponds with the Hellenistic conception of God— and the word is used in this sense by Philo and even in the Acts of the Apostles (7:48) of temples.[41]

Thus the first motif of the speech rests upon Old Testament ideas, expressed in modernized Hellenistic language. As the speech continues, we see a departure from Old Testament ways of thought: God will not be served by human hands, as if he needed anything. Undoubtedly, the service of God does not here mean prayer, but religious office and attendance, i.e., every kind of service in the temple. This use of the word "serve" (*therapeuō*) is, however, almost unknown in the Greek translation of the Bible,[42] but quite familiar in original Greek texts,[43] and in the context with which we are acquainted. The deity (*daimonion*) is too great to need my "service" (*therapeia*), we read in the famous chapter of Xenophon's *Memorabilia*, which contains the teleological proof of God.[44] Piety, so Plato teaches,[45] is certainly a "service to the gods" (*therapeia theōn*), but it must not be taken as though it were useful to the gods or edified them. Philo has clearly used the word having Plato in mind and, like Xenophon, firmly established the fact that God does not stand in need of anything.[46] In the Areopagus speech, also, the exposition of this theme leads in a very Greek manner to the establishing of the fact that God does not stand in need of anything.

The demand for what is "appropriate for a god" (*theoprepes*)[47] is one of the most characteristic features of the idea of God that were developed in Greek philosophy and then absorbed both by Hellenistic Judaism and by the theology of the early Church. Nothing may be said of God that is not worthy of him. Hence the anxiety not to humanize God in any way and the tendency to negative definitions of his being. After a formal enumeration of divine qualities had been made, perhaps based upon older material, on the Stoa,[48] this *via negationis* ("way of negation") in the acknowledging of God became predominant in philosophical theology. When portraying the nature of God, adjectives with the negative *a* are favored; antitheses are also a popular method of emphasizing the meaning of adjectives: thus, invisible, yet seeing all (*Sib. Or.* 3.12), all-embracing, yet embraced by nothing (Philo, *Leg.* 1.44, and elsewhere). God's freedom from any kind of need is one of the most characteristic among these negative qualities and is occasionally represented by a pair of antitheses of this type.[49] The following verse from Euripides is usually quoted as the best example of this in classical poetry (*Herc. fur.* 1345-46):

> For the deity, if he really be such,
> has no wants. These are miserable tales of the poets.

> *deitai gar ho theos, eiper est' orthōs theos,*
> *oudenos. Aoidōn oide dustēnoi logoi.*

From the Eleatic School onwards, the idea that God is not in need of anything is repeated in all the schools of Greek philosophy till the Neo-Pythagoreans and the Neo-Platonists.[50]

The emphasis on Old Testament piety is quite different from this. And this difference has a fundamental meaning that must not be underestimated. The Old Testament lays no importance upon pronouncements upon God's passive being. It emphasizes God's actions and God's demands. Even where God is spoken of as the Supreme Being, we are not concerned primarily with a condition but with the exercising of God's power. Therefore the doctrine of divine qualities, and particularly that doctrine that is acquired by means of the *via negationis,* has no place in the Old Testament. So also there is no emphasis at all in the canonical books of the Old Testament upon God's freedom from need. Attention has rightly been drawn to the fact that Deutero-Isaiah's repeated mocking at idols[51] conceals an unexpressed conception of a God who has no need of any help: the idol must be carried to its place, for it cannot walk; it must be nailed or placed firmly in position, so that it does not totter. But the essential thing here is scorn of images, and not definition of God's being. The same is true of words in a psalm (50:9-10), which tell how God requires no animals sacrifice, but now the reason offered is not that which might have been given by a Greek critic of sacrifice, namely that God needs no appeasement; in true Old Testament style we are told: God is Lord of all animals.

Only twice is it emphasized in the LXX that God needs nothing, but even these two passages are sufficient to prove the Greek origin of the idea; they are found in 2 and 3 Maccabees, thus in late, purely Greek texts which, in language and thought, stand out from the Old Testament. On both occasions temple prayers are involved, and on both occasions, in the sentence concerned, the existence of a temple is justified in face of the fact that God needs nothing: "O Lord of all, who has need of nothing, you were pleased that there be a temple for your habitation among us" (2 Macc 14:35); and "sanctified this place for your name, though you have no need of anything" (3 Macc 2:9).

If the word and the conception "free from need" suddenly appear in this way on the edge of the Greek Bible, we may expect to find them used by Philo and Josephus also. This is, in fact, the case. We have already mentioned that Philo, like the speaker on the Areopagus, introduces the subject of God's freedom from need in connection with the false and the true "service" (*therapeia*) of God.[52] But Josephus lets Solomon say in the second prayer of dedication of the temple, which is conceived in completely Hellenistic style, that men cannot repay God by their works for the blessings which he gives, for he does not need anything.[53]

An idea that was so widespread in Hellenistic doctrine and so readily adopted by Hellenistic Judaism naturally was available for use in Christian thought. But this is a very obvious example of how little the first generations of Christianity had their roots in the Hellenistic world, how much their thought was their own, and how closely their piety was linked to the Bible; for this motif of God's freedom from need, which was so familiar to Hellenism, is foreign to the whole of the New Testament, with the sole exception of the Areopagus speech. But the motif is known and used even in those early Christian writings which were contemporary, or almost contemporary, with the later New Testament writings, but which are distinguished from them by more secular temper and by literary style: namely, *1 Clement*, the *Praedicatio Petri*, and the *Apology* of Aristides.[54] As in the latter of these two writings, the "Epistle" to Diognetus, which has strong affinities with the writings of the Apologists, applies the idea in the form of an antithesis (see above p. 106): God sends us all that we need, but does not himself need the things he gives us.[55] It is, in fact, an antithesis of this kind which now provides the continuation of this thought in the Areopagus speech: "since he himself gives to everyone life and breath and everything" (*autos didous pasi zōēn kai pnoēn kai ta panta*).

The commentators have, on the whole, treated the concluding "and everything" (*kai ta panta*) in a somewhat careless fashion; but some of the copyists obviously did not know what to do with the words and either altered them to *kata panta* (koine) or sought a solution by linking the words with what followed—"and he made everything from one" (*kai ta panta epoiēsen ex henos*). The sense of the words, which at first seem very general, can be understood only if they are taken as a response: God needs nothing and gives us everything. Earlier, we have had the expressions "life and breath" (*zōē kai pnoē*), which have been put together because of their assonance. The tautology is not found elsewhere, but the introduction of "breath" (*pnoē*) might have been occasioned by its similar sound; apart from this, we are reminded here of the account of the creation given in the Old Testament, in which, also, in Gen 2:7, the word *pnoē* is used for the breath which God gave to humans. But this echo of the Old Testament in no way alters the scheme of the whole speech.[56] Also, the first and the second themes (vv. 24-25 and vv. 26-27 respectively) are intended to convey a Hellenistic doctrine of God. The two themes belong together. The end of the first idea—God needs nothing and gives us everything—leads to the second: God has created human beings in order that they may inhabit the earth, and has made it possible for them to have dwellings, seasons and zones of habitation, in order that they should seek after him.

THE THIRD THEME AND CONCLUSION
(ACTS 17:28-29, 30-31)

The second theme concludes with the words "Yet he is not far from each one of us" (*kai ge ou makran apo henos ekastou hēmōn hypar chonta*, 17:27b). What is introduced here as proof[57] is actually the subject of the third theme (namely, the fact that God is related to humanity). So much material on this subject has been collected in the discussion of the last twenty-five years that the purely Hellenistic character of this theme is obvious. God is not far from us—the litotes means, of course: by virtue of his nature, regardless of human behavior, he is very near to each of us.[58] "For in him we have life," it continues, and there can be no question that, for the speaker on the Areopagus, *en autō* could mean "through him." For the conclusion drawn from this and the next sentence is that we human beings are the progeny of God, that is, that we are related to God. Thus *en autō* is at least to be taken as implying a certain panentheism (the divine in everything).[59]

The idea that God is related to men has been familiar in philosophy ever since the spread and popularizing of the Stoic conception of the wise man. As has often been observed, certain expositions of Dio Chrysostom come closest to our passage, according to which the conception of deity is implanted by nature in every reasonable being (*dia tēn xungeneian tēn pros autous*).[60] In this context, we read, however, *hate gar ou makran oud' exō tou theiou diōkis-menoi kath' autous, alla en autōi mesō pephykotes, mallon de sympephykotes ekeinōi*.[61] The first prayer of dedication of the temple, which Josephus ascribes to King Solomon, and which, as already mentioned, is quite hellenistically conceived (see p. 188, n. 47 and p. 189, n. 53), shows that such ideas can easily be taken for granted. According to this, the aim of the temple religion is to establish the conviction in men, "that you are present and not far away" (*hoti parei kai makran ouk aphestēkas*).[62] Thus the relationship is such as to allow even litotes as the form of expressing it. God's nearness to man is further proved in the Areopagus speech with "live and move and have our being" (*zēn, kineisthai,* and *einai*) in God (17:28); here, the most striking verb "move" (*kineisthai*) again points to Stoic ideas of the God who sets everything in motion.[63] The richness of expression, however, the juxtaposition of the three verbs, can now with some certainty be attributed to a veiled quotation from the poets.

Our appreciation of the words has changed since 1913, when the commentary on Acts by the Nestorian Isho'dad of Merv (c. 850) was published.[64] Isho'-dad sees in this passage a strange mixture of traditional and imperfectly understood material and asserts that Paul took both sentences in 17:28 "from certain heathen poets." This would apply then not only to the verse "for we are indeed his offspring" (*tou gar kai genos esmen,* v. 29), which has long been recognized as a quotation from Aratus, but also to the first sentence, "In him we live and move and have our being."[65] Now with reference to this, says Isho'dad, because "the Cretans said as truth about Zeus, that he was a lord; he was lacerated by a wild boar and buried; and behold! his grave is known amongst us.[66] So therefore Minos, son of Zeus, made a laudatory speech on behalf of his father; and he said in it, 'The Cretans carve a tomb for thee, O holy and high, liars, evil beasts and slow bellies! for thou art not dead for ever; thou art alive and risen;[67] for in thee we live and are moved, and have our being.'"[68] John Chrysostom's homily on Tit 1:12, the passage in which the words about the lying Cretans are used in the New Testament,[69] makes it clear that this is not mere phantasy.[70] In support of these mocking words Chrysostom mentions the grave of Zeus alleged to be in Crete, which has called forth the mockery "of the poet," and then quotes from this unnamed poet the words:

> For even a tomb, O king, the Cretans made for you
> who never dies, but shall ever live.
>
> *kai gar taphon, ō ana, seio krētes, etektēnanto*
> *su d' ou thanes, hesai gar aiei.*[71]

These words (and the description of the Cretans as liars) are also found in Callimachus.[72] But if Isho'dad is right, the verses quoted were followed immediately by the saying "in him we live, move and exist,"[73] and the whole passage does not come from Callimachus but from the same poet to whom the verse mocking the people of Crete is to be attributed. According to Clement of Alexandria and Jerome, its composer is the poet Epimenides of Crete.[74] But since there is among his works also a poem "Concerning Minos and Hradamanthuos (*Peri Minō kai Hradamanthuos*),[75] Isho'dad's account of the supposed poet Minos is explained as a misunderstanding either of Isho'dad or of his source.

Thus the speaker on the Areopagus seems to have stated the theme of God's natural relationship with men by means of two quotations from the poets.[76] Only the second has he introduced expressly as such. The formula of quotation with its plural—"as even some of your poets have said" (*tines tōn kath' humas poiētōn*)[77]—need not necessarily refer to several poets but only to the one Aratus, as whose literary property it has already been recognized by Clement of Alexandria (*Strom.* 1.91.5). This manner of quoting vaguely and in the plural shows that the speech is delivered in a cultivated manner,[78] as does also the number of quotations. This is a small indication of an important point. The speech in Acts 17 gives, both from the point of view of form and subject matter, a view of a cultured Christianity that we otherwise know only from the second century. In the New Testament, however, the only evidence of this kind of Christianity is here and, perhaps, in Acts 14:15-17.

The verse used here out of the *Phaenomena* of Aratus, to whose refinement of style Callimachus dedicated an epigram,[79] is found in the introduction to the poem:

> Let us begin with Zeus: Streets and markets, oceans and harbors are full of him; we all need him, and we are of his family. But he in his graciousness shows favorable signs to people; he reminds the peoples of the necessities of life and thus goads them to activity; he tells them when to plough and when to plant.

Then the poet speaks of the stars that show men that the seasons have been ordained for them; at the end of the introduction, Zeus is greeted: "Hail, O father, great object of wonder" (*chaire, pater, mega thauma*), and he is celebrated as the ancestor of the human race. Thus, in more than one respect, the Areopagus speech seems to be similar to these introductory verses of Aratus. Man's origin in God, and the relationship that results, the mention of the earth and the seasons as proof of God's existence (compare p. 189, n. 17)—all this features in both texts. And since the speaker uses this very quotation with a literary turn, it is easy to assume that he really knew Aratus's poem and not only this one-half verse taken from it. A similar verse also occurs in the hymn to Zeus by the Stoic Cleanthes, a contemporary of Aratus. But it is not the aim of Cleanthes, as of Aratus, to trace out God's works upon earth but to assert that it is fitting for humanity to offer praise to God:

It is right to proclaim you (i.e., Zeus) to all mortals,
for they are your offspring, they alone having been allotted an imitation of
a sound, of all the mortal creatures that live and move upon the earth.

se gar pantessi themis thnētoisi prosaudan.
Ek sou gar genos eis' ēchou mimēma lachontes
mounoi, hosa zōei de kai herpei thnēt' epi gaian[80]

It is not possible to establish a closer connection between this quotation and
the Areopagus speech. It is clear, however, how familiar the idea of God's relationship with men was in Hellenistic poetry and philosophy; from them the
idea reached the composer of the Areopagus speech.

The Old Testament cannot even be considered as the place of origin of this
motif. We may recall the idea that man is made in the image of God, but, by
virtue of its origin and range, this idea is to be understood quite differently. In
the story of Genesis (1:27) it is intended to serve as proof of man's lordship
over all the rest of creation. This is said expressly and also emphasized in Sir
17:3. But this superiority is based on his creation, thus upon the past. From it
is derived the lordship over the animals and the command that human blood
shall not be shed (Gen 9:6). But the Old Testament does not therefore say that
this gives man a particularly close connection with God, nor that it follows
that, because he is now alive, he should have his existence and being in God.
The Old Testament does not say this, even when it ascribes to the people of
Israel a certain particularly close relationship with God (although not that
panentheistic one of the Areopagus speech). Therefore we cannot say that this
panentheistic idea of relationship with God "converges"[81] with the Old Testament idea that man is made in the image of God.

This idea of God's relationship with men is, however, as already shown,
certainly Hellenistic.[82] Thus the strangeness of the Areopagus speech in relation to the piety of the Bible and its familiarity with philosophy became especially evident in this theme, not one sentence of which accords with what we
are accustomed to find elsewhere in the Old or New Testament. And that
would still be completely true even if the hypothetical derivation of the sentence "in him live, move and exist" were false. For God's relationship with
men is taught by philosophy in the very same context in which the idea
appears in the Areopagus speech. It lays a basis for correct conception of the
gods and brings about independence of ancient religious forms. Once more,
Dio Chrysostom may be taken as evidence of the first, Seneca of the second:[83]
Dio's twelfth speech has already been quoted (p. 185, n. 21; p. 108), but in the
thirtieth speech he makes a simple countryman come on the scene and, in
contrast to pessimistic assertions about the relationship between God and

man, emphasize the love of the gods for men as for their relatives; he declares that the race of men is descended not from titans and giants but from the gods.[84] Like Aratus and the Paul of the Areopagus speech, he might have cried: "We are of their family."

Here, however, we should make particular reference to the numerous parallels to the Areopagus speech that are found in Seneca. In the forty-first letter we find this reference to man as opposed to cultus, or worship: "We do not need to raise our hands to heaven, nor to ask the temple-ward to allow us to approach nearer to the idol's ear, as if we should then gain a more certain hearing; God is near to thee, with thee, yea, in thee."[85] Here, indeed, the proximity rests more upon the mystic quality of immanence—God is in man—[86] while the speaker on the Areopagus stresses the inherence—man has his life in God; but, in the prologue to the *Questiones naturales*, Seneca has proved man's divine origin in just the same sense as in Acts; the divine is a joy to him and the upper realms are his home.[87] And, according to Lactantius (*Divin. instit.* 6.25.3), Seneca has given in his *Philosophia moralis* a synopsis of ideas to which the speaker on the Areopagus alludes: man should think of God as great and gentle, as a friend and one who is always near (*amicum et semper in proximo*); he should not be honored by sacrifice and the shedding of blood, but by a pure spirit, by a good and moral purpose. Temples should not be set up to him; we should worship him in our own hearts.[88] But, in his ninety-fifth letter, in a survey of the practices of various religions, Seneca very impressively criticizes that service of the gods that the speaker on the Areopagus had rejected (17:25). Some people light their lamps on the Sabbath, but the gods do not need the light, nor do men find any pleasure in the smoke. Others wait upon the gods in the morning and sit at the temple gates; but only human ambition could be bribed by such things. Honoring God consists of knowing him (*deum colit, qui novit*; *Ep.* 95:47). Others bring to Jupiter towels and brushes for bathing, to Juno the mirror—a fine example of the "served by human hands" (*therapeuesthai hypo cheirōn anthrōpinōn*; see Acts 17:25)— God needs no servants, but himself serves the human race; he is everywhere and close to all people (*non quaerit ministros deus, quidni? Ipse humano generi ministrat, ubique et omnibus praesto etc.*; *Ep.* 95:47). And the idea of relationship with God begins, at least, to be perceived here in the concluding reminder of this theological section: you seek the grace of the gods? Then be good! He who emulates them as honored them enough (*satis illos coluit, quisquis imitatus est*; *Ep.* 95.50). Thus the motifs of Acts 17 constantly recur in Seneca's work: rejection of worship and of every service to the gods, the nearness of God to men, man's relatedness to God.

Let us now return to the Areopagus speech. We can see a distinct climax as the relationship with God is described. First, there was the rhetorical understatement—God is not far from us. Then came the words of the first quotation (if Isho'dad informs us correctly): we have our existence in him—that is how the idea of coherence is expressed—and now follows the second quotation, taken from Aratus: "We are of his family." Finally the writer gathers these ideas together in order to draw the conclusion: since we are now of his family, that is, after all that has been said, we are of his nature and bound to him.[89]

Now the sequence of thought returns to where it started. Whereas at the beginning of the speech we found the rejection of any idea that God dwells in temples, now the representation of the deity in images is condemned; beings who are related to God should not think in this way. Images are the works of men and the deity is not concerned with them. It is mild polemic; Deutero-Isaiah (40:19-20; 46:6; and especially 44:9-20) spoke more bitterly and mockingly. Even the Jewish Hellenism of the Wisdom of Solomon (13:10—14:2; 15:7-17) criticizes more sharply; but an echo of what is said there about the material of the images recurs in the Areopagus speech.[90] As is evident, and confirmed by what follows, the writer does not wish to speak in the tone of one accusing the heathen world of their sin, but as one who is enlightening them in their ignorance.

The introduction to the speech is in accordance with this attitude toward the heathen world; the same spirit is evident in the conclusion, which speaks of the past as the time of ignorance. This motif, which ascribes as little guilt as possible to the heathen, has already been used in the introduction (17:23). In the speeches in Acts it appears in three places (3:17; 13:27; 14:16; compare also the *Apology* of Aristides, 17:4), and indeed is used in connection with Jews as well as heathen. Thus we have before us an idea particularly emphasized by the author, and equally characteristic of the author is the further idea that God overlooks those times of ignorance[91] and now ordains that the call to repentance be preached to all men everywhere. For that is indeed the motif of the Christian mission; the book of Acts deals with that mission, and actual instances of this call to repentance occur often from 2:38 onwards. And here, as in 10:42, attention is turned to the future and to the judgment by Jesus, so that in these two verses (17:30-31) past, present, and future appear in close connection with one another.

These concluding words consist of one sentence, the *only Christian* sentence in the Areopagus speech. At last Jesus is alluded to, even though his name is not actually used.[92] The reference to his resurrection and the proclamation of a judgment by him are the only specifically Christian ideas that are imparted to the hearers. Moreover, the hearers are introduced to this other world with the tenderest pedagogical care. First comes the announcement of the divine court, an item of eschatology such as might have been taught by

many a religion and many a preacher of the time. Here, certainly not by accident, Old Testament words are used: "He will judge the world with righteousness" (*krinein tēn oikoumenēn en dikaiosunē*) is a phrase taken from the
Psalms (9:9 [8]; 96:13; 98:9). Then follows the careful introduction of the man
whom he has chosen,[93] with no mention whatever of his name or destiny, and
finally, the least acceptable feature of all, this man's resurrection from the
dead. The manner and meaning of his death are not discussed, nor the significance of his resurrection for the belief of Christians. The resurrection is only
introduced in order to prove that this unnamed man has been chosen. At the
same time, the word *pistis*, which is so completely confined to one meaning in
Christian language ("faith"), is used with the meaning of "proof" or "verifica-
tion," a sense that is quite foreign to the New Testament, although familiar in
literary language. Thus, in the conclusion also, we are once again given the
impression of a kind of speech that, in its form of expression and its line of
thought, is foreign to the New Testament.

The words about the resurrection are the last of the speech. It seems as if
the mockery of a few listeners and the definite agreement of others brought it
to an end. But there is no mention of a major interruption, and this apparently
sudden ending is actually a favorite device of the author, who leaves what is
most important until the end and emphasizes it by means of the contradiction of the listeners (10:44; 22:22; 26:24; perhaps 5:33 and 7:54 are to be similarly understood). The writer certainly did not believe that the speaker was
forced simply by an incident to a premature conclusion. The composition of
the speech makes it abundantly clear that it forms an intended whole, which
reaches an intended ending. So, if we feel that anything is missing, we must
reconcile ourselves to the fact that it is according to the author's will that
whatever is lacking is not expressed here. And this point presents yet another
problem of the speech.

THE SPEECH AND PAUL'S OWN STYLE

What we have before us is a *Hellenistic* speech about the true knowledge of
God. It is, of course, not one that could be delivered orally. It comprises only
ten verses and would take but a few minutes to give. But it is not merely a synopsis. Throughout, it shows the style of a speech to be delivered. There is an
intentional harmony between the beginning and the end; the apostrophe and
the demonstration of proof are vivid; the formation of the sentences demands
that they should be spoken aloud; many groups of words are adorned with
rhetoric.[94] Only, instead of ideas that have been developed, we find only
groups of motifs, and every motif would bear and would merit being extended
for several minutes in the delivery of the speech. The motifs have become

intelligible to us by analogy with Hellenistic philosophy. If our interpretation of it follows only the indications which are to be found in the motifs them-selves, if we do not constantly take into consideration New Testament paral-lels which really belong to another range of ideas, then we can only conclude that the Areopagus speech is a Hellenistic speech with a Christian ending; its theme is knowledge of God, to which every human being can attain, since man's own position in the world and the affinity of his nature with God's inevitably lead him there. Nothing is said of the claim of the Christian mes-sage that true knowledge of God can be possessed and imparted only through revelation. The repentance, to which the hearers are called at the end, is natu-rally to be understood in its Christian sense. It is suggested, however, that repentance consists ultimately of recalling that knowledge of God that, by virtue of his nature, belongs to man.[95] And it is merely as a motif of this repen-tance that the impending judgment by the Risen One is mentioned right at the end. When we consider the Areopagus speech as a whole, we see that it has a rational character that is foreign to the New Testament. In recognizing this fact, we may well draw both historical and literary inferences from it, and to these we shall now turn our attention.

The historical problem is whether the apostle Paul could have made this speech. For it is this question which is first and foremost, rather than whether he made a speech in Athens at all, or whether, to quote the words of a well-known treatise by Ernst Curtius, "a well-informed witness is here faithfully reproducing the event."[96] For this last question must be regarded from the point of view of the sources, the technique, and the literary potentialities of the book of Acts; these aspects we shall consider later. With regard to the first question, we must examine how Paul, the Paul of the genuine epistles, would have regarded the theme of the Areopagus speech.

Curtius has also examined the Pauline epistles, but from a particular point of view. He says of the Areopagus speech, and rightly, that it seeks to establish an historical understanding of the religious life of the Gentile world. And he adds: "Those are considerations which could present themselves only to one whose mind was familiar with Hellenic culture." Taking this as a starting-point, Curtius seeks to prove from Paul's epistles that the apostle was influ-enced by this culture.

But the question as to whether Paul was as familiar with philosophical ideas as the Areopagus speech presupposes is not the vital one. The proof attempted by Curtius did not extend to the real core of the Pauline message, namely the announcement of the new salvation that appeared in Christ, and all that it presupposes. But Curtius was compelled to declare of the hortatory passages of the Pauline epistles, that is of the parenesis, what we today believe with good reason, that they were not composed by Paul, but largely taken over from the tradition of Christian, Jewish, and Greek philosophers. Of course, much of the material is Greek, or rather, belongs to Hellenistic thought.[97] The same is true of the apostle's metaphorical language, which Curtius quotes in the course of his treatise; especially is it true of the metaphor of the body and of the whole series of metaphors connected with the stadium.

In our examination we must begin at a central point and ask how the Paul of the epistles thought about the natural man's knowledge of a relationship with God. For this is the important issue in the Areopagus speech. As we know, Paul has touched upon the subject of our knowledge of God in the first chapter of Romans, but this is in a context which permits of only one interpretation: the apostle intends to show that there is no excuse for those who worship idols, and particularly images (Rom 1:20: "So they are without excuse" [eis to einai autous anapologētous]). Their sin, however, consists in this, that while they did certainly recognize the true God, they did not honor him—they worshiped the creature instead of the creator. And now, to make the magnitude of their sin quite clear, Paul wrote that sentence in Rom 1:20 which has so often been isolated as evidence of an alleged "natural theology" (theologia naturalis) in Paul, over-emphasized and, as a result, misunderstood: "Ever since the creation of the world his invisible nature, namely, his eternal power and diety, has been clearly perceived in the things that have been made" (ta gar aorata autou apo ktiseōs kosmou tois poiēmasin nooumena kathoratai, hē te aidios autou dunamis kai theiotēs). By nooumena kathoratai "it is seen to be recognized," reference is made to the proof of God's existence from what we perceive in the world,[98] a proof so often found in the Stoa: "His being, which we cannot look upon, has been visible in his works to the thinking mind since the creation of the world, indeed as eternal power and deity." But the Stoic proof is only mentioned; it has no value in Paul's eyes for, in fact, the consequence of that knowledge of God was not that men venerated him, but that they conceived a false idea of him. The knowledge that was given to people as a reality, and not merely as a possibility, did not compel men to fall upon their knees. Deum novisse (to know God) and deum colere (to serve God) did not, as Seneca believed (see p. 112), coincide.

The Areopagus speech shows a different conception of the Stoic proof of God; it is the teleological rather than the cosmological proof which stands foremost. By his intentional provision for men God has himself to some extent challenged them to seek him. Thus it happens that they honor him without knowing him by actual revelation ("What therefore you worship as unknown"; ho oun agnoountes eusebeite; 17:23), and this is demonstrated by the altar with the inscription "to an unknown god." The contradiction between the Epistle to the Romans and the Areopagus speech is clear. Admittedly both mention knowledge of God through creation or the ordering of the world, but, according to the speech, this knowledge leads to man's "feeling after" and honoring the God he believes must exist, whereas, according to the Epistle, it leads certainly to the knowledge of God, but at the same time to a misunderstanding of his power, to a refusal to serve God in the true sense, and to man's becoming ensnared in false service of idols. In Rom 1:23, 25 the error of serving idols is spoken of in an indignant tone; but in an admonishing and reproving one in Acts 17:29.

The second evidence of natural man's knowledge of God is provided in the Areopagus speech by man's relationship with God. Paul, on the other hand, is not concerned with this at all. Of course, he has used a succession of new phrases that are reminiscent partly of the language of the mystics, partly of the mysteries, to emphasize the nearness of man to Christ. But here the subject and object of the relationship are different from those in the Areopagus speech: it is not a question of communion with God, but always, in the first place, of communion with Christ; the close relationship with God arises only through Christ. The man who enters into this relationship with the divine world is, above all, however, not simply man, but man redeemed, the bearer of the Holy Spirit, the Christian, who belongs not only to the community but really belongs to Christ. But the speaker on the Areopagus turns to non-Christians and he calls them also the family of God. In a very characteristic way Luther turned these words into poetry. In the Christmas carol *Vom Himmel kam der Engel Schar* (From Heaven Came the Angel Throng) the final verse begins thus:

> *Zu letzt müsst ihr doch haben recht,*
> *Ihr seid nun worden Gotts Geschlecht.*[99]

Those who have "now" become the family of God can only be Christians; the word "now" refers to Christmas, but the people who in the Areopagus speech are called the family of God are the Gentile hearers.

Paul would never have written in this way. He is too deeply convinced that man is estranged from God (Romans 1–3), and, indeed, really estranged, and not simply in that each individual once refused to obey God's commands. This estrangement is written as "sin" (*hamartia*), in the singular, and it is said in Rom 7:17, 20 of this power of sin that it dwells in persons and does with them what it will. Humans are not near to God, but at enmity with God (Rom 5:10); they need reconciliation with God, and this they receive through Christ and not by their own achievement (2 Cor 5:20-21).[100] Paul would never ascribe even to Christians as direct a relationship with God as the speaker on the Areopagus ascribes to men generally, or as is ascribed to Christians in that carol of Luther's and in 1 John 2:5 and, probably, 5:18.[101] He is filled with too great an awe of God who is Lord of all things; he is too thoroughly steeped in the Old Testament idea of God's inaccessibility; it seems to him impossible to apply the predicate "divine" (*theios*) to any man. He lives "in Christ," but not "in God"; he can speak of being transformed into the image of Christ (2 Cor 3:18), but not of apotheosis.

What distinguished Paul of the Acts of the Apostles from the real Paul can be shown by a few more details. The Areopagus speech speaks of times of ignorance; this means the times when men certainly possessed that natural knowledge of God but allowed it to lead them only to honor the unknown god. Now, the Christian message brings them a certain proclamation of God, and to it belongs the news that God will overlook that period when they worshiped ignorantly. Because he now sends to the Gentiles also the message that makes his nature known, the honor previously paid to the Unknown One (more from instinct than from knowledge) is to be mentioned no more. Nothing is said about sin and grace in so many words; the old and the new age are as distinct from one another as ignorance and knowledge. Paul says, however, in the Epistle to the Romans (3:25-26), when dealing with the subject of salvation, that the old age was a time when God was exercising patience. The sins of humanity accumulated but God showed forbearance (*paresis*). Now, and with this the new age begins, he has proclaimed in the death of Christ that atonement (*hilastērion*) has been made for all that is past and that, at the same time, by his grace, the gift of righteousness has been bestowed on all believers. So the old age is to the new as sin is to grace. The division into two ages is the same in Paul and in Acts but, in Romans, the distinction between the two ages has its roots in the Old Testament–Christian idea of the just God with whom man must enter into a covenant-relationship, whereas, in the Areopagus speech, the distinction arises out of the Greek conception of God as the object of human knowledge. We have here two different worlds of thought.

Finally, in this context, we may mention once more the word *pistis*, which is used in the Areopagus speech (17:31) in a manner completely foreign to Paul, in the sense of "proof." God will judge the world through the man whom he has chosen, after he has, by this man's resurrection, "given all people proof" (that he has been chosen) (*pistin paraschōn pasi*). The Western reading, *pistin pareschein*, is confirmed as the infinitive *pareschein* by the Latin, d, and gig. Then, however, it gives a different sense to the whole sentence: "By means of the man whom he has chosen, to give faith (that is, the possibility of faith) to all men, after he has caused him to rise again from the dead." The sentence no longer sounds strange; it becomes a part of a proclamation that is, generally speaking, Christian. But the manuscript D shows once more an anxiety to bring Hellenistic elements in the Areopagus speech into conformity with Christian ideas and so to remove from it whatever is alien.[102]

The speech is as alien to the New Testament (apart from Acts 14:15-17) as it is familiar to Hellenistic, particularly Stoic, philosophy. Analysis has shown that it is not only subsidiary motifs that are derived from it; the main ideas of the speech, knowledge of God and God's relationship with man, are Stoic rather than Christian. But it was not only the Areopagus speech that introduced these ideas into Christianity. Soon after the book of Acts was written, the first epistle of Clement appeared; this, by virtue of its style, its interpretation of the saga of the Phoenix, and its emphasis upon the cosmic harmony belong entirely to Hellenistic literature. This letter, the *Praedicatio Petri,* and the *Shepherd of Hermas* already contain negative definitions of the being of God (compare pp. 105–6), assertions that have been occasioned by the philosophical desire to define the nature of God and not by the desire to conform to his commands. It is the Apologists of the second century, however, who have given prominence to this philosophical theology, this striving after the being of God and the knowledge of God, this attempt to make God accessible through the nature and meaning of the world. The speaker on the Areopagus is the precursor of the Apologists.

But the Church followed them and not Paul. The Church saw no necessity here of refuting a heresy, as in the case of the radical-dualistic, Gnostic conception of man and God. She used the opportunity to make her teaching a part of Hellenistic culture. In this way she avoided the infiltration of heathen myths, but forfeited the numinous solemnity of the biblical proclamation of God, which aims, not at knowing the nature of God, but as subjecting one's self to him in belief. The Church furnished proofs of God's existence and confirmed assertions concerning the qualities of God. She deduced her doctrine of God from her contemplation of the world, and forced eschatology, the core of early Christian preaching, to the place that it takes in the Areopagus speech, namely the end.

The magnitude of this change cannot easily be overestimated, for the whole of ecclesiastical theology was affected by it. As far as the doctrine of God was concerned, it increasingly followed in the steps of the Apologists, and thus of the philosophers, rather than along the lines of Old and New Testament belief in God. Admittedly, Gnosticism compelled ecclesiastical theology to speak philosophically of God, but the fact that it could do so to this extent is an indication of the extent to which it had become hellenized. Speculations about God as the One, as the only substance, negative definitions of the being of God, all show that theologians of the Church thought it supremely important to have the correct conception of God.[103] Herein lay the primary cause, not only of the Monarchical, but also of the Arian dispute, which began with the assertion that "unbegotten being" (*agannēton einai*) was God. All these theological struggles cannot be envisaged without the philosophical-Hellenistic transformation of the idea of God. The first sign of this transformation, however, embedded in the New Testament is the Areopagus speech.

THE SPEECH AND THE BOOK OF ACTS

Embedded in the New Testament—this presents a further problem, one of a *literary nature.* If the Areopagus speech is foreign to the New Testament, is it then also a foreign body in the book of Acts, composed by an editor, traces of whose work can be discerned in all likely passages of the book?

The speech is found within an account of Paul's appearance in Athens; this report can, likewise, be described as unique, particularly on account of its portrayal of the Athenians. At none of Paul's mission centers has the author given such a colorful picture of those to whom Paul preached. Agora and Areopagus, Epicureans and Stoics are mentioned. The Athenians are described in Attic phrases as people who "have no time for anything except to tell or to hear something new";[104] they name the apostle Paul (and this seems to be characteristic for the Athenians) a "clever babbler"[105] and in the accusation that he brings strange gods there is probably an echo of the accusation which was once brought against Socrates.[106] In fact, these few verses are teeming with allusions. This characteristic of the Athenians has rightly been called "the most cultivated feature" appearing anywhere in the New Testament.[107]

At any rate, the account of Paul in Athens was written by someone who was able to choose his style freely. And if, supposedly because he does not preserve such artistic style elsewhere,[108] we say that Luke (to give this name to the author of Acts)[109] was not the writer of this account, then we must ask, on the other hand, whether this alleged editor of Acts has shown such ability to stylize in any other passage. It seems to me that we cannot deduce from this a theory that the work has been revised.

If the question of historicity is provisionally adjourned, we can, however, make out a good case for the derivation of this narrative and the Areopagus speech from the same author, for the description of Athens and the Athenians has obviously been composed as a preface to the speech.

The first thing we are told concerning Paul is of his perturbation about the number of idols in Athens. This is a preparation for the introduction and the third theme of the speech: for the Athenians' acknowledgement of the "reverence for God" (*deisidaimonia*) and the warning against serving idols. Certainly, a difference of judgment seems to be evident here: the narrative does not speak with approval of the Athenians, as does the speech. The difference must not be exaggerated: the perturbation may refer to the task and need not necessarily indicate anger; moreover, it does apply to the images, and they are also criticized in the speech. Nevertheless the difference in tone between 17:16 and 17:22 is bound to strike the reader of Acts, but a similar divergence between narrative and speeches can also be established elsewhere in the book of Acts.[110] Let us remember that the conversion of Paul is reported somewhat differently in the two speeches (22:6-16 and 26:12-18) from the way it is in the narrative (9:1-19). And, although we may read in Paul's speech before the procurator Felix (24:17) the mention of the collection as the real purpose of Paul's journey to Jerusalem, on the other hand there is the fact that the narrative of the journey says nothing about it. Also, the speeches made in the assembly of the apostles (Acts 15:7-21) are not at all in accordance with the tense situation that has previously been described.[111] The reason for these evidently conscious variations is probably that these speeches express distinct complexes of ideas which are important in themselves, and that they therefore dispense with any strict regard for the prevailing historical circumstances. In many cases it may also be that the author is trying to achieve literary variation. In any case, the difference in the way the pagan world is judged (Acts 17) cannot be traced back to a difference of source, but to the conscious aim of the author.

The narrative tells further of Paul's appearance in the synagogue and in the Agora. The synagogue and the Jews, of course, do not feature at all in the speech on the Areopagus, and that is in accordance with the occasion. The Epicureans and the Stoics are mentioned, however, as being among the apostle's listeners, and, in fact, this mention of the philosophers effectively prepares for and characterizes the essential content of the speech, as we have noted in our analysis. One might almost be inclined to include the expression "babbler" (*spermologos*) in this context. This derogatory condemnation of the apostle as a man of catch-phrases would then (by foreshadowing the reverse of the truth) prepare the way for the subsequent quotations from the poets. However, the connection of this is not verifiable, since we cannot be certain that *spermologos* has here the special meaning of "catch-phrase-hunter"; but we are told clearly and expressly in 17:18 that the mention of strange gods is to prepare the way for the speech. The Athenians believe that Paul is preaching of Jesus and of the resurrection; the latter is obviously understood to be a goddess, and this explains the assertion that he is proclaiming "foreign divinities" (*xena daimonia*). It is no accident that the Areopagus speech then reaches its climax in the mention of Jesus and his resurrection, thus again taking up the motif of 17:18.[112]

Acts 17:20 and 21 are a direct preparation for the speech; they show that the Athenians are not repelled but, on the contrary, attracted by something strange, thus even by the proclamation of strange deities. After hearing him in the Agora, they therefore cause the apostle to expound his strange teaching once more and select an illustrious setting, the Areopagus: "And they took hold of him and brought him to the Areopagus" (17:19); "So Paul, standing in the middle of the Areopagus" (17:22).

Admittedly the interpretation which we presuppose here is not uncontested; Ernst Curtius[113] and Sir William Ramsey[114] have given considerable weight to the view that the writer of Acts did not mean at all the "sacred assembly-place upon the hill," but that by Areopagus he was describing the magistracy which conducted its affairs in the Stoa Basileios,[115] thus in the Agora. We have to imagine the seats arranged in a semi-circle, so that Paul could indeed stand "in the middle of the Areopagus," but could "still be audible to the crowd across the marketplace." Indeed, the powers of the court that met on the Areopagus seem later on to have been not solely judicial ones, but probably included also oversight of religious affairs.[116] The Areopagus speech is certainly not a speech of defense, in court, before judges.[117] It mentions neither an accusation nor an impending judgment. Moreover, it really amounts to preaching but in no way seeks to justify the speaker's right to preach, nor does it claim that there is no moral harm or political danger in this sermon. Finally, no imprisonment is reported[118] at the beginning and no verdict at the end; indeed, the very vague verse 17:33 does not even report that Paul was released.

More easily one could believe that, standing in the Agora before the Stoa Basileios, in the circle of the Areopagites, Paul spoke to the people of Athens, somewhat in the position in which he is represented in the Raphael cartoon in the Victoria and Albert Museum in London. In support of this, it is usual to quote the fact that the Areopagus hill itself offered no space for the crowd of hearers, and that the scene occurred therefore in a more suitable place. The account in Acts, however, says nothing about a great crowd; and even if there had been more than twenty people present, then although they would not have found space up on the hill, there would have been room for them on the high, broad ridge south-east of the Areopagus. There the hill does not descend as steeply as toward north and east; there, that is, between the Areopagus and the Acropolis, a considerable number of people would have found a place where they could hear.[119] Thus, considerations of topography do not require the scene to be set in the Agora.

It seems to me, however, that the decision must be reached neither by topographical nor by historical, but by literary considerations. We have first to establish what Luke wishes to convey (quite apart form whether it appears to us as probable or not); only then can we ask whether he used traditions or fashioned the material in his own way and, finally, whether we can regard as historically possible the picture which he in this way produced. We cannot overlook the way in which Luke fashioned the scene, whether correctly from the historical point of view or not. The first exchanges between Paul and the Athenian spokesmen take place in the city; he speaks in the synagogue to the Jews and the "God-fearing" Gentiles, and in the Agora to the passers-by. If, according to 17:19, his partners now take him by the hand and lead him to the Areopagus, we cannot believe that the next scene again takes place in the market-place, before the Royal Colonnade; undoubtedly, a change of locality is taken for granted: thus Luke means the Hill of Ares.[120]

Now, however, arises the literary question, namely Luke's authority in fashioning this scene, that is, what material he used for it. Elsewhere I have tried to show that obviously a record, which may be described as an itinerary, underlies the presentation of Paul's journeys in Acts (13:1—14:28; 15:35—21:16);[121] information about the stations on the journey, the hosts, the preaching and the results of preaching, the founding of communities, disputes and either voluntary or forced departures—all these constantly recur, varying with the situation at the time, and these may therefore be considered as the constituent parts of this itinerary. We cannot imagine that these records, with their concise and impartial style, were written down with the purpose of edifying or of entertaining. Nor are they colorful enough to be regarded as the local traditions of individual communities.

The limits of the itinerary can be roughly defined only by means of stylistic criticism. The recurrence of accounts of the type mentioned can be observed in respect of the individual stations on the journeys. We can also observe how these itinerary accounts diverge from other elements of the narrative, that is, the speeches and the individual stories. The appearance of "we" in the narrative does not greatly help in establishing the limits of the itinerary, however; we cannot suppose that there was one particular source for the so-called "we-passages" (16:10-17; 20:5-15; 21:1-18—the voyage to Rome does not belong to the account of the missionary journey with which we are concerned) and another source (or none at all) for the accounts of other stations. There are various important reasons why we should not distinguish a particular "we-source," as is still frequently done by critical research even today. In the first place, the "we-passages" do not differ, from a lexicographical point of view, from the other sections: Harnack has convincingly showed this.[122] Nor do they differ from the point of view of style; that can easily be seen, for example, in the stations Philippi (16:11-15, first person) and Thessalonica (17:1-9, third person): it is the same type of account, given in the same brief and unemotional style. Nor do the "we-passages" differ from the other sections in subject matter. We read the same sort of account about Philippi (first person) as about Corinth: where Paul lived and where he preached, how long he worked and what success he achieved. Individual stories, like speeches, are similarly divided among "we-stations" and "they-stations."

Of course, there can be no question of determining the limits of the itinerary completely accurately by means of style-criticism, but we can say what obviously does not belong to the itinerary. This is particularly true of the stories that are complete in themselves, whose form even now partly betrays the fact that they were passed on as separate stories in the communities. It is the speeches, then, which, in accordance with the custom of ancient historians, were inserted by the author. Whether in doing so he was able to rely occasionally upon his own or someone else's memory we cannot say, since we have absolutely no information on the subject. The probability is that the speeches were written by the author, with the primary intentions of guiding his readers, rather than extending their knowledge of history. The speeches answer the question: how is one to speak? and not the question: how did that man speak at that time?

Thus, for literary reasons, the Areopagus speech must be regarded as a composition of the author of Acts, and not of someone who revised the whole book. Now, as new evidence in support of this conclusion, we have the results of our analysis of its doctrine. It has been shown that the theology of the Areopagus speech is absolutely foreign to Paul's own theology, that it is, in fact, foreign to the entire New Testament.[123] It has its counterpart only in the few sentences Paul speaks in Lystra (Acts 14:15-17) in order to restrain the crowd from honoring himself and Barnabas as gods.[124] Both speeches were composed by the author, both are intended to be examples of what Luke, writing about the year 90, regards as a pattern for Christian proclamation to the Gentiles. Another indication that both speeches are the work of the author of Acts is the fact that the transition from speech to narrative is again not achieved without some difficulty. The speech in Lystra takes place at the most dramatic moment of an incident that is present in the form of an independent story. This story begins in 14:8 and tells how, as the result of a successful act of healing, Paul and Barnabas are honored in Lystra as if they were gods.[125] This story, which is so characteristic and so vivid, deserved, and originally had, a conclusion which was different from what we now read in 14:18: "and with such words they scarcely restrained the people from sacrificing to them." Here, the insertion of the speech has obviously supplanted the original ending. The Areopagus speech ends in an equally colorless manner in 17:33: "So Paul went out from among them." "This" may refer to the differences of opinion among the listeners that have previously been mentioned;[126] it may, however, simply mean that the apostle was neither insulted nor pressed to stay. But this vague ending to the scene enables the author to add a short account of the result of the speech: some people attached themselves to Paul and were converted, "among them Dionysius the Areopagite and a woman named Damaris and others with them" (17:34).

This account has a special significance. It is obviously intended to show that Paul's success in Athens was slight. Since it seems that in fact no community was founded as a result of the apostle's activities, this indication has to be taken seriously. Attempts have even been made to draw from this point conclusions bearing on the Areopagus speech itself.[127] The failure in Athens, it is alleged, caused Paul to change his method of approach and henceforth simply to preach the cross of Christ in the sense which he described in 1 Cor 1:18-31. It is claimed that he realized he could not hope to achieve much success from adapting himself to the philosophical ideas of the Greeks, especially to the ideas of the people to be converted. Some scholars think that this change of method simply means that Paul is returning to the method he used a long time previously, that what we see in the Areopagus speech was an exception, an experiment. Others believe that Paul discovered his own style only as a result of his failure in Athens. Now this view that Paul underwent a change, which we should almost have to regard as a second conversion, is sheer fantasy. There is not a shred of evidence that such a change did take place in Paul, and, what is more important, both aspects of this suggestion ascribe to Luke a procedure which it is quite impossible to envisage. Apart from the little speech in Acts 14:15-17, the Areopagus speech is Paul's only sermon to the Gentiles recorded in the book of Acts; the greatest apostle to the Gentiles would then, in this portrayal of his work, be represented only by an unsuccessful speech to the Gentiles, one which, as the apostle himself realized, was to be regarded as a failure. This seems to me to be too high a price to pay for the historicity of the Areopagus speech! No, Luke wrote this speech as an example of a typical sermon to Gentiles and put it in the setting of Athens; in doing so, he did not allow himself to be influenced by the poor results which Paul actually achieved in Athens.

As we saw, he also composed at any rate the major part of the narrative introduction, for it was written with the speech in mind and, in view of the details of the place that it gives, may be regarded as a unique passage. The question now arises as to whether we can see traces of the itinerary (or whatever we like to call the account which the author had at his disposal) in the whole section dealing with Athens.[128] In the introductory scene there occurs a sentence which does not show the same literary style as the rest of the account, but describes Paul's activities in Athens in a simple and compressed style (17:17): "So he argued in the synagogue with the Jews and the devout persons, and in the market place every day with those who chanced to be there." This is how Acts, doubtless following that account, describes Paul's preaching activities elsewhere in the book as well: the verb "argue" (*dialegesthai*) is used in connection with Thessalonica, Corinth, Ephesus, and Troas (17:2; 18:4, 19; 19:8-9; 20:7, 9).[129] The synagogue also is regularly mentioned in these contexts, except in Troas: the reference to the Agora is peculiar to the account concerning Athens, but is no more remarkable than that to the *Hellenes* in Corinth (18:4). That one sentence (17:17), therefore, seems to belong to the itinerary. No doubt that is also the case with the final sentence (17:34), which describes the poor results and gives the names of the two converts. For a legend about the conversion of the distinguished Areopagite Dionysius would have a quite different appearance. There is therefore some doubt as to whether the "joined him and believed" (*kollēthentes aut episteusan*) means an actual conversion to Christianity or simply a readiness, perhaps, to agree with the sermon; for nothing is said about the founding of a Christian community.[130] The same question can be raised in respect of Acts 13:12, where Luke uses the same word "believed" (*episteusen*) to describe the success of the Christian sermon before the proconsul Sergius Paulus in Paphos. It is doubtful whether these distinguished figures, the high-ranking official in Paphos and the Areopagite in Athens, became Christians permanently, since we hear no more either of them or of the founding of Christian communities in connection with their conversion. This is not to say, however, that the Areopagite Dionysius was not mentioned in the itinerary of Paul's journeys. He and Damaris were obviously described in these notes as being willing listeners; therefore Luke thought it right that they should be mentioned here.

As is well known, the mention of the Areopagite's name here caused one of the later writers among the ancients, a mystic-Neoplatonist theologian, to have his works published under the same name. This pseudo-Dionysius had keen insight: he chose as the patron-author of his synthesis of mystical Hellenism and Christianity the man who, according to the Acts of the Apostles, was said to have been converted by a synthesis of rational Hellenism and the Christian missionary message, namely the Areopagus speech.

We cannot say what other accounts about Athens, beside these two observations (Acts 17:17 and 34), may have existed in the itinerary. We might hazard a guess that other people, who received Paul's sermon less kindly, were mentioned before the "some men" in 17:34, and we could produce similar examples out of Luke's actual account.[131] But such conjectures cannot really be systematically proved.

Perhaps, also, the mention of the Areopagite in the itinerary had a particular effect upon the author of Acts. Perhaps it caused him to set the scene of the speech on the Areopagus, thus giving a classical pulpit to the classical sermon—for he wanted the speech to be regarded as such. All the historical questions which we raise concerning the suitability of the place would then have worried him as little as the fact that, at that time, Paul had practically no success in Athens. The scene that he portrayed was not intended to be understood in the context of that missionary journey; he did not want to raise

Athens—which had almost closed its ears to the sermon—above Corinth, the station where Paul was successful. He wanted to give us a picture that would be over and above the historical; and, for him, Athens was obviously still the symbol of Greek culture.

He knew from those accounts of the journeys that, as we are told in 1 Thess 3:1, when making his first journey to Greece, Paul had actually been in Athens, but this journey to Greece was, in Luke's eyes, an event affecting the entire world. His whole handling of the account in Acts 16:6-10 aims at emphasizing how divine providence was instrumental in causing this journey to take place: the journey was not planned—Paul was compelled to make it, by the leading of the Spirit and by a nocturnal vision. Undoubtedly Luke, who participated to some extent in the Greek world of culture, realized the importance of the event that occurred as the Christian apostle entered Greece. Paul's appearance in Athens is, for the author, the focal point of this great event in the history of evangelism and religion. Therefore Luke conjures up in a few sentences the whole individuality of Athens as it was at that time, in order to give the right background to the apostle's sermon; for this reason he brings the apostle to an illustrious place, sanctified by a great tradition, and for this reason he lets Paul speak more of the Gentile way of recognizing God than of the Christian way. Of course, this God is none other than the Father of Jesus Christ; the apostle really knows him, while his listeners only suspect his existence. This introduction, which is, of course, really intended to lead to the Christian message of salvation, is attractive to the listeners because it is something new. The apostle's words signify not a judgment upon the lost state of the Gentiles, but rather a fulfillment of their unconscious longings.

Paul might have been portrayed differently. He could have offered the gospel as a complete contrast. He would in that case have made his appearance in the city of wonderful temples and splendid images with the coarse story of a savior on the gallows.[132] In that case, he would have spoken, not of man related to God, but of man sold to sin, not of the free wise man with all his pride, but of the man freed by Christ for loving service. The author would then have been fairer to the true Paul than he has been in the Areopagus speech, but he would not have rendered to the Christianity of his own day and of the future the service which his book was intended to render, that is to say, he would not have shown how the gospel went out into the world and how it must be proclaimed to this world. So let his Paul preach, preach in one of the most distinguished places in Greece, in the way that he thought the Greeks ought to be preached to at that time: with philosophical proofs, with comparative acknowledgements to Greek monotheism, and pressing into service the words of wisdom spoken by Greek poets.

In fact, Luke strayed too far from the Paul who was the theologian of the paradoxes of grace and faith; nevertheless, he gave for the future the signal for the Christian message to be spread abroad by means of Hellenistic culture. And if it has been justly said that succeeding generations of Christians misunderstood the real Paul, they understood the speaker on the Areopagus created by Luke. By "Paul on the Areopagus" is meant not an historical, but a symbolic encounter. The Areopagus speech became a symbol of Christian theology in the environment of Greek culture.

8

Paul in Athens

The author of the book of Acts in the New Testament wanted to describe the first Christian mission but really only presented Paul's journeys. These seemed to him to be significant for the future, since they showed the spread of belief in Christianity from Jerusalem toward Rome. Obviously he had a source for these journeys. Many investigators thought they could restore this source by concentrating on those parts of the work that are written in the "we-style" (16:10-17; 20:5-15; 21:1-18; 27:1—28:16). Adolf von Harnack, in particular, has proved in modern times that we cannot be certain that this theory of the "we-source" is justified: he has shown that what we find in the "we-passages" and in the other parts of the account of the journeys is, from the lexicographical standpoint, the same.

We might argue that the vocabulary used belongs to the author of the whole work and that the style of the whole is therefore, to some extent, leveled out. But the argument from the lexicographical standpoint is supported and confirmed by other considerations. All the scanty accounts which the book gives of the missionary stations—whether they are "we-passages" or not—fit in with the same scheme. The arrival and accommodation of the missionaries are always dealt with, also the point of contact for their evangelism which they seek (and generally find within the Jewish community), their preaching, the disturbance of their activities (usually by the Jews), and the results, which include the names of new converts. This sort of information is too dull to be legend, too detailed to be fiction. Its colorless nature also prevents us from assuming that the author of the book composed it himself on the basis of information he had. He writes differently, at least where he can expand freely. So we have before us fragments of a source, of an itinerary, which must ultimately be ascribed to one of the company on the journey.

In view of this, it no longer matters whether the "we" was really to be found in the itinerary or whether it was inserted by the writer of Acts in order to indicate his part in the journey. It is sufficient that this writer possessed such a source and used it in accordance with his own purposes. He abbreviated it

where he was not interested in the stations (as in 16:6-8 and 20:2-3). He ampli-
fied it where he either knew more about them or wanted to say more about
them. The former is the case where the writer includes in his account stories
which are isolated but which were already well known. The latter occurs
where he inserts speeches by his hero Paul: in the synagogue at Antioch in
Pisidia (chap. 13), on the Areopagus in Athens (chap. 17), and on the shore of
Miletus to the elders of the congregation of Ephesus (chap. 20).

These speeches have been constantly examined from the point of view of
their historicity—that is to say, of whether they ever actually took place. We
might have known from Thucydides or Josephus that at least this cannot be
the first question to ask about such speeches. We must first ask what the
author of the book intends to convey by them. In Antioch Paul makes a speech
that in construction and content is reminiscent of Peter's speeches in Acts 2, 3,
and 10, and there is nothing in either of these speeches that would be characteristic of either apostle. The author's intention is obvious. He wants to show
how the Christian message should be preached in his day: in the last decades
of the first century. In giving only one sermon addressed to Gentiles by the
great apostle to the Gentiles, namely the Areopagus speech in Athens, his primary purpose is to give an example of how the Christian missionary should
approach cultured Gentiles.

This intention is seen in the choice of setting. Paul first founded a great
Greek missionary center in Corinth; he stayed there eighteen months and
gathered a considerable community. According to Acts 17:32-34, Paul seems
to have had no particular success in Athens. Few people are mentioned as
having been won by him, and it is only after many decades that we hear of a
Christian community in Athens. Even so, Athens means more than Corinth to
the author of Acts. Corinth is the gateway to the world, Athens the gateway to
wisdom. In Corinth the nations land from both sides of the Mediterranean
and give the city an international character, and it is an historical fact that this
stream of culture was favorable to the Christian community. For the author,
however, Athens still harbors something that is Greek; Athens still has a feeling for the unknown and a curiosity to hear something new. In fact, it was
probably this intellectualism that resisted the simple message of Christian
salvation. But the clash of these two worlds, namely that of the successors of
the Athenian philosophers and that of the preacher of the gospel, as a subject
is particularly attractive to the writer of this narrative; it gives something of
significance to Paul's short stay in Athens and symbolical meaning to the
scene on the Areopagus.

In a short characterization of the city and its inhabitants (one which, with
regard to both style and content, has no parallel in the New Testament), the
author has shown what he himself thought about Athens. We have previously

been told, in the style of the itinerary, that Paul spoke in the synagogue and in the Agora. Now we read:

> Some also of the Epicurean and Stoic philosophers met him. And some said, "What would this babbler say?" Others said, "He seems to be a preacher of foreign divinities"—because he preached Jesus and the resurrection. And they took hold of him and brought him to the Areopagus, saying, "May we know what this new teaching is which you present? For you bring some strange things to our ears; we wish to know therefore what these things mean." Now all the Athenians and the foreigners who lived there spent their time in nothing except telling or hearing something new. (Acts 17:18-21)

The localizing of Paul's sermon on the Areopagus also belongs to this colorful portrayal of the scene in Athens. For it is certainly the ancient, sacred assembly-place northwest of the Acropolis which is meant. Admittedly Ernst Curtius and Sir William Ramsey have come to the conclusion that Paul could not possibly have made this speech on the Areopagus, and many others have since said the same thing. It has been argued that the Hill of Ares is too small for such a crowd of people, and also that such a speech, which was of a non-legal nature, belongs not to the old place of judgment but to the Agora. In the marketplace, before the Royal Colonnade, there would probably have been seats for the use of members of the Areopagus when they were engaged in their business of examining or administering. Paul could have spoken there, standing between the Areopagites and yet addressing the whole crowd.

But that topographical argument is invalid. The space—not on the narrow hill but on the ridge lying southeast of it toward the Acropolis—would have been sufficient for the number of listeners which the account gives us to understand were present. The first thing for us to ask is not where Paul could speak best, but where the author of Acts imagined him to be. There can be no doubt that the scene reproduced above makes it quite clear that the people who were curious to hear him led him, not to the Agora, to that place before the Royal Colonnade, but that they went away from the Agora with him, so that the Areopagus is in fact the place where the sermon was preached.

To help to provide the scene with local color, the speech is introduced with a reference to the famous inscription on the altar: "To an unknown god." There is evidence in various writers that it was said of the Athenians—either in admiration or mockery—that they were so pious that they set up altars to gods whom they did not know. Presumably, unknown gods were honored in order that none should be overlooked. But the fear or anxiety reflected in the inscription becomes, for the speaker on the Areopagus, a presentiment of the Great Unknown, whom Paul has come to the city to proclaim.

The speech itself is particularly remarkable because it contains so little that is Christian.[1] Jesus and the coming judgment are mentioned only at the end, and even then the name of Jesus is avoided. It is a Hellenistic speech about recognizing God. The author of the book of Acts, who composed it, has prepared the way for it in the narrative: in the reference to the idols, in the introduction of the Epicureans and Stoics, and perhaps also in the mention of the derisive name "babbler," which the Athenians dubbed the apostle. The philosophical questions received a philosophical answer because the knowledge of God is not proved by the Old Testament or Christian revelation. The proofs of the presence of God, which are here paraded anew, are rather those which had been known to philosophy for a long time; the human knowledge of the ingenious arrangement of the world order and the consciousness of the natural relation of humanity to God (not limited to Christians) should convince one of the existence of God and of the close relationship between God and humanity. And this relationship to God is proved with citations from one, or as we may now assume, from two authors: Epimenides and Aratus.[2]

This then was what the author imagined a model Christian sermon to educated Gentiles was like at the end of the first Christian century. All this has very little to do with Paul, the Paul of the epistles. Paul preached the paradox of grace and faith; the sermon on the Areopagus, however, speaks of sound reason; Paul deals with the revelation in Christ, the sermon with the evidence of God in the arrangement of the world and in the thoughts of humanity. That which was preached on the Areopagus, according to the book of Acts, will be repeated in the second century by the representatives of an educated philosophical Christianity, the Apologists, in a much more wordy and much more learned manner. This Christian theology has then, however, become more Stoic than biblical. At any rate, one is not justified in giving Paul's sermon on the Areopagus a Christian meaning until one is able to concede that even Paul could have said something similar at one time. The real parallels to this sermon are to be found not in the epistles of Paul, but in the writings of Cicero and Seneca and in those of their Greek predecessors. It is true, no doubt, that Paul on occasion also followed a stoic train of thought. In this case we have to deal, however, with thoughts that play a minor role in Paul's theology. The author of the book of Acts, however, had no desire to use the sermon on the Areopagus to parade nonessentials and what was merely opportune. It is the only sermon to the Gentiles in which he mentions of the great Apostle of the Gentiles. This scene would be typical of the mission to the Gentiles.

And the scene is typical. It is not typical of the historical Paul, however, but of the mission from a generation after his death. One sees in what an uncultivated form the Christian gospel was carried to the West; one also senses the measure in which the theology of the ancient church was based on Stoic rather than on Christian suppositions. The process of reconstitution was necessary if the educated people of the Roman empire were to grasp it; it had to be said in their own language and in terms they could understand. At the beginning of this process of reconstitution, however, stands the sermon on the Areopagus of the book of Acts—and therein lies its historical significance.[3]

9

The Apostolic Council

The rivalry of different sources still makes it difficult for us to assess the so-called Apostolic Council. Many commentators associate Acts 11:29-30 with the two accounts, Gal 2:1-10 and Acts 15:1-29. Here, they say, the same event must be described as in Galatians 2, for Paul knows nothing in Gal 1:20-24 of any visit to Jerusalem before the conference of the apostles. To touch briefly on this,[1] it certainly seems to me that Acts 11:29-30 is an innocent allusion, intended to wind up the information about Agabus and perhaps used by the author in the wrong place. In any case, the important thing reported in these verses is simply the collection; they are not intended to report any thoroughgoing apostolic conference.

A further complication in the question of the source arises out of the β-text of Acts 15:1-5 (to give as neutral a name as possible to the so-called Western text). This text contains a sharper presentation of the conflict. Christian Pharisees from Judea who, according to this account, promoted dissension in Antioch by their insistence on circumcision and moral observances request Paul, who holds fast to his own view, to go with a few companions to Jerusalem and there allow himself to "be advised." But, as the β-text continued, it precludes the idea that any aspersion upon Paul is intended here, for the contribution to the discussion[2] made by the β-text minimizes the dispute, rather than magnifying it. We can thus regard the corrections provided by the β-text in 15:1-5 as supplements to and summaries of the somewhat general "popular" text, amplifications such as β often provides, rather than the emergence of a new point of view.

There remain, therefore, the accounts in Galatians 2 and Acts 15, but it is remarkable that the peculiarities of these are seldom fully appreciated and that our understanding of Acts 15, especially, suffers from the fact that the comparison with Galatians 2 is brought in too soon. This account must first be appreciated for its own sake. Indeed, this is important, and I find it difficult to understand why attention has not been drawn more often and more forcefully to its very strange character. Only a few commentators (especially Loisy) have even noticed what is so striking.

The course of the narrative is as follows: a serious dispute breaks out in Antioch because Christians coming from Judea are teaching the "brethren" that circumcision is necessary to the salvation of Gentile Christians. It is decided that Paul and Barnabas shall be sent to the "apostles and the elders" in Jerusalem and shall put the dispute before them. The envoys are kindly received by the community and their leaders, and they made known (as they had done already on their way to Jerusalem) the results of the mission to the Gentiles. Here also, however, the Christian Pharisees insist that Gentile Christians shall be circumcised and fulfill their obligations to the law. "The apostles and the elders were gathered together to consider this matter" (15:6). We see from v. 12 that the community is present; they are also present according to the mss. 614 and syr[h]. As in Antioch, a dispute arises until Peter stands up and makes a speech. And this speech, which is supposed to settle the question of circumcision for Gentile Christians, has recourse to Peter's experience with Cornelius![3] "Brethren, you know that in the early days God made choice among you, that by my mouth the Gentiles should hear the word of the gospel and believe" (15:7). Therefore, because God gave the Holy Spirit to Cornelius and his family, without their first becoming Jews, other Gentile Christians ought not to have the yoke of the law laid upon them either.

There is much that is remarkable in this speech, especially the fact that the reference to Acts 10:1-48, which, in itself, it quite vague, cannot be understood by Peter's hearers, but can be understood by the readers of the book. The story of Cornelius has great significance for the book; this explains the expression "in the early days" (*aph' hēmerōn archaiōn*) which lends classical dignity to the story. We can see that the narrative of Cornelius is the work of the writer Luke,[4] for, by including the vision of Peter, the reference to this vision in 10:27-29, the speech, and the account of the justification of Peter in 2:1-42, he has extended the story of Cornelius and given it fundamental significance.[5] Originally, it was the simple story of a conversion, without further significance. Peter enters Cornelius's house, just as Philip enters the Ethiopian's chariot (8:31). Luke saw the story as evidence of the fact that the conversion of the Gentiles depended upon the will of God and not upon a decision by Peter or by Paul. But who in the "Apostolic Council" knows that? Only the readers of the book know and understand it. So Peter's speech is founded upon the literary work of the author and can be understood only in the context of this work. The ending of the speech is also remarkable, asserting as it does that the law has always been unbearable, even for Jews. Loisy's remark "Paul could not have said it better" does not seem to me quite right.[6] Paul does not place the emphasis where it is placed in this passage. Paul also means that the law was not fulfilled by men, but it was not annulled for that reason, but because Christ has dealt with it. It is thus the theology of Luke that we have here, for the words are not in the least appropriate to the Peter of the Antiochan dispute (Gal 2:11-14).

No discussion follows Peter's speech. With a colorless transitional statement[7] the author introduces the account given by Paul and Barnabas of the signs that God gave and the miracles that he caused to be performed among the Gentiles. What they said would be of great pertinence, and would furnish a decisive contribution toward settling the dispute about circumcision— arguing not from principle but from the actual fact that God had associated himself with this kind of mission. But the two missionaries tell us nothing at all of this account, on which everything depends here, and which would have decided the issue! The commentators (Overbeck, Wendt) are surprised that Paul left the fundamental defense of his point of view to be made by Peter and James, while limiting himself to an account, but the far more remarkable fact, that we hear nothing whatever about this account, is scarcely mentioned in the commentaries.[8]

And yet this is extremely striking in an author who, in Acts 15:1-5, gives considerable attention to the way the plot develops and in doing so has already spoken of an account given by the missionaries. The settlement should now have followed; God's deeds in the mission should have reduced to silence every opposition to this type of evangelizing! Why does this not happen? Why do we hear nothing of what Paul and Barnabas say? There seems to be only one answer—because God's acts in the mission to the Gentiles have already been related, not in this gathering of the apostles, but in the book of Acts. The listeners in Jerusalem do not know of them yet, as do the readers of this book. Thus for the second time we are led to see that the portrayal of the Apostolic Council in Acts 15 is a literary rendering, and is significant as such, but not in its understanding of historical events.

James's speech follows; it is characteristic of James that he uses the Semitic form of Peter's name; he has been known to readers since the fleeting mention of him in 12:17 in connection with the legend of the releasing of Peter, but Luke has not yet expressly introduced James,[9] and even now he is delineated only by means of the content of his speech. His speech, again, is surprising. The missionaries' words, which must have been of the utmost importance to the impending decision, seem to have been forgotten. James, also, speaks about Cornelius! But the readers cannot have understood this incident out of the past any better now than when Peter referred to it. James, even more than Peter, makes allusions that can be intelligible only to those who are familiar with the episode—that is, to the readers of the book. "Symeon has recorded how God took care to win a people out of the Gentiles for his name"; that is all that is said about the story of Cornelius. Who would recognize the allusion if he did not know the story already? There follows scriptural evidence for the inference which is intended to be drawn from the story of Cornelius; this evidence lies in the fact that it is God's will to embrace the Gentiles "who are called by my name."

Out of this quotation (Amos 9:11-12) arises the proposal not to "burden" Gentile converts to Christianity, but to charge them simply to abide by the four well-known ordinances. In the same strain it is written in the so-called "decree" (15:28): "It seemed good to the Holy Ghost, and to us, to lay upon you no greater burden than this, the most essential one: that you shall refrain from sacrificing to idols, from blood, from that which is strangled and from fornication." Thus the contents of the decree are regarded virtually as a concession by the people of Jerusalem to the Gentile Christians, and not the reverse. No particular burden is to be laid upon Gentile believers. The four points are those which go without saying: these conditions will be necessary especially if Jewish and Gentile Christians are to associate with one another, and they will surprise no one.

Acts 15:21 is also to be understood in this sense. Although straightforward from the linguistic and textual points of view, in context and meaning it is one of the most difficult verses in the New Testament. It certainly cannot mean that the wide dissemination of the Mosaic law makes it necessary that Gentile Christians should draw near to Judaism and that this would be achieved by obedience to the four ordinances. Luke does not understand the ordinances as such an approach! They are intended to make possible a release from the burden of the law, not to introduce a part of it (in default of the whole law) into Gentile Christian practice. The simplest meaning of the verse seems to be that Moses also is proclaimed to the world without our assistance.[10] We should really expect this idea to be introduced by a "but." Yet, because of the *gar* which gives the proof, it is possible to suppose that a little midrash has been applied here to the quotation from the prophet,[11] saying that the ruins of David's fallen tabernacle shall really be set up again, so that "the rest of men may seek the Lord" (15:17), *then* (15:21) Moses will be proclaimed to the world.

So James's speech means that, long ago, God wanted to accept the Gentiles into the Christian community. Both the story of Cornelius and also the Scriptures are evidence of this. The ordinances of the Apostolic Decree are felt to be along these lines; but this is usually overlooked in commentaries on the speech, because the commentator thinks of the words of Paul in Gal 2:6: "those in authority have imposed nothing further upon me."

Thus if we examine the actual contents of Acts 15:1-29, we arrive at the following conclusion: Luke knows of a conflict about the circumcision of the

Gentile Christians in Antioch, which was arbitrated in Jerusalem. But he does not simply reproduce a tradition about the events in Jerusalem.[12] He considers the events to be as he has outlined them in 15:12. His concern is literary and theological. His main thought, that the unconditional admission of the Gentiles to salvation is not the work of men but of God, he has taken from the story of Cornelius. In Acts 15 he reintroduces this idea by means of two speeches, both of which refer to the story of Cornelius interpreted in the sense taken by Luke, but refer to it in a way which can be understood only by readers of the book and not by participators in the Apostolic Council.

At the end of the "council" comes the "decree" with its four clauses,[13] which is envisaged entirely as a concession to Gentile Christians. Luke wanted to acquire a conclusion. In doing so, he was following the custom of the ancient historians of incorporating into their work the text of documents, either genuine or fictitious (compare in Acts also 23:26-30). Now he really seems to have known this document with the four clauses, and not to have reconstructed it. The fact that it was addressed simply to Antioch, Syria, and Cilicia is evidence of this; when Luke then undertakes in 16:4 to make the decree part of his narrative he causes it to be introduced into Lycaonia by Paul. Luke evidently ascribes positive value to the clauses, for he quotes them again in 21:25. Paul must have known these formulae ever since the Apostolic Council took place. The repetition affects him less than the reader, upon whom these conditions of peace—for as such Luke regards them—are to be particularly impressed. Luke must somehow have come to know about them, and felt that they were fruitful; he therefore used them as a conclusion for his account of the Apostolic Council. From the literary point of view, they fitted in well with the way in which Luke tells of the event: a "decree" belongs to the end of a convention with several speakers (the name "council" is appropriate only to Acts 15, not to Galatians 2). On the other hand, historical criticism leads to a different conclusion. Now, for the first time, we are justified in turning our attention, with regard to this question, to the Epistle to the Galatians. His representation of the agreement between Paul and those in authority in Jerusalem makes it at least improbable that Paul would simply have omitted a formulated conclusion, which would have provided the end of the pronouncement. But the events related in Gal 2:11-12 would have been quite impossible if a universal ruling on the question of food has been made at the same time as other problems came under consideration.

This critical analysis of Acts 15:1-29 has therefore produced two conclusions.

1. *Literary:* We need no division into sources in order to understand the text. We need only be clear as to Luke's intention and follow the indication that he gives in twice mentioning the story of Cornelius. The

thesis that he has upheld by his treatment is fulfilled here;[14] God himself, by causing the Gentile centurion to be accepted into Christianity, has revealed his will that the gospel should be freely carried to the Gentiles. This, not the course taken by the convention, is important to Luke. He simply tells the story of what went before and adds to the end the decree with its four clauses, which he had come across somewhere in Antioch, Syria, or Cilicia.

2. *Historical:* We thus have only one account of the meeting between Paul and those in authority in Jerusalem, that of Paul in Galatians 2. We are not justified in correcting it according to the account in Acts. It is only the motives for the journey to Jerusalem that are essentially different: Paul refers to a revelation, Luke to a decision made by the community, but both can ultimately be reconciled. Luke's treatment of the event is only literary-theological and can make no claim to historical value. The final result, the Apostolic Decree, did not originate in this meeting.

Thus we are able to solve many of the difficulties in the way of an understanding of Galatians 2. Especially, we need no longer assume that there were two separate gatherings, because the "privately" (*kat' idian*) in Gal 2:2 does not accord with the "assembly" (*plēthos*) gathering in Acts 15:12. Also, we no longer need the very strained exegesis of the words in Gal 2:6—"they have imposed nothing upon me"—it is rather that the Apostolic Decree has been imposed upon the communities. Paul gives a description which is certainly disturbed by many kinds of "nervous" interpolations (vv. 3, 4b, 6b, 8), but the chief content is quite clear: "I laid my gospel before them in a private discussion, and indeed (only) before those in authority," for I wanted to submit myself to their judgment. "But to those false brethren who had forced their way in" (I never met them at all?—or at least) "for the moment I did not give way,[15] so that the truth of the gospel may remain with you. But nothing was imposed upon me by those in authority; on the contrary," they have been convinced of the blessing of God, which confirms my methods of evangelizing, "and they have given the hand of fellowship to me and to Barnabas, that we should go to the gentiles, and they to the circumcision. Now we ought to think of the poor, which I have also endeavored to do."

It is a passage that, despite all the agitation we see in Paul, really contains no difficult historical problem, as long as we are not compelled to regard Acts 15 as a serious rival source. My intention has been to make it clear that there is no need to do so if we acknowledge the real intention of Luke, that is, his literary and theological concern.

10

The Conversion of Cornelius

The story of the centurion Cornelius in Acts 10:1—11:18 obviously has a special importance in the Book of Acts. This fact clearly emerges from the detailed apology with which Peter justifies his attitude before the Jewish Christians in Jerusalem. It is also obvious from the emphasis with which both speakers in the "Apostolic Council," Peter and James, refer to the conversion of Cornelius as decisive evidence of the acceptance of the Gentiles by God. Why the writer of Acts—I call him Luke—favors the story in this way presents a problem which can be solved only if we discover what material Luke had at his disposal and how he treated it.[1]

LUKE'S DEVELOPMENT OF THE STORY

The story of the centurion Cornelius was certainly not invented by Luke, for he enriched it by additions which are recognizable as such because they clash, to some extent, with the original story. This must have been born in tradition—presumably in the tradition of those Hellenistic communities which would have been interested in a story set in this particular locality and with this particular content. We must see first how Luke dealt with this story.

Peter's Speech in Jerusalem

The speech in which Peter justifies himself before the authorities in Jerusalem is certainly Luke's own work, for the Jewish Christians charge Peter with associating and eating with Gentiles. In the story itself, this act of eating together does not play an essential part at all. In the old tradition, Cornelius is a Gentile, but a devout and God-fearing man who, because of these virtues, is honored by God with a special message brought by an angel. The tradition speaks of him most sympathetically, and it is unlikely that it would have perceived any necessity for Peter to defend himself for having associated with this man. Someone who wanted to give major importance to the story added the defense. In view of Acts 11:1-18, we must assume that this was Luke.

Peter's account differs in various details from the account in Acts 10,[2] but especially in one point: the Holy Spirit is manifested (by means of the "speaking in tongues") to all Gentile believers. According to 10:44, this happened at the end of Peter's sermon; according to 11:15, it was just as he had begun to speak. According to the second account, there would be no place for Peter's speech. This "contradiction" must not, however, be used as the basis for a division into two sources,[3] but is to be ascribed to the author. A speech can obviously be regarded by the author as an insertion or addition that does not necessarily affect the course of the narrative. The break made by Stephen's speech in the obvious connection between 6:15 and 7:55 makes it clear that Luke takes this point of view. Here Luke is acting as a literary historian; not as an historian in our sense, who wants to show what has really happened, but as an ancient writer, who singles out what is significant and possibly emphasizes it by means of speeches. Again, in the retelling of the story in 11:14, the angel's message to Cornelius points forward to his salvation by means of Peter's words, whereas in 10:5, 32 we read only that he is to send for Simon. This is connected with the method of composition: since the legend itself does not at this point disclose what the outcome is to be, tension arises when, in the retelling of the story, both the message and the ultimate purpose of the angel's appearance are included. In the same way, in 26:16-18, the voice from heaven that converts Paul also announces his missionary task. In the actual legend of the conversion the Lord makes this announcement to Ananias (9:15-16), and in the first repetition (22:14-15) by Ananias to Paul.[4]

Peter's Speech in Cornelius's House

Peter's speech (10:34-43) was certainly contributed by the author himself. A speech that is so long, relatively speaking, cannot have had any place in a legend told among Christians about the conversion of a centurion. Moreover, the analogy of the other speeches in Acts shows that they are literary compositions by the author, directed at the readers, and intended to show them the importance of an event or to impress upon them certain tenets of belief. We shall never be able to discover for certain whether Luke knew either that a speech was made on this occasion or what was said. Nor is it necessary to go into such questions, for Luke would not, in any case, have been bound by such knowledge. Indeed, we have already established that in 11:15 he does not abide at all by the fact that he has, himself, given an account of a longer speech.

Finally, this speech in Cornelius's house, with the exception of the introduction, does not include any reference to the particular question of the conversion of the Gentiles, but is composed on a pattern similar to that of Peter's other speeches and of Paul's speech in Antioch (13:16-41).[5] All, after they have been linked with the occasion, continue along the lines of a scheme that consists of kerygma (in this case 10:37-41), proof from the scriptures (10:43a), and exhortation to repentance (10:42, 43b). By developing the same scheme several times, Luke wants to show his readers what Christian preaching is and ought to be. It is a literary-theological, not an historical task, which he wants to fulfill here as in other passages. This can be seen in the way in which he begins in 10:36: "You know the message"—a literary phrase which could scarcely be appropriate to use with Cornelius who, although he evidently knows something of the Old Testament, as 10:1-4 indicates, knows nothing about Jesus Christ.[6]

The Vision

It is probable that Luke also contributed the vision (Acts 10:9-16) which shows the apostle clean and unclean animals and answers his refusal to eat of them with the sentence: "What God has made clean, you must not call profane." Obviously the vision is intended to give Peter courage. The question is whether this means courage to eat both clean and unclean animals or, if we take the scene figuratively, courage to associate and eat with Gentiles. In our text, as a result of the vision, we are now told in 10:28b that there is no distinction between people who are (from the religious point of view) clean and those who are unclean; the vision is thus understood in a figurative sense. This is the conclusion reached by most of the more recent commentators with regard to 10:28b. Others, Bauernfeind particularly, have taken another sense, close to or underlying the figurative one, which gives as the meaning of Peter's vision: "In such a case you may—indeed you must—disregard all rules about eating with Gentiles."[7]

There are in fact various valid points of view in support of this interpretation. In the first place, we are told in 10:10 that Peter became hungry and wanted to eat. This suggests that the command "kill and eat" is meant quite literally and that the food from heaven, which is intentionally mixed with unclean animals, is to serve as earthly food. Next, the account of the vision (11:5-10), which is given in Peter's defense, seems to supply the direct answer to the reproach in 11:3 that Peter has eaten with the uncircumcised: obviously, this has involved eating that which is unclean. Since, as we have seen from 10:28b, Luke has interpreted the vision differently, as referring to the distinction between men and not between foods, a reference to foods was apparently inherent in the vision right from the start. Now we must remember that, according to Gal 2:11-14, Peter later found himself in a difficult situation as regards food: in Antioch he allowed himself to be persuaded to give up his usual custom of eating with Gentiles. In connection with the discussion of this question Peter, or others who knew about it, may have quoted the vision of the clean and unclean animals. In that case, it would be one of Peter's actual experiences, presumably from the later period, when the conflict about the food question was fierce. Luke—we have yet to see why—added the vision to the story of Cornelius and thus shows how the apostle was both encouraged and justified. A further observation endorses this view.

Narrative Interruptions

If the vision is set apart as Luke's own composition, 10:27-29a must also be regarded as such, since they refer to the vision. And now we can see that the context becomes distinctly clearer if we read: "Stand up! I am only a mortal" (10:26). "Now may I ask why you sent for me?" (10:29b). After Peter's greeting, Cornelius has to say why he did so. Verses 27-29a thus cause an interruption to the narrative. If, on the basis of other considerations, these verses are omitted, the story becomes more compact.

The same thing is true in another connection. Verses 24-25 give the impression that Cornelius lingered with relatives and friends in his house and "when Peter was at the door" met him (after passing through the room, at most through a courtyard), so that the falling to his knees took place in the vicinity of the door. Continuing with "And as he talked with him, he went in" (*kai synomilôn autô eisêlthen*) in 10:27, therefore, sounds strange, because there seems to be no place for a conversation. That is not a modern idea; the version given in D and in some of its dependents has altered the situation considerably: "and after he had called together his relatives and closest friends, he waited. But, when Peter drew near to Caesarea, one of the slaves (Cornelius's messengers from among Peter's companions), who had gone on in advance, announced that he (Peter) had arrived. Then Cornelius jumped up and when he met him . . . ."

Now, the falling down at Peter's feet takes place somewhere outside (Zahn even thinks it means outside the town). Then Peter goes in, finds the people assembled and addresses them. In this form of the text there is no more mention of the conversing (*synomilein*). So it is obvious that this *synomilein* appeared impossible to the author of the "Western" special text. Indeed, it was the impossibility of it that probably prompted the author of this form of the text to produce his own version. Thus we see here the artificiality of the situation as described by the Egyptian text of 10:27-29; and again we find support for the theory that the original story did not contain this account but that this, together with Peter's vision in the Cornelius narrative, was added by Luke.

The four points we have established probably do not account for the whole extent of Luke's own composition. One might ask, for example, whether Peter's Christian companions who traveled to Caesarea with him as witnesses of God's acceptance of the Gentiles were perhaps Luke's addition to the account (10:23b; 10:45; 11:12b); this is suggested by the fact that they testify, in 10:45, to what Luke wishes to underline, namely to the pouring out of the gift of the Spirit upon the Gentiles also. They are thus mentioned particularly (11:1-18) in the paragraph which belongs entirely to Luke; here we learn that there were six of them and that they came to Jerusalem with Peter in order to confirm Peter's evidence. We could also point to the conclusion of the main account, in the remarkable verse (10:48): "He commanded, however, that they should be baptized in the name of Jesus Christ." We might think the account would have to conclude with the actual baptism by the apostle. Perhaps this expected ending has simply been supplanted by the concluding sentence: "Then they asked him to stay with them a few days longer." For it is possible that this account is not so unimportant in the case of Cornelius as might otherwise appear, and that, to Luke, it expresses more than a description of the actual ceremony of the baptism would have done. It shows, in fact, that Peter has entered upon a relationship with Cornelius that is so real as to entail sharing a common table with him. We may suppose that the old story concluded with the baptism itself, but Luke's version ends with *epimeinai* ("remain"). This leads on to the question of the meaning of this version.

THE INTENTION OF THE EPISODE

Let us take stock once more of the results of this analysis.[8] A story about the centurion Cornelius, which was current in the community, tells how Cornelius was commanded by an angel to send for Peter from Joppa. Peter, instructed by a voice from heaven, accepts the invitation; he finds Cornelius and his household assembled, and they break forth into an ecstatic "speaking in tongues" when they hear his words. This he takes as divine confirmation of their belief and he does not hesitate to baptize Cornelius and his household. Luke has added the vision of Peter, the mention of it before Cornelius, the speech and Peter's justification, besides, probably, the content of 10:48b and the mention of Peter's Jewish Christian companions.[9]

What moved the author to make this compilation? In order to answer this question, we must consider the last treatment in Acts of the conversion of Cornelius, the reference to it in the so-called Apostolic Council. How is it possible that in all the literature which has been published on the subject of Acts 15 the most striking peculiarity of this account is not commented on at all? The commentators, who always think only of the comparison with Galatians 2, make practically no reference to the strange way in which this scene of the "Apostolic Council" is elaborated. It arises out of a complaint by Jewish Christians regarding the gospel as preached by Paul, but, in the section 15:6-18, nothing more at all is said about this complaint. During the discussion, the only speeches reported are those of Peter, and of James the brother of the Lord. Peter quotes his experience of a good while ago, of how, in accordance with the will of God, he converted Gentiles to the gospel. In this way the speaker provides a link with the story of Cornelius and gives to it—as a regularizing tradition "of a good while ago"—a classical meaning. Now James also quotes Peter's experience—that is to say, the conversion of Cornelius—and interprets it by means of words from the Old Testament as saying that God has gained for himself a nation from among the Gentiles. Between these two speeches stands the sentence: "Now the whole community was silent[10] and listened as Paul and Barnabas told of all the signs and wonders which, through them, God had made to come to pass among the Gentiles" (15:12). This is rather a slight point if it is to be the crux of the whole discussion. A decision has to be made as to whether Gentiles shall be admitted to the community; this, Paul, as a missionary, has already been doing for some years. The only speeches reported deal, however, with the conversion of Cornelius, which was confirmed by God a number of years previously. The words "in the early days" (*aph' hēmerōn archaiōn*;15:7) are certainly spoken with a particular intention and with slight exaggeration, in order to stress the fact that the decision came from God some time ago and was made known to the first of the apostles. We may ask why this decision was not applied to the dispute regarding Paul's evangelizing, if this could have settled the question. On the other hand, we may ask why the real point at issue, after being introduced in such detail (15:1-15), now almost disappears out of the narrative until verse 15:12, which, however, leaves the essential question still unanswered. The "signs and wonders" referred to here can be regarded as divine approbation of this type of mission to the Gentiles; this is not expressed in so many words— and what is said here has also been intimated already in the introduction (15:4). It is clear from textual criticism,[11] reconstruction of the scene from the literary angle,[12] and modern literary criticism[13] that the appearance of Paul and Barnabas seemed relatively insignificant to those who came afterwards, while originally it must have been the chief concern.

The strange nature of this account cannot, however, be explained either by attributing the account to two sources or by arguing from historical circumstances; for neither theories based on literary criticism[14] nor those arising out of historical considerations[15] can explain the fact that in Acts 15 we are told for the first time of what appears to be a considerable conflict, and that the account then deviates completely from the subject of the dispute[16] in order to quote the conversion of Cornelius and to clarify this allusion by means of two speeches. Only a literary explanation drawn from the author's ideas and intentions can help here. To him (rather than to an editor or to the actual history itself) we must attribute the recollection of Cornelius's conversion to settle the dispute concerning Paul's mission. To follow up this intention he does not need the eloquence of Paul, who might have introduced the success of his mission into the discussion as a kind of decision by God. Luke certainly does not want to give the impression that a man, even a great apostle, has won the decision for himself and his work by means of a struggle. Even Peter, whose experience is quoted here as a "classic" one, is not the final authority. It is not to be said even of him that he introduced conversion of the Gentiles into the Church without regard for the law. This was done not *by* him, but *in* him, through God. "You know that long ago God made the decision among you that the Gentiles should hear the word of the gospel by my lips and should believe," says Peter; "Symeon has shown how God took care to win from among the Gentiles a people for his name," we read in James's speech. This, then, is what the reference to the conversion of Cornelius means. It is not a conversion-story of the usual type, nor is it meant to show that Peter is glorified by the consequences of the knowledge which he gained through a vision. It shows the revelation of God's will that the Gentiles should be received into the Church without obligation to the law. This is what the story of Cornelius means, at least for Luke.

THE ORIGINAL NARRATIVE AND LUKE'S VERSION

From this point in the examination we can survey both the meaning of Luke's version and the character of the original narrative.

Luke wanted to show how the will of God was made known to Peter in the conversion of Cornelius; it was because of this same will that the Gentiles were called, and just how this came about Luke proposed to relate immediately afterwards (11:20-21) in several examples concerning (unnamed) people in Antioch. Here, however, the classic example was to be described, the decisive first manifestation of this will. This is how Luke regards the story of Cornelius, and as such he makes Peter quote it ("in the early days," 15:7), and James ("how God first looked favorably," 15:14). Therefore, right at the beginning of the story of Cornelius, God must speak words of authority to Peter, telling him to go to the Gentiles. A mere sermon preached to a "God-fearing Gentile" would not in itself have had any far-reaching significance. Philip had no hesitation in climbing into the Ethiopian's carriage and expounding the scriptures to him (8:31-39). Apparently it means much more for Peter to enter the Gentile house.

Luke borrowed the revelation that orders him to do so from the vision which was told of the first of the apostles, and which was probably related wherever in the Christian community clean and unclean foods were discussed. Luke does not, however, interpret it in the sense of removing the distinction between *foods*. To him it was (according to 10:28) a sign that God no longer wished there to be any distinction between "clean and unclean" *people*. Luke then makes the apostle expound this knowledge straight away to the people assembled in Cornelius's house (10:28-29), although the hearers can scarcely suspect the significance of these ideas, far less their motivation. It is, rather, for the reader to appreciate their significance—and also for those Jewish Christian witnesses from Joppa, whom Luke himself probably provided as companions for the apostle.

Along with the significance which Luke gives to the epoch-making story are two other factors: first, the mention of the relationship which Peter assumes with the Gentile centurion, the "talking with" (*synomilein*) in 10:27 which is difficult to envisage from the context; and second, the request made by the new Christians and obviously granted by Peter that the apostle should stay longer, a request which has forced the ritual of baptism into the background. Peter is to spread abroad this new truth wherever opportunity offers—by associating with the centurion, as also with the community which is being formed at his house. Luke does not regard Cornelius as the main character, and Cornelius's adoption of the Christian faith is not the essential content of the story; it is Peter whom we find in the center of the narrative from Acts 10:1 to 11:18, Peter, his newly-acquired knowledge, and his deference of it. For, obviously, the insertion of the paragraph 11:1-18 is intelligible only if seen from this point of view. It is not the centurion's belief which is being proved, but the apostle's right to enter the house of uncircumcised men—and then not in order to convert the uncircumcised to Christ, but in order to eat with them. This new truth is expressly proclaimed at the end of the paragraph in question: "Thus God has granted to the Gentiles also a repentance unto life" (11:18). This is proclaimed in Acts even before the conversion of the Gentiles in Antioch and Paul's evangelizing comes under discussion. The new truth is to emerge from the conversion of Cornelius. This is why Luke has elaborated the story.

Of the four major additions by the author Luke (the vision, the words of introduction, Peter's sermon, and the justification) only the sermon in 10:34-43 seems to have nothing to do with the point of view raised here. It is really composed, as shown on pp. 141–42 in accordance with the scheme which governs the other sermons by Peter, as well as the one by Paul in Acts 13. It is also part of this scheme that, at the beginning of every sermon, consideration should be given to the contemporary situation. Now by "situation" Luke understands not the moment when Cornelius and his household are waiting for the apostle's proclamation, but the revelation which has been given to Peter. Although he has already declared it in 10:28-29, that revelation must be repeated here in more general form: "In truth, I now understand that God is no longer a respecter of persons, but that he who fears God and works righteousness is pleasing to him—in every nation." The climax, as a negative pronouncement in 10:28b ("there are no 'unclean' persons") gives way to a positive one in 10:35 ("in every nation there are those who are pleasing to God"), is intentional and not to be regarded as antithesis.[17] Once more we see what Luke's version is aiming at.

Even if Peter's sermon does not contain any further features pointing in this direction, the fact that Luke inserts a speech here at all still deserves our attention. He does this only in the case of events which are worthy of special emphasis (Pentecost, the healing of the lame man, Paul's dispute with the Jews in Antioch), or of events which he would like to emphasize in this way. This is the case in Athens, where the success of Paul's mission is slight, but the appearance of the Christian apostle in an exalted place seems to Luke so symbolical that he furnishes the event with a speech. So here too the occasion is not, historically speaking, of great significance: it is simply a sermon given before a household, and the conversion of the "God-fearing" Gentile. But we know well enough that Luke wishes this event to be regarded as one of great moment, through which, long before the time of Paul, and in a way which transcends the bounds of man's imagination, God revealed his will that the Gentiles should be received in. This is why Luke makes Peter deliver a speech in Cornelius's house.

Now, once more, we return to what we must suppose to be the original form of the story of Cornelius as set out on p. 144. If we delete Luke's additions to it, we are left with a straightforward legend of a conversion, comparable in its simple beauty with the legend of the Ethiopian eunuch. Evidently the communities used this form of "pietistic" narrative to record the conversions of men of particular standing. The emphasis on Cornelius's piety is, in fact, characteristic. While in Luke's version the gulf between Peter and the centurion is made as great as possible, so that the bridging of this gulf can be presented as a significant event, the legend, in biblical style, calls special attention to the prayers and good deeds of Cornelius, which are known before God; it portrays him as a "God-fearing man," thus as one who is, in any case, close to the religion of the Bible, and it makes him receive as a reward for his pious life[18] the message from the angel telling him to send for Peter. And now everything happens according to the angel's instructions: Cornelius's messengers, carefully selected, reach Joppa and ask for Peter; he is directed by the Holy Spirit not to avoid the messengers but to travel with them without hesitation "for I have sent them." The original account of the messengers' arrival in Joppa is obviously cloaked by the elaborated version, that is, by the addition of the vision,[19] but I should not wish to join Bauernfeind (p. 143) in the view "that in the pre-Lukan tradition the exhortation of the Spirit in v. 20 was rather more forceful."[20] It was not Peter who was the chief character in the old legend, but

Cornelius.[21] There was therefore no need to create a complete counterpart to Cornelius's vision of the angel; the simple directing of the Spirit was sufficient for Peter. Obviously, where the legend deals with Peter, there are no serious fundamental considerations to be surmounted. This arises from the fact that the Jewish Christian, Peter, receives the Gentile messengers into his house without this procedure being acknowledged as significant or controvertible. The text of the legend seems now to have continued in an equally simple manner, free from fundamental problems—it is Luke's elaborated version which is interested in principles. Thus the old story related, in swift sequence: Peter's arrival in Caesarea; the beginning of his proclamation; the gift of the Holy Spirit (the "speaking with tongues") to the hearers; the baptism (p. 144). In the legend, everything comes from God: God wishes to receive the pious centurion; God causes Cornelius to send for Peter; he commands the apostle to go with the messengers; he shortens the future Christian's period of development to maturity by sending him the Holy Spirit when he has scarcely been instructed.

The legend in its original form was simple and, we might say, innocent of any deeper meaning. It forms a parallel to the legend of the Ethiopian (Acts 8:26-39), in which the implications of the Christian preacher's companionship with the Gentile as he journeyed and also of the latter's baptism are not fully appreciated. This Ethiopian may also be numbered among the "God-fearers," as his visit to the temple and reading of the Book of Isaiah suggest. Verse 40 is certainly Luke's own composition, adding information as to the whereabouts of Philip, who has disappeared in the manner of genuine legend. Verse 37, with the baptismal confession, is, however, a post-Lukan insertion made by a ("Western"?) editor who was conscious of the absence of such a confession.

The parallel is important for the historical question. Both these "innocent" stories of conversion, which were not based on principles but gave factual accounts, were current in the communities; obviously, they reproduced historical events, expressed, of course, in the style of "legend." When did these things happen? It is hardly conceivable that such an "innocent" association of leading men of the early community with God-fearing Gentiles should, on each occasion, have led to baptism just at a time when the question of uncircumcised Christians had already been raised in Antioch as a serious problem and had been dealt with in Jerusalem in the so-called "Apostolic Council." So we must assume that there was a period of time previously during which such isolated cases could have occurred, by chance and not in order to defend a principle, that is, in the occasional manner in which the cases quoted in Acts 11:20-21 probably did originally occur. As far as we can see, Luke has correctly placed the stories of the Ethiopian and Cornelius: they belong between the death of Stephen and the beginning of Paul's mission. But now, as we have seen, Luke has elevated the story of Cornelius in order to make it represent a principle, and in so doing *he* has created an "historical" difficulty; for how is it possible that Peter, who has been instructed in this way by a vision, still discusses the question of uncircumcised Christians at all (Gal 2:1-21)? And, with reference to the question of Jewish and Gentile Christians eating together, how could Peter behave in the manner described in Gal 2:11-14?

The "historical" dilemma no longer exists if we do not regard Luke's compilation as history, at least not as history that took place in accordance with this sequence of events. Here, as elsewhere, Luke has abandoned an exact reproduction of history for the sake of a higher historical truth. We have seen how this truth consists of the idea that the incorporating of the Gentiles into the Church without subjecting them to the law originated neither with Paul, nor with Peter, but with God.

PART III
THE TEXT OF ACTS

11

The Text of Acts

While there are many problems, any one of which might be singled out as "the next task" of New Testament scholarship, the text of Acts is to me a particularly conspicuous one. I feel justified in calling attention to it by a treatment which of necessity can be only of a preliminary and tentative nature.[1]

To be sure, the objection may be raised that the problem of the text of Acts has been sufficiently dealt with in the discussions of Codex D.[2] But the question to which I wish to call attention was minimized rather than emphasized by the debate on the so-called Western text. It is the question whether the text of Acts deserves the same confidence as the text of the Gospels and of the letters of Paul. There is reason to believe that a special literary fate has befallen Acts—a fate which created a special kind of text, a fate which forces us to approach the textual problem of Acts differently from the way we approach that of other New Testament writings.

THE WESTERN TEXT

Before submitting proof for this proposition, I must on my part briefly touch on the problem of the Western text. Although much has been said about Codex D and its parallels, I believe that the method of form criticism still has a contribution to make to the evaluation of this text type.

In the case of writings like Acts the form-critical method raises the question not only of the sources but also of the "small units" which, deriving from popular tradition, may have been incorporated into the text. As a matter of fact, all parts of Acts include brief narratives of various kinds that beyond doubt circulated in the churches before the composition of Acts.[3] One sees that from their "closed," well-knit form; one sees it also from the fact that these small units do not fit easily into the literary framework.

When these old narratives retain their original, closely knit, and finished form, they stand out noticeably against their context. In such cases seams are bound to show between Luke's own work and the narratives he incorporates.[4]

Now, if in one text-type these seams are still visible, while in another they are covered up, the latter is doubtless the later text-type, for it shows traces of editorial leveling, a stage which the earlier text-type has not yet reached.

In the light of this insight, great significance for the evaluation of the text of D attaches to the observation that in some passages the D text definitely aims at eliminating or at least at covering up those seams. I give some examples:

1. Acts 3:11 is a frequently discussed passage.[5] The narrative has just described how the paralytic, healed by Peter and John, went with them into the temple, that is, the inner forecourt. "While he clung to Peter and John, all the people ran together to them in the portico called Solomon's, astounded." This hall is situated on the temple square but not within the forecourt. Therefore, there should have been a statement that the apostles had left the temple along with the healed paralytic. But the omission is intelligible, for v. 10 obviously is the conclusion of the old narrative. The statement of the successful healing here is the conclusion typical of the miracle story. Peter's subsequent speech with the necessary introduction was added by Luke in a style much less concerned with detail. The Western text has removed the difficulty by stating the departure from the temple, and we read in D: "When Peter and John went out, he clung to them and went with them."

2. Acts 10:25.[6] Within the story of the centurion Cornelius, the most significant story of a Gentile conversion in Acts, we also read of Peter's vision (Acts 10:9-16). This vision encourages Peter to share table-fellowship with the Gentiles, but it has nothing at all to do with Cornelius and his conversion. If we consider these verses as an addition by the author to the older material, the same holds true of vv. 27-29, the brief report on the vision.[7] One still sees clearly that v. 30 was the continuation of v. 26, for, after his welcome of Peter, Cornelius must explain why he sent for Peter. Thus the insertion of vv. 27-29 raised difficulties which the author did not completely smooth out. Codex D and the Harkleian Syriac,[8] however, did smooth them out. They state that a slave of Cornelius's was sent ahead to announce the apostle's arrival to Cornelius. Cornelius leaps to his feet, meets Peter, and falls at his feet.

3. Acts 14:7. An itinerary, that is, a list of stopping-places, lodgings, and missionary successes, is obviously behind the account of Paul's journeys, even in chaps. 13 and 14. This itinerary in 14:7 names the stations Lystra and Derbe together and adds "and there they preached the gospel." But Luke still wishes to report a story about Lystra, and does so in vv. 8-18. For this the reader must be transported back to

Lystra, since the report had already proceeded to Derbe. What the report presupposes, D has expressly stated; here 14:7 says, "But Paul and Barnabas stayed at Lystra." It is a subsequent addition. If it were the original text, this note would be found in v. 6, and the travel station Derbe would not be mentioned until v. 20, that is, after the conclusion of the Lystra episode.

4. Acts 14:18-19. At the end of the Lystra episode another case of unevenness is to be found. The population of Lystra had hardly been calmed down when the Jews from the other cities appeared and stoned Paul and Barnabas. According to the Western text, here represented by syr[h] and the Harkleian Syriac,[9] the first thing that happens is that the people return to their homes; then follows a stay of the apostles in Lystra (this item is also in D), and only then do the Jews from the neighboring cities appear. This, too, is an improvement, doubtless a secondary correction.

5. Acts 16:35. In connection with Paul's stay at Philippi there are two stories that, in the usual text, are not related to each other—the story of the shamed magistrates and the story of the jailer. It is important to observe that the magistrates in the morning following upon the night of the earthquake say nothing at all about this catastrophe. But according to D they are afraid because of it, and this fear becomes the cause of Paul's release. Once more the D text covers up a seam, in this case a seam between two narrative units.

6. In 20:12 there is in the usual text a similar gap that the Western text closed. The gap is caused by the fact that the author, with the phrase "thus he went away," makes the transition to the travelogue, while the next sentence ("they took the lad away alive, and were not a little comforted") still belongs to the Eutychus story. The text of D, smoothing out the transition, adds a farewell greeting to the departing apostle by the persons who take the boy home.

These examples are enough to show that the Western text endeavors to smooth out roughness that resulted from the characteristic method by which Acts was composed. These Western readings are nothing other than corrections of the text, and they thus clearly demonstrate their secondary character. It is impossible to suppose that a redactor, by taking the opposite course, transformed the Western into the usual text.

Certain other corrections, made by the Western text to eliminate factual difficulties contained in the usual text, reveal their secondary character even more convincingly. Acts 15:33 in the Egyptian text is an example of such a difficulty. The statement that both Judas and Silas return from Antioch to Jerusalem causes the difficulty. This is not quite possible, for, according to v. 40,

Silas is still in Antioch. Now the Western text offers the information in v. 34 that only Judas returned (and this correction passed into some representatives of the Antiochian text). If this were not a subsequent correction but the original text, why should v. 33 first record the departure of both Judas and Silas? Thus it is clear that v. 34 is a later supplement.[10]

In similar fashion the Western text in 12:22 states an additional reason for the veneration accorded to Herod by the people, namely, his reconciliation to the people of Tyre. If this were a part of the original text, v. 20 would have stated the nature of the controversy and v. 21 the manner of reconciliation. As we now read the Western text in its various representatives, it strikes us in every way as an incomplete, inadequate correction.

Thus we must conclude that from the so-called Western text we may at best accept some individual readings that, on the basis of separate analysis and for specific reasons, prove superior. As a type, the Western text has no claim to be considered as the original text.

EGYPTIAN WITNESSES

But what about the text of the Egyptian witnesses, the type of text on which today the critical editions are usually based? It is a question whether this text deserves the same confidence in Acts which it so rightfully enjoys in the Gospels and in the Pauline letters.

I am under the impression that nowadays New Testament exegetes come to terms with this text much too readily and accept in the bargain certain objectionable features which in any other text type they would reject as corruptions. It is a question whether the early textual history of Acts was really so safe that no thought of textual shortcomings can arise.

Luke wrote two books. He composed them for a reading audience that was not the audience of Mark and Matthew. When an author writes a dedication like Luke 1:1-4—a dedication whose style and choice of words are closely akin to the opening of many literary, secular writings—he has in mind readers who will understand and appreciate such a prologue. Few, if any, of the rank and file of the early Christians belonged to this class of readers. We may think of a few individual, cultured Christians—like Theophilus, if he actually was a Christian. But chiefly we must think of interested, sympathizing pagans who were not yet baptized and, finally, of "pure" pagans who, it was hoped, might be won by such literary propaganda. Luke's words are the only New Testament books written with such readers in mind.

But there is a great difference between the two books. Acts presupposes throughout an audience accustomed to literature. This may be seen in the choice of words, the structure of the sentences, the inserted speeches, and the emphasis on the sympathy shown by the authorities and by high circles.

All this is not as obvious in the Gospel of Luke as in Acts. Its style is not by any means so literary as that of Acts; such speeches as Acts presents are entirely lacking (for the "teachings" of Jesus consist of traditional groups of sayings). Much less independent literary effort is expended on the Gospel of Luke than on Acts; the former follows a literary genre which already was well-established in the Christian churches, the Gospel genre. It contains the traditional materials concerning the life of Jesus—to be sure, in a new and peculiar redaction.

Because the Gospel of Luke as a whole does not deviate from the customary type, it was eagerly accepted by the Christian churches. Soon there were churches that possessed and used the first "volume" of the Lukan works as "the Gospel of Jesus Christ." But this does not hold true of Acts. There was a need to furnish every Christian community in written form with the traditions about Jesus that hitherto has been handed on by preachers and teachers. The same need did not exist for the story that Acts told. Thus we must assume that during the first two-thirds of the second century Acts did not belong to the books used for regular reading in the churches. As far as we know, Acts is never quoted in this period. Marcion did not have it in his canon.[11] Perhaps he knew it as a separate writing—it would cause no surprise, since he was a man of some culture—but he rejected it. Acts is as yet not intimately familiar to the churches.

The Gospel of Luke, in this period, probably led a dual existence. First, with the second "volume," Acts, it belonged to the literary reading public that we characterized above. In the "book trade," it was probably known under the title *Praxeis Iēsous* (Acts of Jesus), which corresponded to the title of the second volume. Before this title may have stood the name of the author in the genitive case, for it is difficult to imagine that the name of the author remained a secret while the person to whom the work was dedicated was stated. This consideration lends more credibility than is usually warranted to the ecclesiastical tradition concerning the authorship of Luke, for both writings, Gospel and Acts, were offered to the literary reading public from the very beginning under the name of Luke as author.

During this period the Gospel of Luke existed in a different form in the churches. Here it was simply called "the Gospel of Jesus Christ," and it was one of the ecclesiastical writings employed for reading in church. For the preservation of the text this had distinct advantages. The book was being read continually; care was taken to produce correct copies, and the text was safeguarded against accidents. This the interests of the Church demanded.

Acts, however, at that time, existed in only one form—in the "book trade." Its text, unlike that of the Gospel, was not read to a community that would have been interested in the preservation of the authentic text. It was exposed to the typically varied fate of the literary text. Proof for all this is precisely the fact of redaction, which is known to us from the witness of the Western text. Thus the fact must be taken into consideration that during this early period other changes, too, were made in the text of Acts, and that no traces of the authentic text at certain points are preserved in any single manuscript. For our manuscripts descend from manuscripts that had already been in ecclesiastical use. But Acts did not become a regular, ecclesiastical reading-book until the end of this period, that is, the last third of the second century. That was when all apostolic possessions were carefully gathered together. Before this happened, the decisive textual changes had already been made.

Thus it is our right and our obligation to ask again and again whether the text of Acts is as reliably preserved as is the text of the Gospel of Luke. The difference in text evaluation corresponds to and depends upon the difference in the early history of the two books. The one was, at an early date, taken into the care of the Church, which was interested in the faithful preservation of its wording. The other, for a long time, remained outside of the circle of the ecclesiastical reading-books and within the circle of the literary reading public, exposed to its textual dangers.

UNCERTAIN PASSAGES

I shall now attempt to list such passages in which the text in its usual wording appears to be questionable. This first effort is chiefly an appeal to other scholars to help. Perhaps, within a generation or two, we shall achieve a degree of agreement.

One of the most impossible clauses in the entire book of Acts is the introduction to the quotation from the Psalms in the prayer of the congregation, 4:25:

> *ho tou patros hēmōn dia pneumatos hagiou stomatos Dauid paidos sou eipōn.* . . .

> Who by the mouth of our father David, your servant, didst say by the Holy Spirit. . . .

The stylistic pleonasm is perhaps due to the rival claims of two different text forms. Or, it may be due simply to someone's desire to emphasize in the quotation of Scripture not only the human speaker but also the Holy Spirit as the source of all inspired speech. If we expunge *pneumatos hagiou* ("Holy Spirit") and perhaps also *tou patros hēmōn* ("our father"), a good sense results. But now it is important to observe that mention is made of the Holy Spirit in 1:2 as well, in the most difficult part of the introductory sentence. Here is must be construed either with the commands of Jesus, which is almost impossible, or with the call of the apostles, which is still more difficult. Jesus has no need of the Holy Spirit, either for his commands or for the choosing of his apostles. Here and in 4:25 the text may have been influenced by a view that might be called a theology of the Holy Spirit.[12]

An entirely different example is the much-debated list of nations in the Pentecost story. It is difficult to explain why in 2:9 Judea is listed between Mesopotamia and Cappadocia, for the broad "prophetic" meaning of Judea, to which Lake and Cadbury point in *The Beginnings of Christianity*,[13] can hardly be presupposed here. It seems most advisable to postulate an early error and to assume that the original reading was *Galatian* (Galatia) or, with the same meaning, *Gallian* instead of *Ioudaian* (Judea). As to the other hypotheses, Tertullian's "Armenia" or *Libuan* (Libya) is paleographically less probable, and Idumea is geographically too distant. For Galatia, which fits well geographically, since it is immediately followed by the names of other countries of Asia Minor, Judea may have been substituted by an unthinking copyist, especially since Judea is always close to the mind of a Bible reader. There is, of course, no specifically paleographical reason for this substitution.

In 5:13-14, too, we are confronted with a grave exegetical difficulty which is vividly brought out in *The Beginnings of Christianity*:[14] "None of the rest dared join them, but the people held them in high honor. And more than ever believers were added to the Lord." It is hardly possible to extract any definite meaning from the phrase "of the rest." But what if the enigmatic *tōn de loipōn* ("but the rest") should have come from *tōn archontōn* ("the officials")? The number of letters is the same, and the changes—at least from A to Δ and from X to Λ—are easily understood. "Of the leaders no one dared join them, but the people held them in high honor and more than ever believers were added to the Lord." Thus the sentence becomes intelligible.[15]

Two older conjectures should be referred to briefly. I cannot quite convince myself that the high priest, in the general description of 5:17, must "rise" in order to initiate a persecution of the Christians with the Sadducees. Therefore, the reading *Hannas* (Annas) for *anastas* ("rise") seems to me still worth mentioning. Also, the synagogue of the "Freedmen" in 6:9, in spite of certain analogies, is still puzzling, and I wonder if we should not read *Libuōn* ("Libyans") for *Libertinōn* ("Freedmen").

There are other passages whose readings cause hesitation, though I am unable to suggest definite solutions. In Peter's speech before Cornelius, 10:36 is enigmatic in its lack of connection with vv. 35 and 37. It is best understood as a doublet to v. 37 (but in that case we must read *ton logon hon*).

Many will agree that there is some textual corruption in 13:27. Perhaps the simplest solution is to construe not "him" but "the voices of the prophets" as the object of *agnoēsantes* ("did not recognize").

Asiatic Jews are mentioned in 24:18, but nothing further is mentioned about them. Here at least a predicate must be supplied (perhaps: "they caused a disturbance"), unless, as a part of the Latin textual tradition suggests, a few lines have dropped out.

In 26:20 there is an occurrence in the accusative case of "the whole land of Judea," but it is impossible to construe it properly. The assumption of a Semitism, that is, an accusative between two datives,[16] is not very probable. The dropping-out of *eis* (after *Hierosolumois* [Jerusalem], and then haplographically identified with the ending *-ois*) is more credible (see the Antiochian text).

The text of 26:16 is utterly impossible:

martyra hōn te eides me hōn te ophthēsomai soi.

to . . . bear witness to the things in which you have seen me and to those in which I will appear to you.

The heavenly voice promises Paul not that Christ shall again appear to him but that much shall be shown him. Obviously the clause was corrupted through the influence of the preceding *ōphthēn* ("I have appeared").

In certain passages of Acts it may be permissible for internal reasons to prefer a more poorly attested variant. Examples are *epistamenos* ("being familiar") in 26:3; and 16:8, where the variant *dielthontes* ("pass through"; D, gig, vulg) for *parelthontes* ("passed by") appears logically justified.

Finally, we must in this connection mention the much-debated passage in 15:21. Its meaning is clear; but in the context, it is obscure. Perhaps the simplest solution is the assumption that v. 21 is a marginal gloss[17] to the final words of the passage from Amos just quoted: commenting on the prophecy that the pagans, too, shall seek God (vv. 17-18), a reader remarked in the margin that there are numerous followers of the Law in all the cities of the world outside of Palestine. This solution has the further advantage that now James's speech actually concludes with the terms of the Apostolic Decree.

I have not by any means given a complete list of all uncertain passages. The chief purpose of this brief sketch was simply to show (1) that the textual criticism of Acts must not be restricted to the question of the evaluation of the Western text; (2) that the exegetes of Acts, instead of aiming at an explanation of many impossible readings, should rather attempt conjectural improvements of such readings; and (3) that the history of Acts before its acceptance into the New Testament entitles us to resort to such conjectures.

Notes

1. Acts in the Setting of the History of Early Christian Literature

[1.] This is a reference to corresponding studies on Luke's Gospel to have been found in the *Urchristliche Literaturgeschichte*, which was planned. Dibelius went into the question of authorship in his *A Fresh Approach to the New Testament and Early Christian Literature* (New York: Scribner, 1936), as he does also in many essays in this collection. [—H.G.]

[2.] This point is not considered in the present essay, nor are the speeches dealt with as is proposed below (p. 7). These themes were apparently reserved for concluding studies which are not found in the manuscript. But elsewhere Dibelius examines the question broached above: see pp. 124–28; 60–61; 81–82 above. [—H.G.]

3. Acts 3:1, 3-4, 11; 4:13, 19; 8:14.

4. Josephus, *C. Ap.* 2.1 (§§1-2). "In the former book, my most honored Epaphroditus, I demonstrated our antiquity. . . . But now I shall begin . . ." (*dia men oun tou proterou bibliou, timiōtate moi Epaphrodite, peri te tēs archaiotētos hēmōn epedeixa. . . . arxomai de nun . . .*)

5. Josephus, *Ant.* 8.1.1 (§§1-2). "We have already treated David and his virtue . . . in the previous book. And when Solomon his son . . ." (*peri men oun Dauidou kai tēs aretēs autou . . . en tēi pro tautēs biblōi dedēlōkamen. Solomōnos de tou paidos autou . . .*).

6. It is really only 1:9-11 which can be considered as telling a story in Old Testament style; everything else is framework provided by Luke. It may be due to this editing that we cannot rightly see whether the story begins in 1:4 or 1:6; 1:5 in this form is probably Lukan; at any rate, 11:16 reproduces the same words and, apart from these two examples, the words are not found anywhere else.

[7.] Compare pp. 66–67 above.

[8.] For a recent discussion and bibliography, see Joseph A. Fitzmyer, *Acts of the Apostles*, AB 31 (New York: Doubleday, 1998), 80–89.

[9.] On the we-passages, see Fitzmyer, *Acts*, 98–103, 109–11; and A.J.M. "The 'We'-Passages in Acts: On the Horns of a Dilemma," *ZNW* 93 (2002) 78–98.

[10.] In a review of Jackson and Lake, *The Beginnings of Christianity*, Part I, *Prolegomena*, Dibelius comments: "I can report with the fullest agreement that here (2.158ff.)

at last the 'we' is regarded for once not as a signpost in the search for sources but as a problem which makes analysis more difficult" (*TLZ* 48 [1923] 150). [—H.G.]

[11]. Dibelius never carried this out; compare note 2, above. [—H.G.]

12. Acts 13:42 is the final comment in connection with the speech; in 13:43 the source is used again; thus the conclusion of the service in the synagogue is described for the second time. Had the speech not been added in 14:15-17, the story would probably not have come to such an insipid ending: "they scarcely restrained the people from sacrificing to them" (*molis katepausan tous ochlous tou mē thyein autois*). After the Areopagus speech (and after Paul has already gone *ek mesou autēn*), certain converts are spoken of in 17:34; thus the source again comes into use.

13. The traditions concerning the name of the sorcerer, Bar-Jesus or Elymas, clash; also, according to 13:6, it is the missionaries who encounter the sorcerer, but, according to 13:7, the proconsul who sends for them.

14. With regard to the end of the story and the extension of it by means of the speech, see note 12 above.

15. It would be difficult to decide what relationship there is between the preceding story of the healing of the girl, and this story of release on the one hand, and the source on the other.

16. This anecdote, of a very secular nature, is found sandwiched in a so-called collective account (19:11-13, 17-19), as a special instance of what has been reported in general terms. The development of a tradition works in the reverse way: at the beginning the individual event is related; and it is the literary form which later generalizes the events; it is not surprising therefore that the story loses its beginning as a result of being embedded in a collective account. [The fifth of the isolated stories was inadvertently not mentioned in the author's manuscript, but undoubtedly he had the awakening of Eutychus (20:7-12) in mind; compare pp. 43-44—H.G.]

17. 13:1-3 does not belong to the source, for here Paul is still called Saul; the source calls him Paul, as, indeed, he was called from birth on, and Luke therefore had to achieve the changeover from one name to another within the story of Elymas, by means of the usual formula. To the work of editing are due the three formal renunciations of the Jews (13:46-47; 18:6; 28:25-28), which can be allocated so conveniently to Asia Minor, Greece, and Italy. In the description of Athens (17:18-21) the way is so clearly prepared for the Areopagus speech that we can safely attribute this famous section to the author, that is, to Luke. Most of the accounts from Corinth, on the other hand, with their factual character, are to be attributed to the source. But what of the section concerning Apollos (18:24-28) or the account about Demetrius (19:23-40), in which Paul does not appear at all? We have no means of deciding such questions (see also note 15).

18. The most important ideas are: (1) "grace" (*charis*) within the itinerary (13:43; 14:3; 14:26; 15:40), but also twice in the speech, 20:24, 32; and 11:23; solely the work of the author; (2) "boldly" (*parrēsiazesthai*) (13:46; 14:3; 19:8; but also 9:27, 28); at least one of the two verses is an observation by the author; and (3) "exhort" (*parakalein*) (14:22; 16:40 [?]; 20:1-2; but also 11:23).

19. One not improbable theory sees the intervention of the Holy Spirit in the illness which, according to Gal 4:13-14, overtook the apostle and delayed him in Galatia. Only we must not take "land of Galatia" to mean simply the district of Galatia with Ancyra and Pessinus; how could Paul have come so far east on the way to Bithynia? On his way,

however, were Amorion, Orkistos, and Nakoleia—and these could have belonged to "the land of Galatia" (*Galatikē chōra*), in so far, presumably, as Celtic was spoken there also. Compare Lake, *The Beginnings of Christianity*, 5.236–37.

20. Adolf von Harnack, *Luke the Physician* (New York: Putnam, 1907), 28ff.; in *Die Apostelgeschichte* (Leipzig: Hinrichs, 1908) 131ff., he concludes that Luke the doctor is the author of Acts, that he wrote a considerable part of the second half (from 16:6 onwards) as an eyewitness, the rest being based on stories provided by people who took part.

21. Eduard Norden, *Agnostos Theos: Untersuchungen zur Formengeschichte religiöser Rede* (Leipzig: Teubner), 316–27. Only Norden is not clear as to the doubt about the origin of the "I" in the Jewish texts.

22. Norden, *Agnostos Theos*, 319.

23. See the survey of the position of scholarship in Otto Eissfeldt, *The Old Testament: An Introduction*, trans. P. R. Ackroyd (New York: Harper, 1965), 541–57.

24. 18:2 the "standing-still" of the world—"I"-style; 19:1-2 the midwife—19:1: first person singular, 19:2: third person singular and plural, but in the middle of the second paragraph: first plural. In 15:1 the (supposed) author, James, then speaks in the first person.

25. *Frgmt.* 2 (Klostermann) = Epiphanius, *Haer.* 30.13. [Ed.] See J. K. Elliott, *The Apocryphal New Testament* (Oxford: Clarendon, 1993), 14.

26. Wilhelm Schneemelcher, *New Testament Apocrypha*, rev. ed. (Louisville: Westminster John Knox, 1991–92).

27. *Acts of John*, 18-19, 60-61 ("I"), 62 [Ed.] See Elliot, *Apocryphal New Testament*, 311, 328; *Acts of Philip* 33, 63.

28. I have not counted the anecdote of Paul and the viper (28:3-6), which is told in a completely secular fashion. There is no good reason for taking it as a story about someone else that has been applied to Paul. On the other hand, it does not sound like Christian tradition concerning Paul; Christians would require a Christian conclusion to the story of how Paul was taken at first to be a criminal, for whom Justice was lying in wait, and then for a god; as, for example, in 14:14-20, where horror is expressed at the idolizing of men.

29. Norden, *Agnostos Theos*, 313–14, 323–24.

2. THE FIRST CHRISTIAN HISTORIAN

[1.] Compare Vernon K. Robbins, "Prefaces in Greco-Roman Biography and Luke-Acts," in *SBLSP 1978* (Missoula, Mont.: Scholars, 1978), 2.193–207; and Loveday Alexander, *The Preface to Luke's Gospel: Literary Convention and Social Context in Luke 1.1-4 and Acts 1.1*, SNTSMS 78 (Cambridge: Cambridge Univ. Press, 1993).

[2.] Compare Gregory E. Sterling, *Historiography and Self-definition: Josephos, Luke-Acts, and Apologetic Historiography*, NovTSup 64 (Leiden: Brill, 1992).

[3.] On sources in Acts, see Joseph A. Fitzmyer, *Acts of the Apostles*, AB 31 (New York: Doubleday, 1998), 80–89.

[4.] See Gregory E. Sterling, "'Athletes of Virtue: An Analysis of the Summaries in Acts' (2:41-47; 4:32-35; 5:12-16)," *JBL* 113 (1994) 679–96.

[5.] On the Areopagus speech, see the detailed analysis in chap. 7 of this volume.

[6.] On the composition of the speeches, see chap. 5 of this volume.

3. THE BOOK OF ACTS AS AN HISTORICAL SOURCE

1. Important for the argument of these considerations are the works of Eduard Meyer, *Ursprung und Anfänge des Christentums,* vol. 3 (Stuttgart: Cotta, 1923); Alfred Loisy, *Les Actes des Apôtres,* (Paris: Nourry, 1920); and Otto Bauernfeind, *Kommentar und Studien zur Apostelgeschichte,* edited by Volker Mitelmann, WUNT 22 (Tübingen: Mohr/Siebeck, 1980).

2. I first applied this method of considering the Acts of the Apostles in *Euchäristerion: Studien zur Religion und Literatur des Alten und Neuen Testaments,* 2 vols., FRLANT 36 (Göttingen: Vandenhoeck & Ruprecht, 1923), 2.27-49 (see chap. 4 below); and in *A Fresh Approach to the New Testament and Early Christian Literature,* ILCK (New York: Scribner, 1936); German ed. vol. 2 (1926; rev. ed. 1975).

3. If, as we shall see, the account of the sea-voyage demands a completely different assessment, it is only the passages in Acts 16:10-17; 20:5-15; 21:1-18 that have to be considered as far as a "we-source" is concerned—thus quite a small part of the account of Paul's missionary journeys (Acts 13–21).

4. This proof from the vocabulary was first put forward by Adolf von Harnack, *Luke the Physician: The Author of the Third Gospel and the Acts of the Apostles,* 2d ed., trans. J. R. Wilkinson, CTL 20 (New York: Putnam, 1909).

5. The itinerary leads to Lystra and then straight on to Derbe (Acts 14:6). In order to insert a story from Lystra, Luke was obliged to return to this station expressly in order to do so.

6. On February 19, 1944, in the Heidelberg Academy of Sciences, I delivered a lecture on "The Speeches in Acts and Ancient Historiography" (chapter 5 below).

7. See Adolf Jülicher and Erich Fascher, *Einleitung in das Neue Testament,* Grundriss der theologischen Wissenschaft (Tübingen: Mohr/Siebeck, 1931), 437.

8. Compare Acts 27:43-44: the centurion wants to preserve Paul's life and therefore prevents the murdering of all prisoners, which was planned during the shipwreck; he tells those who can do so to swim to land, the rest to cling to the wreckage. We are not told what Paul does. The words "wishing to save Paul" were thus, obviously, added to a completed account.

9. This was proved by Paul Wendland, *Die urchristlichen Literaturformen,* HNT (Tübingen: Mohr/Siebeck, 1912), 324; and *Kritische Analyse der Apostelgeschichte,* AKGWG 15/2 (Berlin: Weidmann, 1914), 53ff. [Ed.] For the continuation of this debate, see Joseph A. Fitzmyer, *Acts of the Apostles,* AB 31 (New York: Doubleday, 1998), 98–103.

[10.] The value of Acts as an historical source is again briefly dealt with by Dibelius in the small volume, *Paul,* which appeared posthumously and was completed and published by Werner Georg Kümmel, trans. Frank Clark (Philadelphia: Westminster, 1953), 9–13. On pp. 67–84, by making use both of the Pauline epistles and of Acts, Dibelius gives a picture of the apostle's missionary activities.

4. STYLE CRITICISM OF THE BOOK OF ACTS

1. In addition to my *From Tradition to Gospel,* trans. Bertram Lee Woolf (New York: Scribner, 1965), compare Karl Ludwig Schmidt, *Der Rahmen der Geschichte Jesu* (1919); Rudolf Bultmann, *The History of the Synoptic Tradition,* trans. John Marsh (Peabody, Mass.: Hendrickson, 1994); Martin Albertz, *Die synoptischen Streitgespräche* (Berlin:

Trowitzsch, 1921); Georg Bertram, *Die Leidensgeschichte Jesu und der Christuskult,* FRLANT 15 (Göttingen: Vandenhoeck & Ruprecht, 1922). [Ed.] See also Klaus Koch, *The Growth of the Biblical Tradition: The Form-Critical Method,* trans. S. M. Cupitt (New York: Scribner, 1969); Edgar V. McKnight, *What Is Form Criticism?* GBS (Philadelphia: Fortress Press, 1969); and James L. Bailey and Lyle D. Vander Broek, *Literary Forms in the New Testament* (Louisville: Westminster John Knox, 1992).

2. Eduard Meyer, *Ursprung und Anfänge des Christentums,* 3 vols. (Stuttgart: Cotta, 1921) 1.2ff.

3. Ultimately that is also true of the absorbing work of Schütz, for the blocks of tradition separated by him have received their unity and their characteristics partly from the work of the author; Roland Schütz, *Apostel und Jünger: Eine quellenkritische und geschichtliche Untersuchung über die Entstehung des Christentums* (Giessen: Töpelmann, 1921).

4. I have tried to prove this in connection with Acts 4:24-28 in "Herodes und Pilatus," *ZNW* 16 (1915) 123–26 [113–26]; and in connection with the speeches in Acts 2, 3, 10, and 13 in my *From Tradition to Gospel,* 16–20. Of course, we cannot deny that records of actual speeches may have reached Luke. There is evidence, however, in the speeches in Acts, of an attempt to create types, to give examples and models of Christian sermons, far more than to attempt to recall particular persons and what was said by them on specific occasions.

5. In the Synoptic Gospels, apart from the story of the Passion, legendary interests play only a small part; compare my *From Tradition to Gospel,* 49–51, 105.

[6.] For a current bibliography and discussion of the we-passages, see Joseph A. Fitzmyer, *Acts of the Apostles,* AB 31 (New York: Doubleday, 1998), 98–103, 109–11.

7. The appearance of "we" (Acts 11:28) in the Western text can be explained in both ways. Compare also Eduard Norden, *Agnostos Theos: Untersuchungen zur Formgeschichte religiöser Rede* (Leipzig: Teubner, 1913) 327–31.

8. Adolf von Harnack, *Luke the Physician: The Author of the Third Gospel and the Acts of the Apostles,* trans. J. R. Wilkinson, ed. W. D. Morrison, CTL (New York: Putnam, 1907).

9. Compare 16:11-15 (first person) with 17:1-9 (third person) for style, color, and accuracy of the narrative.

10. This does not exclude the possibility that the writer had information concerning these factors at his disposal. In the story of his experiences during sickness, Aelius Aristides allows many things to have been ordered by divine inspiration, without giving any description at all of the means by which they came about.

11. In such an examination it is best not to touch on the question of authorship, since to do so is likely to blur our judgment of the style. We shall therefore neither assert nor combat the possibility that the writer of the itinerary was the same author who wrote a generation later, and who composed the Acts of the Apostles. Nor shall we attempt to say to what extent that writer of the itinerary was an eyewitness. These questions should be considered only when the problems of tradition and composition have been solved.

12. Acts 13:42 is the final observation on the speech. In 13:43 the itinerary obviously continues, its thread being broken off, perhaps, in 13:14; *ekathisan* ("sat down") is quite pointless and was introduced, no doubt, in order to lead into the speech. The itinerary could thus be reconstructed something like this: "They went on the sabbath day into the synagogue and preached. When the meeting of the synagogue broke up . . ."

13. The words *tines de andres* ("But some men," 17:34) are parallels to the phrase *kai tines elegon* ("And some said," 17:18). "Mocking" and "believing" were in juxtaposition. The speech has separated them.

14. The paragraph about the Apostolic Council (15:1-34) does not come into the picture and creates its own problem. The itinerary becomes noticeable for the first time in 13:4, for the lists of names in 13:1 and the ordination (13:2-3), which represents a later conception of office, obviously do not belong to it. The first mention of Paul by name in the itinerary comes, however, in 13:13 with the words *hoi peri Paulon* ("those accompanying Paul"). The itinerary calls the apostle, in what follows as well, by the name Paul, which was the name by which the world knew him, and which this Jew of the Dispersion probably bore from his birth, together with the Jewish name Saul. But since, up to this point, Luke had mentioned only the name Saul, in the Elymas-episode that was inserted between 13:4-5 and 13:13, he was obliged to introduce the name used in the itinerary. The fact that he does so in 13:9, by means of the formula *ho kai*, with which we are familiar after seeing many instances of it, thus arises from the source and not from the subject matter.

15. Norden, *Agnostos Theos*, 313–27.

16. From this example we can see particularly clearly how discussion of the matter of authorship and of the "we-question" can confuse a critical analysis of style. Nothing at all can be learnt about the author from these chapters of literature. He may possibly have accompanied the apostle (and there is a hint of this in the "we"); in that case he has invested his own memories with a literary veil and suppressed what was individual in favor of the conventional, but it is also conceivable that he gained possession of a short account of the events from somewhere else, secured credibility for the section provided by the witness by the word of the word "we," and then extended the account to a literary composition. "The important points are . . . first of all, why the writer of Acts lingers here in such detail on these technical matters and in other parts of his book does not do so at all; and, moreover, whether a conscious literary intention is concealed by this extremely careful description of motifs which already belong to literary convention. . . ."; review of Eduard Meyer, *Ursprung und Anfänge des Christentums*, vol. 3, in *DLZ* (1924) 1636–37.

17. The story (28:1-10) is written throughout in such a way as to tend toward the personal glorification of Paul. There is a complete lack of any religious point that might in some way correspond with the devotional interest in the legend. The dominating idea is that the one who is apparently pursued by the *Dikē* is finally taken by the barbarians to be a god; but this thought is non-Christian (and non-Jewish), because it presents deification as a claim to glory on the part of the person concerned. The Christian treatment of the story in Acts 14:15 is not suggested here at all. The fact that the Pauline episodes in Acts 27 have probably been inserted into a narrative about a sea-voyage has been recognized by Eduard Schwartz, *Zur Chronologie des Paulus*, NKGWG (Berlin: Weidmann, 1907), 17; Wellhausen, *Kritische Analyse der Apostelgeschichte*, AKGWG 15.2 (Berlin: Weidmann, 1914), 53–54; and Paul Wendland, *Die urchristliche Literaturformen*, 2d ed., HNT (Tübingen: Mohr/Siebeck, 1912), 324, n. 4. The Pauline episodes in Acts 27 represent the Pauline motif worked into the conventional scheme. The fact that in 27:43-44 we are not told by what means Paul was saved seems to me to be one of the various points which make the position of this Pauline motif somewhat doubtful. And yet we are to believe that the whole scheme was conceived for Paul's benefit. The last scene is

the parallel to 13:46-47; 18:6-7; but Paul's concluding words do not at all reflect the Jewish attitude to the gospel, which, though divided, was not altogether favorable.

18. Just as, with this intention, the author places abrupt accounts next to one another, so in 4:34-35. he gives a generalized description of the self-denial practiced by individuals and is not worried by the fact that, because of this method of generalizing, the individuality of this particular sort of heroism is lost, together with the value of recoding it. In a similar way, the effect of Mark's description in 3:11-12. is according to a pattern. [Since 1938—according to a letter received by the editor (Greeven)—Dibelius had been seeking in another direction for an explanation of the hardships described in 5:13-14. He offered his solution—a conjecture—in 1941: see p. 159.]

19. Compare the commentary by Preuschen in *Die Apostelgeschichte*, HNT (Tübingen: Mohr/Siebeck, 1912); the analysis by Wellhausen, *Kritische Analyse*, 2; and Johannes Weiss, *Earliest Christianity: A History of the Period A.D. 30–150*, trans. Frederick C. Grant, 2 vols. (New York: Harper, 1959), 143–45, 169–70.

20. Compare Luke 3:15; 3:19-20; 8:1-3; 9:9; 21:37-38.

21. Both lists are superfluous to the context, since only Stephen is required from the first list, only Barnabas and Saul from the second; thus they are, in some way, traditional. The object of giving the first list, however, is obviously to name representatives of the Hellenists at the meals served to widows; so it is he who first finds a use for the list.

22. The significant date as regards the conversion of the Gentiles is, in Acts, that time when the story of Cornelius takes place; see 11:18 [and p. 116f.]; thus in 11:20 Luke allows an account to appear which does not correspond with his plan.

23. In the attempt to introduce Agabus, in preparation for 21:10, the author mentions his prophecy in 11:28; with it he links a mention of the Pauline collection but mistakenly makes the help happen at this point; see 11:30; 12:25 [Dibelius describes both passages and 16:5 in *TLZ* 59 (1934) 247, as "pragmatic observations by the author," as distinct from "application of the material"], and compare my arguments in *Wochenschrift für klassische Philologie* 36 (1919), esp. 5ff.

[24.] See Frans Nierynck, "Miracle Stories in the Acts of the Apostles: An Introduction," in *Les Actes des Apôtres: Traditions, Rédaction, Théologie*, edited by J. Kremer, BETL 48 (Gembloux: Duculot, 1979), 169–213; and John J. Pilch, "Healing in Luke-Acts," in idem, *Healing in the New Testament: Insights from Medical and Mediterranean Anthropology* (Minneapolis: Fortress Press, 2000), 89–117.

25. Acts 9:43 is, of course, a pragmatic observation by the author in preparation for 10:5-6.

26. Concerning the technique of miracles, see my *From Tradition to Gospel*, 81. The frequently stressed connection with the story of Jairus (Mark 5:40) rests solely upon the similarity of subject and not upon borrowing; for it includes the motif of secrecy that Luke, in his version of the story of Jairus in 8:53, has left out. The act of taking the hand belongs, however, in the Gospels, to the technique of the miracle, but here it serves only to help the child to stand after the miracle has taken place. It is particularly significant that witnesses to the so-called Western text have supplied the technique of the miracle, which is lacking, by introducing the name Jesus into the words that work the miracles. The original story of Aeneas also contained details connected with the working of the miracle: see the mention of eight years in 9:33. [Ed.] On healing techniques, see Gerd Theissen, *Miracle Stories of the Early Christian Tradition*, trans. Francis McDonagh, ed.

John Riches (Philadelphia: Fortress Press, 1983), 62–65. On healing in general, see John
J. Pilch, *Healing in the New Testament*.

27. We may well adopt the ancient Latins' understanding of the "popular" text;
Theodor Zahn, *Die Urausgabe der Apostelgeschichte des Lucas*, Forschungen zur
Geschichte des neutestamentlichen Kanons und der altkirchlichen Literatur 9 (Leipzig:
Deichert, 1914), 68: *et ostendentes pallia et vestimenta quae faciebat illis Dorcas*.

28. After the centurion has shown the apostle his respect and Peter has refused it, it
is for Cornelius to say how it came about that he sent the message and is now welcoming Peter; thus 10:30 follows 10:26 [for more detail see 143]. The present text first substantiates the *synomilein* ("conversing") of Peter with Cornelius, then lets him enter (we
should imagine from 10:25 that they had met at the door) and then justify himself. It is
significant again how D, among others, conceals the actual place of meeting: informed
by a slave that the apostle is approaching the town, Cornelius runs to meet Peter, i.e.,
they meet in the street.

29. If Schütz, *Apostel und Jünger*, 40, reads an edifying moral into it (the power of
God is to be seen in the apostles as an inheritance from Jesus), this is possible only
because he includes Peter's speech (3:12-26) in the story, and so does not separate the
author's work from tradition. Otherwise his characterizing of the story as a miracle-story of the usual type is undoubtedly correct.

30. The mutual fastening of the eyes that causes the miracle to take place (vv. 4-5) is
solely conceivable between only two, of course, and not three persons.

31. Again D and the ancient Latins omit the place of meeting, for they let the apostles leave the temple with the man who has been healed.

32. Compare Karl Ludwig Schmidt, *Die Pfingsterzählung und das Pfingstereignis*,
ARU 1/2 (Leipzig: Hinrich, 1919), 23–24.

33. The frequently discussed *erēmos* ("desert," 8:26) may well be interpreted thus; we
cannot know whether the road was really desert; but, as the scene of the legend, it was
devoid of people, and barren, and Philip went there only because of a special command
from God.

[34.] For similar comments see Dibelius, "Literatur zur Formgeschichte des Neuen
Testaments ausserhalb den Evangelien," *TRu* 3 (1931) 235 [207–42]. [—H.G.]

35. The sparseness of expressing *pisteuein* ("belief")—with neither amplification nor
mention of baptism—leads Zahn in his commentary to decide that the significance of
the whole episode is not primarily to tell of a conversion, but merely a moral success.
But if the story does not tell of conversion in the same way as Luke writes of it elsewhere,
what we then see is the style of a tradition which was originally isolated.

36. Acts 8:5-8 is a kind of general summary, giving no details connected with the
events and with no individual content, but with the Lukan motif of joy in the conclusion
(13:52; 15:3). Simon's activity is subsequently introduced by *proüpērchen* ("previously").

37. Compare Schwartz, *Chronologie*, 279, n. 3; Preuschen, *Die Apostelgeschichte*;
Wellhausen, *Kritische Analyse*, 15.

38. According to v. 24 we should imagine that a most vigorous cursing had just taken
place. Instead we read a severe sermon with a comparatively mild curse at the beginning. Here, also, D has the solution: it concludes: "he did not cease weeping."

39. In v. 7, as in v. 9, the length of the speech is emphasized. Of the two passages, v. 7
is the one that creates difficulty, for it is not related at all to v. 8. The phrase *houtōs
exēlthen* ("thus departed") in v. 11 presents an anticipation of the departure, which is

difficult to interpret. Obviously v. 12 belongs directly to v. 10. Then, however, we become suspicious of the accounts of worship in v. 7; they also may well be Christian embellishment. If we suppose that already, before Luke, Christians had applied this anecdote to Paul, we must surely allow for the possibility that part of this embellishment can be ascribed to them and not in the first place to the author of Acts.

40. Strictly speaking, the motif rests upon v. 7 and is completely isolated; it must, therefore, have arisen out of the original form of the tradition. In that case, this cannot be understood apologetically—as proof that Christians did not practice immorality at the Eucharist—there must, rather, be a reference here to the chief motif: in spite of the fact that the lamps were burning, he fell asleep (this can hardly mean that because the lamps were smoking he sat by the window: thus Zahn).

[41.] In the original publication, Dibelius identified these two forms as "A" and "J" for Acts and Josephus in what follows—which I take to be more of a distraction to the reader than a help.

42. Verse 20 describes something of a general nature: *ēn de thymomachōn* ("Now he was angry"); with *parēsan* ("came") we have a definite event, which was certainly originally motivated by the account of the object of the dispute. The mention of Blastus marks the complete transition to description of individual events. If we do not know the reason for the dispute, naturally we do not understand the meaning of *edēmēgorei* ("made an oration") in v. 21 either; the speech has settled the dispute. It is particularly characteristic of D and other witnesses to the Western text that they supply this want. They supply the completion *katallagentos de autou tois Turiois* ("but he was reconciled to the Tyrians") subsequently, however, in v. 22 (D, others similarly), instead of telling in v. 21 of the dispute and its settlement. This is a proof that we have here a correction of the unintelligible "popular" text and not original tradition.

43. If Josephus were dependent upon Acts (Zahn, *Die Urausgabe,* 236ff.), this would concern only the anecdotes and not the books. But even the anecdotes have no direct connection with one another; for we can hardly believe that the *angelos kyriou* ("angel of the Lord"), which executes the punishment has been made into the owl that announces it and that Josephus (and also his source?) would therefore have called the owl *angelos kakōn* ("messenger of disaster"). On the other hand, if Schütz (*Apostel und Jünger,* 63) takes as a significant difference between Josephus and Acts the fact that the Christian writer lets the angel of the Lord prevail where, according to the Jewish historian, men, women, and children all begin to lament, then we should again have to ask whether this detail in Josephus was not introduced by the author really for practical reasons. In that case it would not be relevant to our attempt to distinguish between the different traditions.

44. See above, p. 37.

45. See above, p. 36.

46. In the Western text there is again an attempt to conceal the seams as far as possible. In v. 7 a better transition from itinerary to story is made with the words: "but Paul and Barnabas lingered in Lystra"; the Western text also brings the episode to a better conclusion by allowing the crowd to go home at the end of v. 18. But that is naturally only an expedient; there is as little point to the story here as in the "popular" text.

47. Western witnesses have preserved this interest still better; some vouch for the lame man's piety or tell that he liked to listen to Paul; one even, the Latin Gigas, says that he came to be a believer; in this instance, the formula of healing contains the name of

Jesus. This could all be taken as a remnant of the original legendary style, but the large number of variants indicates that we are dealing with the different ways of completing the text that were occasioned by *echei pistin* ("had faith," v. 9).

48. The difference between this story of healing and that told from Jerusalem in chapter 3 lies in the appearance of the devotional and the personal element. It is the typical difference between "legend" and "tale," and it seems to me to be a reversion to a superseded way of thinking when Schütz applies the question of "primary or secondary" here (*Apostel und Jünger*, 50–51).

[49.] Compare on this subject Zahn's discussion in "Acta-Kommentar," *TLZ* 47 (1922) 4; also Dibelius, "Literatur zur Formgeschichte," 234–35. [—HG]

50. They think finally that Peter's angel is standing outside. Although the maid has not seen the apostle, those who are assembled together obviously suppose that he of whom they are speaking resembles Peter in voice and appearance. Thus, for the first time in early Christianity, we find an example of that belief which is very important in the history of religion, the belief that the angel appears in the form of the human being who is under his protection. For more on this subject see my *Der Hirt des Hermas*, HNT 4, Suppl. Vol. (Tübingen: Mohr/Siebeck, 1923), in the excursus on *Vision* 5.7.

51. The famous seven steps that D names in v. 10 could actually be the original ones. But anyone telling the story in such detail would also have given the name of the street in what follows. Thus we ascribe the steps to the well-informed writer who elaborated the material, to whom the D-text owes so much.

52. The fact that an old miracle-motif, or perhaps several of them, is used here (see especially Euripides' *Bacchae* 432–654; also Schütz, *Apostel und Jünger*, 51–52) shows how much the ethos of a narrative depends on its style.

53. Again the Western text fills all gaps; according to this text in v. 35 the magistrates, "in thinking about the earthquake," decide to release the disciples, and in v. 39 confess "we did not know that you were innocent"—that too is a reference to what has happened, as Ephraim also understood it according to the Armenian Catena (Zahn, *Die Urausgabe*, 303, *Apparat*).

54. In v. 32 the apostles are already preaching to the prison guard and his family; only then does he take them with him (v. 33) and wash them. Now follows the baptism of the guard and his family, and only then, in v. 34, does he take the prisoners into his house! Everything becomes intelligible if we leave out the preaching and baptism.

55. The author's attempt to introduce the baptism—where it was not mentioned in the old tradition—seems to be evident in another part of this tradition, the conversion of Saul, 9:1-19. The baptism is mentioned here in v. 18; we read first "he regained his sight" and then "he took food and was strengthened." These stages of physical recovery must originally have belonged together; Luke added the baptism here in order to parallel inward with outward "enlightenment" and to place it at the end of the fasting. On the other hand, the old story can scarcely have ended with physical recovery. It is much more obvious that the author is endeavoring to weave the story into his own composition. We therefore find greater difficulties in analyzing it, and it seems to me that we ought also to take into account Acts 22 and 26. This story may therefore be put aside for the present.

5. THE SPEECHES IN ACTS AND ANCIENT HISTORIOGRAPHY

1. Compare Wolfgang Schadewaldt, "Die Anfänge der Geschichtsschreibung bei den Griechen," *Die Antike* 10 (1934) 146. [Ed.] For current discussions and bibliography see: F. F. Bruce, "The Significance of the Speeches for Interpreting Acts," *SWJT* 33 (1990–91) 20–28; G. H. R. Horsley, "Speeches and Dialogue in Acts," *NTS* 32 (1986) 609–14; Edward Schweizer, "Concerning the Speeches in Acts," *Studies in Luke-Acts*, edited by Leander E. Keck and J. Louis Martyn (Philadelphia: Fortress Press, 1980), 208–16; Joseph A. Fitzmyer, *Acts of the Apostles*, AB 31 (New York: Doubleday, 1998), 103–8, 111–13.

2. Otto Regenbogen, "Thukydides als politischer Denker," *Das humanistische Gymnasium* 44 (1933) 3. I am indebted to Regenbogen for valuable advice in preparing this work, also to Hans Schaefer, with whom I was able to discuss the material after completing the work.

3. Joseph Vogt, "Tacitus und die Unparteilichkeit des Historikers," in *Studien zu Tacitus*, Würzburger Studien zur Altertumswissenschaft 9 (Stuttgart: Kohlhammer, 1936), 10 n.23.

4. Compare Martin Braun, *Griechischer, Roman, und hellenistische Geschichtsschreibung*, Frankfurter Studien zur Religion und Kultur der Antike 6 (Frankfurt: Klostermann, 1934); Hans Sprödowsky, *Die Hellenisierung der Geschichte von Joseph in Ägypten bei Flavius Josephus*, Greifswalder Beiträge zur Literatur- und Stilforschung 18 (Greifswald: Dallmeyer, 1937).

5. The fact that the evangelist Matthew changes the words in Mark's account of the Last Supper "they drank all of it" (Mark 14:23) into words spoken by Jesus "Drink of it, all of you" (Matt 26:27) is an example of how independent the attitude is—even of an author who employs no type of literary technique—toward the authentic text. Matthew has also dramatized the betrayal by Judas (which is merely reported in Mark 14:10) by making Judas address the high priest in direct speech: *ti thelete moi dounai, kagō humin paradōsō auton* (Matt 26:15); and, in the same way, he has introduced the healing on the sabbath with direct speech: "And they asked him, 'Is it lawful to heal on the sabbath?'" (*kai epērōtēsan auton legontes. ei exestin tois sabbasin therapeusai;* [Matt 12:10]—as against Mark 3:2 *kai paretēroun auton ei tois sabbasin therapeusei auton*).

6. Of the works dealing with this subject in the last decade I mention: Max Pohlenz *Thukydidesstudien I*, NGWG.PH (1919–20) 117ff.; Ed. Schwartz, *Gnomon* 2 (1926) 79ff.; Wolfgang Schadewaldt, *Die Geschichtsschreibung des Thukydides* (1929), 22ff.; Ernst Kapp, *Gnomon* 6 (1930) 91ff.; August Deffner, *Die Rede bei Herodot und ihre Weiterbildung bei Thukydides* (Munich: Salesianischen Offizin, 1933); Regenbogen, "Thukydides als politischer Denker"; August Grosskinsky, *Das Programm des Thukydides* (Berlin: Junker und Dünnhaupt, 1936); M. Pohlenz, *Göttingische gelehrte Anzeigen* 198 (1936) 281ff.; Harald Patzer, *Das Problem der Geschichtsschreibung des Thukydides und die thukydideische Frage*, NDF 129 (Berlin: Junker und Dünnhaupt, 1937); Franz Egermann, *DLZ* (1937) 1474; Helmut Berve, "Thukydides" (*Auf d. Wege z. nationalpolit. Gymn.* 5 (1938) 21ff.; Otto Luschnat, *Die Felderrnreden im Geschichtswerk des Thukydides*, Philologus Supplementband 34.2 (Leipzig: Dieterich, 1942).

7. It is a matter of controversy whether *akripeia* means the authenticity of the speeches (Grosskinsky, Patzer) or the aim of the historiographical method generally (Egermann), which cannot be achieved in the speeches, but rather in the reporting of facts.

8. This is said especially by Pohlenz, *Thukydidesstudien I,* 117ff.

9. Dionysius of Halicarnassus, *Pomp.* 3.20 (2.240, Usener-Radermacher).

10. Compare Heinrich Gottlieb Strebel, *Wertung und Wirkund des Thukydideischen Geschichtswerkes in der griechisch-römischen Literatur* (Speyer: Pilger, 1935).

11. According to Duris (*Fr. Gr. Hist.* [Jacoby], II, A, 76, F, 1), *mimēsis* (dramatic vividness) and *hēdonē* (entertainment) are required. Compare also Cicero, *Fam.* 5.12.4: "for the untroubled recollection of a past sorrow has a charm of its own" (*habet enim praeteriti doloris secura recordation delectationem*). The construction of the two main works of Sallust is characteristic of the *misēsis.* Both in the *Bellum Jugurtha* and in the *Bellum Catilinae* we follow an action which rises and falls, has a climax in the middle, and a catastrophe at the end. The analyses in Richard Reitzenstein, *Hellenistische Wundererzählungen* (Leipzig: Teubner, 1906), 87–88, are certainly exaggerated; see Kurt Latte, *Sallust,* NWA 2.4 (Leipzig: Teubner, 1935), 30.

12. Thus we find in Cicero, beside admiration of the great historian, also the characteristic criticism (*Brutus,* 287): "'Thucydides,' you say 'we strive to imitate.' Very well, if you are writing history; but not if you are considering pleading a legal case" (*"Thucydidem" inquit, "imitatamur." Optime, si historiam scribere, non si causas dicere cogitatis*). Or *Opt. gen.* 5.15 with reference to Thucydides: *Aliud est enim explicare res gestas narrando, aliud argumentando criminari crimeuve dissolvere.*

13. In *Bellum Catilinae* there is a long speech by Catiline both at the beginning and also at the end (20.2-17; 58.1-21); the fall of the action is denoted by the two speeches by Caesar and Cato, who says of Caesar's speech: "good and elegant language" (*bene et composite disseruit*) (51.1-43; 52.2-36); in 54 there then follows a comparison by the author between the two speakers, and this is introduced (at the end of 53 by the characteristic words: "since the subject has brought them before me, it is not my intention to pass in silence, but to describe, to the best of my ability, the disposition and manners of each" (*quos quoniam res obtulerat, silentio praeterire non fuit concilium, quin utriusque naturam et mores, quantum ingenio possem, aperirem*). In *Bellum Jugurtha* it is striking how Jugurtha's Roman and African opponents launch forth into long speeches, while he himself speaks only briefly and in *oratio oblique.* In this speech we read, with reference to the short instructions to the messengers (22.2-4): *accepta oratione.* Thus a full-length *oratio* really is in question, and it is due to the author if the speech is only briefly reported to the reader.

14. Compare Karl Münscher, *Xenophon in der griechisch-römischen Literatur,* Philologus Supplementband 13.2 (Leipzig: Dieterich, 1920), 181.

15. *Peri logou askēseōs;* Dio Chrysostom, *Or.* 18.14 (2.255, v. Arnim).

16. Compare Münscher, *Xenophon,* 116. Even Xenophon's speeches have not, however, escaped criticism. Dionysius of Halicarnassus says in *De imitatione* 3.2 (II, 208, Usener-Radermacher) that he lets philosophical speeches be made by "unskilled and barbarous men" (*andres idiōtai kai barbaroi*), with the result that the "proper" (*prepon*) is lacking.

17. Otto Regenbogen drew my attention to the speeches in the *Hellenica.* I have counted more than a dozen speeches in the *Hellenica* of the kind described, while the number of long speeches to be found there is about ten.

18. As we may conclude from the criticism of Polybius (12.25i.5), the speeches in *Timaeus* were of this kind. Polybius observes that the historian should not compose speeches merely in order to demonstrate his skill. The speeches of Dionysius of

Halicarnassus also belong, mainly, to this group; compare Joseph Flierle, *Über Nachahmungen des Demosthenes, Thukydides und Xenophon in den Reden der römischen Archäologie des Dionysius v. Halikarnass* (Munich: Straub, 1890).

19. Here we might mention Josephus, for example, who, according to his own description in *War* 3.8.5 (§§361-382), when in a highly precarious situation, still finds time to make a speech against suicide. Also, he avoids the drama of the recognition scene in the Old Testament story of Joseph, favoring instead detailed speeches (*Ant.* 2.6.8-9 §§140-159), which contain many "truths"; compare Sprödowsky, *Die Hellenisierung.*

20. Eduard Meyer, *Ursprung und Anfänge des Christentums,* 3.2 (reference to Herodotus); Jülicher and Fascher, *Einleitung in das Neue Testament,* 7th ed. (Tübingen: Mohr/Siebeck, 1931), 437 (Thucydides and Livy); Cadbury in *The Beginnings of Christianity* (1933), 5.405–6 (Josephus, Thucydides, Polybius, Dio Cassius, Tacitus).

21. Compare Dibelius, *A Fresh Approach to the New Testament and Early Christian Literature,* ILCK (New York: Scribner, 1936), 62–64, 261–64.

22. F. Blass, A. Debrunner, and Robert W. Funk, *A Greek Grammar of the New Testament* (Chicago: Univ. of Chicago Press, 1961), §§485–87.

23. Johannes Weiss, "Beiträge zur paulinischen Rhetorik," in *Theologische Studien: Herrn Wirkl. Oberkonsistorialrath Professor D. Bernhard Weiss zu seinem 70 Geburtstage dargebracht,* ed. C. R. Gregory (Göttingen: Vandenhoeck and Ruprecht, 1897); Wilamowitz-Möllendorf in "Die griechische Literatur und Sprache," in *Kultur der Gegenwart* (Berlin: Teubner, 1912), 1/8:232–33; Rudolf Bultmann, *Der Stil der paulinischen Predigt und die kynischstoische Diatribe,* FRLANT 13 (Göttingen: Vandenhoeck & Ruprecht, 1910).

24. Compare a proem of related style, but of definitely Christian formulation, like that of Papias to his "explanation of the Lord's sayings" (*logiōn kyriakōn exēgēseis*): "I shall not regret to subjoin to my interpretations, also for your benefit, whatever I have at any time accurately ascertained and treasured up in my memory, as I have received it from the elders and have recorded it in order to give additional confirmation of the truth, by my testimony. For I have never, like many, . . . but those that are given from the Lord, to our faith, and that came forth from the truth itself"; *oude tois tas allotrias entolas mnēmoneuousin (scil. echairon), alla tois tas para tou kyriou tē pistei dedomenas kai ap' autēs paraginomenas tēs alētheias* (Papias in Eusebius, *Hist. eccl.* 3.39.3).

25. There are two proofs of this, apart from the probability inherent in the content: 1. The Acts of the Apostles was not received by the communities into the canon at the same time as Luke's Gospel, and does not make its appearance as a canonical book until about 180; 2. The text of Acts has had much more drastic revision than that of any other book of the New Testament (see the so-called Western text); from this it is clear that this text was "free" for a long time, that is, that it was not subjected to that control which is exercised upon a book as a whole when it is used for any length of time publicly in the service of God: in that case, although minor variations may arise, the occurrence of more serious alterations in the text is prevented. I have dealt with this problem, which has been only touched upon here, in my essay, "The Text of Acts," chap. 11

26. Compare my treatise, "Sylte Criticism of the Book of Acts" (chap. 4 above).

27. In respect of Antioch, we read "contradicted . . . reviled" (*antelegon . . . blasphēmmountes*), without more detailed information; of Corinth, "they opposed and reviled him" (*antitassomenōn de autōn kai blasphēmountōn*) gives no definite report of

what was said (D has given more information), and, in respect of Rome, "those who did not believe" (*hoi de ēpistoun*) is the only thing that is introduced to the discredit of the Jews and in justification of the words of Paul which follow.

28. We may also disagree as to what can be called "speeches." Here, for example, the words of the Resurrected One (1:4-5, 7-8) are not included in this number, although, as will be seen, their function is similar to that of the speeches. Nor have I counted passages such as 6:2-4 and 18:14-15. Paul's words to the crew of the ship (27:21-26), which are really in the style of a speech, are included, but not his injunction to eat (27:33-34.).

29. Acts 1:16-22; 2:14-36, 38-39; 3:12-26; 4:8-12, 19, 20; 5:29-32; 10:34-43; 11:5-17; 15:7-11.

30. Acts 13:16-41; 14:15-17; 17:22-31; 20:18-35; 22:1-21; 24:10-21; 26:2-23, 25-27; 27:21-26; 28:17-20.

31. Gamaliel (5:35-39); Demetrius to his fellow-craftsmen (19:25-27); the town-clerk in Ephesus (19:35-40); Tertullus (24:2-8); Festus (25:24-27).

32. If the words of 24:6b, 7, 8a—which are found in the Western text, and which the Antiochan-Byzantine text omits—are to be regarded as genuine, Tertullus is referring to the evidence of Lysias, not to Paul. While elsewhere I regard the so-called Western readings mainly as elaborations of or as improvements on the original, I should like in this case cautiously to suggest that they are original (see also Ropes in *The Beginnings of Christianity*, vol. 3), for the Egyptian text includes the following improbable features: 1. The accumulation of the relative particles *hos, hon, par' hou* (24:6, 8). 2. The reference by Tertullus to Paul's evidence. But, on the other hand, the way is well prepared for the proconsul's final decision in 24:22 by the application of the *par ou* to the tribune Lysias which is necessary in the Western text. The contradiction which exists in some measure between the verses in question and the account in 21:27—22:24 is no proof against the authenticity of those verses, for there are many discrepancies of this kind between speech and narrative in Acts (see pp. 75–76 above). It may well be, however, that it was because this contradiction was observed that the verses were omitted.

33. With reference to all that follows compare my essay "Paul on the Areopagus," chap 7.

34. Emanuel Hirsch thinks there were written models for the account of Athens ("Die drei Berichte der Apostelgeschichte über die Bekehrung des Paulus," *ZNW* 28 [1929] 305–12). There is evidence against this view in the fact that this account is firmly related to the Areopagus speech; compare the "idol-filled city" (*kateidōlos polis*) with the altar to the unknown god, the reference to philosophers with the proof given in the speech (vv. 24-27), perhaps also the *spermologos* with the quotation from the poets in v. 28, the emphasis upon Jesus and the "*Anastasis*" in the conclusion to the speech.

35. Compare my essay "Paul on the Areopagus" (chap. 7 below). Wilhelm Schmid has contradicted my interpretation almost word for word in *Philologus* 101 (1942) 79–120, but has created for his understanding of the speech a basis that I cannot recognize. First of all, he establishes what Paul had to say in this sermon to the Gentiles. In so doing, he takes Paul to be a systematic theologian, who "must have . . . formed his own clear conception of the relationship of Christian theology to that of the Gentiles" (110). He interprets the speech with this idea as starting-point, imagines gaps where the speech gives no reason to do so, and even completes the text with a specifically Chris-tian section (113). The whole procedure condemns itself; I shall elaborate on this later.

36. Schmid, *op. cit.*, 100ff., borrows from biblical tradition the idea of the dispersion of mankind as a result of the fall. He fails to recognize the fact that Acts 17:26 is written in a very optimistic strain and that man's habitation of the earth's surface is regarded as the gift of God and not as the "result of the overthrow of God's plan" (p. 100).

37. In an essay, "Paulus und die Stoa," *ZNW* 42 (1949) 69–104, about which, with the author's kind permission, I should like to give my opinion, Max Pohlenz contrasts the Paul of the epistles with the Paul of the Acts. In an arresting and convincing manner he shows that the Paul of the Epistle to the Romans "moves according to that way of thought which was prescribed for him by birth and education," but that Hellenistic ideas appear in his thought "only on the fringes and considerably transposed." "The speaker on the Areopagus, on the other hand, transplants himself intentionally into the Gentile way of thought." In the course of his exposition Pohlenz raises various objections to my interpretation of Acts 17:26-27 which, however, have not convinced me (but compare below p. 84 and p. 184, n. 84). He would prefer to combine *epoiēsen* in v. 26 with *katoikein* (God has caused all nations to dwell), in which case *ex henos* is to be taken as "neuter, in the philosophical sense." I think that, in a biblical author, *epoiēsen te ex henos pan ethnos anthrōpōn* can only be taken as referring to the derivation of the whole human race from Adam (*ex henos*) and that *epoiēsen* then obviously means "he has created." Nor can I convince myself that the *prostetagmenoi kairoi* and the *horothesiai* refer to the development of the nations in relation to time (?) and space but, for reasons given in my essay, should prefer to keep the interpretation of seasons and zones of habitation, especially in view of the fact that Pohlenz's understanding of *kairoi* is extremely vague. This difference of opinion does not lessen my agreement with the essay as a whole, or my gratitude to its author.

38. Schmid rightly observes: "What were such completely uncalled-for intimations supposed to mean to Paul's hearers, who wanted to have the person and teaching of Christ explained to them?" (p. 113). But we are not entitled to supply what is lacking and must be content simply to establish the fact that the Areopagus speech contains only this one Christian sentence. This, also, is an indication that speeches of this kind are regarded as being intended primarily for cultivated readers, for only they could appreciate the relationship with Hellenistic philosophy.

39. On the other hand, Schmid says, *op. cit.*, pp. 115–16: "Even though we may think in modest terms of Luke's literary and intellectual gifts, we ought not to do him the injustice of stating that it was his intention to present an "example of the Christian proclamation" to Gentile listeners merely by means of the accumulation of genuine fragments, which we have before us."

40. Concerning the altar to the unknown god see my essay "Paul on the Areopagus" (chap. 7 below). In connection with the treatment of the motif I can quote Schmid, who writes, *op. cit.*, p. 97: "This whole section is pervaded by that half-ironical charm which is peculiar to Greek *dialexeis*, and which we should certainly not expect to find in an apostle who is otherwise so passionately zealous." We are therefore all the more justified in ascribing this treatment to the author of Acts.

41. Compare p. 52 above.

42. Apart from biographical encomiums, we might also remember in this connection that, according to Lucian, Peregrinus, a philosopher of questionable repute, makes a speech shortly before his death, in which he describes his life, together with all the dangers he has undergone: Lucian, *De peregrini morte* 32. Perhaps we may infer from

this that the inclusion in speeches of retrospects such as these is in accordance with tradition (although Lucian's account is colored by satire).

43. Compare my commentary on 1 Thessalonians (Tübingen: Mohr/Siebeck, 1937), 8–11. H. Schulze has emphasized the connection between the speech in Acts 20 and 1 Thessalonians, though with pronounced exaggeration (he parallels 1 Thess 2:16 and 4:13a with Acts 20:20; 1 Thess 2:8 with Acts 20:24; "Die Unterlagen für die Abschiedsrede zu Milet in Apostelgeschichte 20:18-38," *TSK* 73 (1900) 119–25. This connection does not depend, however, upon Luke's knowledge of 1 Thessalonians, but upon the fact that, in Thessalonians, Paul is dealing with the same missionary situation as Luke is here.

44. In his commentary, Wendt calls vv. 26-27 and 33-35 "clumsy elements."

45. Compare Dibelius and Heinrich Greeven, *The Pastoral Epistles*, trans. Philip Buttolph and Adela Yarbro, ed. Helmut Koester, Hermeneia (Philadelphia: Fortress Press, 1972), 16–18.

46. It is hard to imagine all this being published in a text unless events had by now lifted it all out of the realm of uncertainty, that is, unless the apostle had already been put to death. It seems to me impossible, therefore, that the Acts should have appeared during the last years of Paul's life.

47. We must here touch on the question of whether the juxtaposition of three accounts which do not completely tally does not lead us to conclude that there were different sources for the book of Acts. Many scholars believe that there were, and Hirsch has now given detailed proof of this in "Die drei Berichte." In his opinion, chap. 26 is Paul's account, for it contains that understanding of the conversion that we have in Gal 1:15-16. Hirsch believes that chap. 9 is the account that was current in the Damascus community, for we are told exactly where Paul stayed in Damascus and the name of his host. According to Hirsch, chap. 22 is intended to furnish a compromise between the accounts in chaps. 9 and 26. As Hirsch plainly asserts, this judgment presupposes that the two accounts, in 9 and in 26, "are incompatible." That is just the question. Hirsch, quite rightly, sees the chief discrepancy in the fact that the call to become a missionary to the Gentiles is given to Paul in chap. 26 only by the voice from heaven; in chap. 9 there is only the Lord's command to Ananias and, in chap. 22, though hinted at in the words of Ananias, the charge is openly given for the first time in the vision in the temple. The question is whether these variations may all be attributed to Luke. Once we have seen that we are concerned primarily with what the account is intended to signify, rather than with its historical reliability, then we can conclude that they are to be attributed to him.

48. Caesar's speech to his soldiers in Cassius Dio 38.36-46 was suggested by Caesar, *Bell. gal.* 1.40. But in Cassius Dio we do not find any developing of those essential ideas that are indicated in Caesar, and only general points of view are put forward. Compare Hermann Peter, *Die geschichtliche Literatur der römischen Kaiserzeit bis Theodosius I. und ihre Quellen*, 2 vols. (Hildesheim: Olms, 1897), 2.301.

49. Acts 7:58b; 8:1. The very first comment interrupts the description of the martyrdom in such a way that "they stoned" (*elithoboloun*) has to be repeated [in 7:59]. So the author seems to have introduced his own reference to Paul into an account of the martyrdom that was already in existence.

50. The speech which comes after the healing of the lame man is interrupted by the priests and the captain of the temple (4:1); the prayer of the community ends with an earthquake (4:31); Peter's discourse in the house of Cornelius becomes the occasion of an

inspiring of the hearers by the Holy Spirit (10:44); Paul's declaration before the Sanhedrin is ended by the dissension between the Pharisees and Sadducees (23:7).

51. Xenophon's *Hellenica* 6.5.37 may be regarded as a kind of parallel: by "at that the Athenians shouted" (*entautha mentoi hoi Athēnaioi epethorybēsan*) acclamations of agreement are meant. Josephus gives the impression that Herod does not allow Tiro to finish his speech (*Ant.* 16.11.5 [§§384-386]).

[52.] After this academy lecture was delivered (1944) and before it was printed (1949), Dibelius published (1947) a more detailed analysis of the Cornelius-story, "The Conversion of Cornelius," chap 10. [—H.G.]

53. In Acts 10:2 Cornelius is referred to as "one who fears God" (*phoboumenos ton theon*): thus he belongs to the "Godfearers" (*phoboumeno*) or "worshipers" (*sebomenoi*), that is, to those who were permitted to come to the synagogue as visitors; but, since he is uncircumcised (Acts 11:3), Luke regards him as a Gentile.

54. Concern for the vision has occasioned the initial words of 10:19, which interrupt the continuity considerably, and because of this it is clear to us today that the vision (10:9-16) has been inserted into a complete story. Acts 10:17b, 18, 19b, 20 should probably follow 10:8.

55. I should like to say: "if we deny the historicity of these speeches," but we cannot go so far. Luke may have known of individual occasions when Paul spoke there. He may also have had information about the "general sense" (*xumpasa gnōmē*) of the speaker or of the speech in individual instances; he may even have been an eyewitness, but we cannot say where or when this was the case. Nor are we able in this case to attribute the speeches to the itinerary, which was undoubtedly used in Acts 13–21, for if this source recorded any speeches that had been made, then they would have been found in the itinerary more often. The selecting of the occasion and the elaboration of the speech is in each case the work of the author.

56. Martin Dibelius, *From Tradition to Gospel,* trans. Bertram Lee Woolf (New York: Scribner, 1971), 16–17.

57. Acts 2:14-21 interpretation of the speaking with tongues; 3:12 the miracle worked upon the lame man; 10:34-35 God makes no distinctions; 13:17-22 survey of the history of Israel (compare p. 68).

58. More recent commentators either lay stress upon the idea that God's presence is not confined to the temple (Wikenhauser), or think there is evidence that the people were ungrateful and disobedient (Preuschen, not with reference to the accusation, but from the plan of the book generally: the way is being prepared for taking the gospel to the Gentiles; Overbeck holds a similar view). Most find indications of both motifs, the disobedience of the Jews and the conditional nature of temple worship (H. J. Holtzmann; Wendt, with emphasis upon the second motif; Bauernfeind). Wilhelm Mundle thinks that the speaker quotes examples from the Old Testament as being typical illustrations of what happened to Jesus and the Christians ("Die Stephanusrede Apg. 7: Eine Märtyrerapologie," *ZNW* 20 [1921] 133–47). Compare, on the other hand, Hermann Wolfgang Beyer, who writes: Stephen probably speaks "in the way in which, in the synagogue, on feast-days, it was customary to interpret the history of God and the chosen people"; and Otto Dibelius: "Jewish teachers and preachers were accustomed to speak as he speaks here": only at the end does the speaker become a prophet and proclaim that the Temple does not constitute God's last word to me.

59. On the subject of Stephen's martyrdom compare Hans-Werner Surkau, *Martyrien in jüdischer und frühchristlicher Zeit*, FRLANT 54 (Göttingen: Vandenhoeck & Ruprecht, 1938), 105–19. I do not share Surkau's opinion and should myself consider it necessary to remove from 7:54—8:2, in order to obtain the text of the martyrdom, only those sentences referring to Paul and the persecution. In that case, the duplication of "they stoned" (*elithoboloun*; 7:58, 59) would automatically disappear. It is possible, however, for the two last utterances of Stephen (7:59, 60) to co-exist. [Ed.] See also *TRu* 3 (1931) 232–34. [—H.G.]

60. Concerning the linguistic relationship of Stephen's speech with the Lukan writings compare Mundle, "Die Stephanusrede," 135.

61. Commentators differ as to whether Felix merited this praise in view of his action in connection with the Sicarii, or whether it was simply idle flattery (see the various quotations in Lösch's essay which is referred to in the next note). If it is not the orator Tertullus but the writer Luke speaking here, then the question is of little importance.

62. It is certainly to Stephan Lösch's credit that he has established this in "Die Dankesrede des Tertullus," *TQ* 112 (1931) 295–319; but the closest connection with the official language of the legal papyri does not justify the conclusion which Lösch clearly advocates, namely that this speech was not composed by the author but that it was actually made by the orator Tertullus. This cannot be proved by the style, and the author's usual custom is against such a suggestion.

63. Compare Lösch, "Die Dankesrede," 317.

64. In comparison with 22:3-5, we notice how emphasis is laid on Paul's associations with Jerusalem; compare the reference to education "in this city," to Gamaliel, the high priest, and the vision in the temple. All this is appropriate in a speech that was made right above the temple court.

65. See below p. 83.

66. Of course these verses can be taken as belonging together only if 1:4-11 are regarded as one scene. That, however, seems to me to be correct, since neither 1:6 nor 1:9 indicates a change of locality, so that in the preceding verses also the situation must be the Mount of Olives (see 1:12).

67. That has often been said; M. Schneckenburger writes in *Über den Zweck der Apostelgeschichte: Zugleich eine Ergänzung der neueren Commentare* (Bern: Fischer, 1841), 191–92: "This verse . . . is, as many commentators have long ago observed, the theme throughout the book of Acts."

68. The speeches in Athens and Miletus are in the middle of the account from the itinerary (which, I am convinced, was not by any means limited to the "we-passages"). The martyrdom of Stephen and the legend of Cornelius were evidently current in the communities as independent stories. It is only with reference to chaps. 21 and 22 that the origin of the account cannot be established. Did these chapters stand originally in the source, or was Luke an eyewitness?

[69.] Compare p. 121 and p. 199, n. 112. [—H.G.]

[70.] For the relationship of the three accounts compare also *TRu* 3 (1931) 235. [—H.G.]

71. In Josephus *Ant.* 2.3.1 (§22), Reuben wants to restrain his brothers from killing Joseph, and, in order to do so, argues that the proposed deed would cause sorrow to their father and plunge Joseph's mother into immeasurable grief at the loss of her son. But his mother is already dead, as Josephus tells it in *Ant.* 1.21.3 (§343)! In Appian's

Lybica 64 §283, is found a reference by the speaker Publius Cornelius to the speech that Scipio has made a short time before in the camp before the envoys from Carthage. The speaker in Rome cannot, however, know of this speech yet! Moreover, Censorinus then makes a speech in the same place that begins graciously (in 86 §§404ff.); but in 90 §423, after the resumption of the narrative, it results in a threat. In Cassius Dio, also, discrepancies between speech and narrative are found; see E. Schwartz, Pauly-Wissowa 3:1719.

72. Acts 2:40 "and he testified with many other words" (*heterois te logois pleiosin diemartuato*). Compare Xenophon, *Hellenica* 2.4.42, "he said this and other more as well" (*eipōn de tauta kai alla toiauta*); Polybius, 3.111.11, "these things and others like them he spoke" (*tauta de kai toutois paraplēsia dialechtheis*); 21.14.4, "and he spoke many other things" (*polla de kai hetera . . . dielechthē*); Appian, *Sam.* 10.6, "but Appian spoke many similar things" (*alla te polla homoia toutois ho Appios eipōn*); *Bell. civ.* 3.63 (§257), "after Antony had said much more" (*toiade polla eipōn ho Antōnios*).

73. Thus, for example, the question as to how Carthaginians and Romans came to an understanding plays no part in Cassius Dio. In the secret parley of Sulla and Bocchus, at least the presence of an interpreter is mentioned by Sallust (*Bell. Jurg.* 109.4). We should, however, recall a well-known exception in one instance where the language question is taken into account, although it is not a case of a speech but of a letter: the Spartan officer Hippocrates writes in the Laconic dialect to his home town; Xenophon, *Hellenica* 1.1.23; "The ships are gone. Mindarus is dead. The men are starving. We do not know what to do" (*errei ta kala. Mindaros apessua. peinōnti tōndres. aporiomes ti chrē dran*).

74. Compare Justin 38.3.11.

75. Compare Hans Oppermann, *Cäsar*, NWA 2.2 (Leipzig: Teubner, 1933), 73.

76. Compare Appian, *Hist. Rom., Hisp.* 40 §162; 87 §§377-378; 95 §§412-413; *Syr.* 3 §§12-13. And in *Bell. civ.*: 2.37 §§146-147; 55 §§227-228; 3.28 §§109-110; 44 §§180-81; 72 §§296-97; 86-87 §§356ff.

77. The change from indirect to direct speech takes place in the words of the resurrected Christ in Acts 1:4. The same thing is found in Acts 25:4-5, the change being in the reverse direction in Acts 23:23-24.

78. Compare Appian, *Bell. civ.* 2.58 §238, where the author records both admiration and disapproval of Caesar; or *Sam.* 10.15, where after two suggestions regarding Fabricius's answer have been given, we read: "one cannot separate between the two" (*hopoterōs d' oun apekrinato*).

79. We shall deal in the last section of this essay with the possibility that the speeches contain definite echoes of works of "great" literature. [Compare pp. 83–86.]

80. Such an application is, of course, not out of the question. The oft-quoted speech by Claudius about the Gauls (compare p. 50) shows that in this instance Tacitus has not so much used his imagination freely but has revised freely. But the writer lacks all interest in preserving the original text and therefore his version can be of no help in determining sources. Compare also p. 181, n. 55.

81. Compare Sallust, *Bell. Cat.* 51.5-6; Josephus, *War* 5.9.4 (§§376-399); Tacitus, *Annals* 11.24.

82. I have quoted this in detail in order to assist in the removal of an old error which is seen even in the great American work on the Acts; compare Foakes-Jackson and Lake, *The Beginnings of Christianity* (1922) 2.356: "In this passage Josephus describes the insurrection of Theudas in the procuratorship of Fadus *and goes on to tell* how the

sons of Judas of Galilee . . . were executed." The words I have placed in italics give a false impression of the closeness of the connection.

83. Compare the essay "Paul on the Areopagus," chap. 6.

84. Max Pohlenz, "Paulus und die Stoa," *ZNW* 42 (1949) 69–104. The reference is to an account in the commentary on Acts, published in 1913, by the Nestorian, Ischo'dad of Merv, who lived in the ninth century. He says that the sentence quoted above also originated in literature, in the work of one called "Minos." One was able to conclude by an indirect method that he was alluding to the poem *Peri Minō kai Hradamanthuos* by Epimenides of Crete. Pohlenz has made it seem probable that a much more far-reaching error exists here than I (following Zahn and Lake) had supposed, see above, pp. 108–11.

85. "Bad company ruins good morals" (*phtheirousin ēthē chrēsata homiliai kakai*). The words "do not be deceived" (*mē planasthe*), when used by Paul, serve to introduce a truth already known (1 Cor 6:9; Gal 6:7); similarly in Ignatius (*Eph.* 16.1; *Philad.* 3.3). James evidently uses them in 1:16-17 to introduce a hexameter; these are not literary quotations, however, but popular applications of ancient wisdom. The difference between the Areopagus speech and these texts is obvious.

86. All the most reliable witnesses have the saying only in 26:14. Of course, some have added it afterwards in other places, even in both places. The fact that in Acts 9 it sometimes appears after v. 4 and sometimes after v. 5 confirms the assumption that it is a later addition.

87. In addition to the more recent commentaries, compare Wilhelm Nestle, "Anklänge an Euripides in der Apostelgeschichte," *Philologus* 59 (1900) 46–57; Friedrich Smend, "Untersuchungen zu den Acta-Darstellungen von der Bekehrung des Paulus," *Angelos* 1 (1925) 34–45; Werner Georg Kümmel, *Römer 7 und die Bekehrung des Paulus,* Untersuchungen zum Neuen Testament 17 (Leipzig: Hinrichs, 1929), 155–57; Otto Weinreich, *Gebet und Wunder: Zwei Abhandlungen zur Religions- und Literatur-Geschichte* (Stuttgart: Kohlhammer, 1929), 168–70; Hans Windisch, "Die Christusepiphanie von Damaskus und ihre religionsgeschichtlichen Parallelen," *ZNW* 31 (1932) 1–23; Albrecht Oepke, "Probleme der vorchristlichen Zeit des Paulus," *TSK* 105 (1933) 387–424; Lothar Schmid, "*kentron*," in *TDNT* (1965) 3:663–68. Evidence that, in later antiquity, the words were regarded as a saying is found in Julian, *Or.* 8.246b: "or as the proverb says, 'kick against the goads'" (*mēde, ho phēsin hē paroimia, pros kentra laktizein*).

[88.] Dibelius erroneously read this as *kentra* ("goads") instead of *kyma* ("wave").

89. Aeschylus (*Agamemnon* 1624) has already been mentioned. Compare also some words from an inscription found in Asia Minor; A. H. Smith, "Notes on a Tour in Asia Minor," *JHS* 8 (1887) 261, *laktizeis pros kentra, ptro[s a]ntia kumata mochtheis*.

90. Sophocles, *frgmt.* 622 (Nauck), *kōtilos d'anēr labōn, panourga chersi kentra kdeuei polin*—Kümmel, *Römer 7 und die Bekehrung des Paulus*, has especially emphasized these possibilities.

91. Kümmel quotes Sophocles (*Oedipus Rex* 807–809): "and the old man, seeing this, watched till I passed and from his carriage brought down right on my head the double-pointed goad" (*kai m' ho presbys hōs hora ochou parasteichonta tērēsas, meson kara diplois kentroisi mou kathiketo*).

92. In *Bacchae* 45, Dionysus says of Pentheus that he is one "who fights against the gods, as far as I am concerned" (*hos theomachei ta kat' eme*); Tiresias confesses of

himself, in 325, "I will not be persuaded by your words to fight against the god" (*kou theomachēsō*); and finally, Agave says of her son in 1255–56, "But all he can do is fight with the gods" (*alla theomachein monon oios t' ekeinos*).

93. But it must be emphasized that in Epictetus 3.24.24 *theomachēsō* and *theomachia* are used unhesitatingly, in lively language, of the unstoic revolt against fate; thus the words are more widely used than our examples would lead us to believe.

94. It is a question of the opposition to the "new" god (*Bacchae* 216, 219, 256, 272) and of the "preacher of foreign divinities" (*xenōn daimoniōn katangelous*) in Acts 17:18; then of the similarity between the motifs of the stories of releases (Acts 4, 5, 12, and 16) and the release scene in the *Bacchae* 576–637, which has been dealt with by Weinreich in *Gebet und Wunder*. These, however, are simply related motifs that, important as they are, are not sufficient to prove any immediate connection between Acts and the *Bacchae*.

6. Paul in the Book of Acts

1. The beginning is round about 6:12; proof of the existence of an older text is particularly to be observed in the fact that the verses 6:15 and 7:55 (excluding the long speech which intervenes) belong together. 7:58b, also, is obviously an insertion, as the repetition of "stoned" (*elithoboloun*) in 7:59 shows; similarly, 8:1 and 8:2 conclude the whole with the burial and lamentation.

2. Compare Hans-Werner Surkau, *Martyrien in jüdischer und frühchristlicher Zeit*, FRLANT 54 (Göttingen: Vandenhoeck & Ruprecht, 1938), 109–10. Whether the repletion of the "last words" is due to the existence of two traditions remains undecided.

3. With regard to the activities of the witnesses according to the Mishnah (see *Sanhedrin* 6:4). In Stephen's case, it is a question of mob-law, and the event, therefore, does not take place as the Mishnah prescribes. [Ed.] See Torrey Seland, *Establishment Violence in Philo and Luke: A Study of Non-Conformity to the Torah and Jewish Vigilante Reactions*, BibIntSer 15 (Leiden: Brill, 1995).

4. Compare note 1 above.

5. Similarly, 8:1, 4 link up with 11:19; 8:40 links up with 21:8.

6. According to Gal 1:18 and 2:1, the conversion took place fifteen to seventeen years before the council with the original apostles, thus between the years 32 and 35; in Acts 12 we are already in the year 44 (death of Herod Agrippa I).

7. What is said of Paul in Gal 1:23—"now preaching the faith he once tried to destroy" (*nun euangelizetai tēn pistin ēn pote eporthei*)—must fall partly in these years.

8. Acts 15:1-35, the portrayal of the Apostolic Council, does not really belong to the accounts concerning Paul. Apart from the journey there and back, Paul is spoken of in only one sentence (15:12) and mentioned in the decree (15:25-26).

9. If the Epistle to the Galatians is directed at communities in this region and, at the time when the letter was written, Paul had already been there twice (Gal 4:13), he must already have founded the communities at that time.

10. Alfred Wikenhauser, *Die Apostelgeschichte*, 4th ed., RNT 5 (Regensburg: Pustet, 1961), 185.

11. The "we" of the report which goes as far as Philippi begins in Troas; the narrator's home is thus in Macedonia. Perhaps there is some truth in the supposition, which at first appears somewhat rationalistic, according to which either the vision in the dream

reflects the actual arrival of a Macedonian, or is confirmed by his subsequent arrival. If this supposition is correct, it would seem to be conceivable that it is the recording of the divine revelation which is important to the author, who therefore allows external circumstances to take a back place. [Ed.] Compare also Dibelius and Kümmel, *Paul*, trans. Frank Clarke (London: Longmans, Green, 1953), 76.

12. Of course, the silence on the matter of the collection may have been due to a source that mentioned the names of those who accompanied Paul on the journey but did not say why they traveled with him. Elsewhere, however, Luke revises the information given by his sources, so that ultimately the silence on this matter must be traced back to Luke.

13. Let us add the observation here that the account of the rising of the silversmiths (19:23-40) certainly names Paul's mission as its cause, but never allows Paul himself to come into action (see 19:30). It does not belong, then, to the accounts about Paul.

14. Eduard Norden has shown this, *Agnostos Theos: Untersuchungen zur Formengeschichte religiöser Rede* (Stuttgart: Teubner, 1912), 313–27.

15. The somewhat artificial way in which these notes have been inserted into the portrayal of the voyage is shown by the fact that in what follows no further regard is paid to Paul. It is said in 27:43-44 that some of the shipwrecked men swim to land, some save themselves on planks, others on other remnants of the ship. But we are not told how Paul reached land.

7. Paul on the Areopagus

1. Ernst Curtius, "Paulus in Athen," *Sitzungsberichte der Berliner Akademie* (1893) 935–38; Adolf von Harnack, *Ist die Rede des Paulus in Athen ein ursprünglicher Bestandteil der Apostelgeschichte?* TU 39 (Leipzig: Hinrich, 1913), 39; Alfred Wikenhauser, *Die Apostelgeschichte und ihr Geschichtswert*, NTAbh 8 (Münster: Aschendorff, 1921), 390–94; Eduard Meyer, *Ursprung und Anfänge des Christentums*, vol. 3: *Die Apostelgeschichte und die Anfänge des Christentums* (Stuttgart: Cotta, 1923), 89–108.

2. Eduard Norden, *Agnostos Theos: Untersuchungen zur Formgeschichte religiöser Rede* (Leipzig: Teubner, 1913), 3–83; Alfred Loisy, *Les Actes des Apôtres* (Paris: Nourry, 1920), 660–84. We need scarcely mention how much our understanding of the Areopagus speech owes to the former book.

[3.] One may find the views of Dibelius's student, Hans Conzelmann, in "The Address of Paul on the Areopagus," in *Studies in Luke-Acts*, ed. Leander E. Keck and J. Louis Martyn (Philadelphia: Fortress Press, 1980), 217–30.

4. Instead of *prostetagmenous* ("ordered"), we find *protetagmenous* ("fixed") in D (but not in d) and in other minor witnesses. Apparently this is a change which is intended to establish the meaning of the sentence as being indisputably "historical," for it is only when *kairoi* means "epochs" of the nations that "predestination" makes any sense. Instead of *ton theon* ("the god"), the Western texts have *to theion* ("the divine") and the corresponding corrections in v. 27. The Western texts are not unanimous, however, about the framing of the word, and the so-called *koine*-text offers *ton kyrion* ("the Lord"); thus both *theion* and *kyrion* presuppose that there was originally a *theon*, and the neuter *theion* arises from v. 29. There it is appropriate. Here, where we are thinking of the true, personal God, the masculine is more fitting.

5. Compare Acts 2:36 "whole house of Israel" (*pas oikos Israēl*); Rom 11:26 "all Israel" (*pas Israēl*); and, if these examples are rejected on account of their Hebraism, Eph 2:21 "whole structure" (*pasa oikodomē*); and the inscription of Antiochus of Commagene, *OGIS* (1903) 1.383.87, *aitines . . . basileiai pasēi koinōn agathōn aitiai katestēsan*. See further my commentary on Eph 2:21, *An die Kolosser; Epheser; An Philemon*, 2d rev. ed. HNT 12 (Tübingen: Mohr/Siebeck), 1927.

6. Oscar Holtzmann, *Das neue Testament*, 2 vols. (Giessen: Töpelmann, 1926), 1.410.

7. *"les saisons de leur prospérité"*; E. Jacquier, *Les Actes des Apôtres*, 2d ed., EBib (Paris: Gabalda, 1926), 533.

8. Similarly according to Kirsopp Lake in *The Beginnings of Christianity*, 5 vols. (London: Macmillan, 1933), 4.216.

9. Compare Aelius Aristides, *In Jovem*, 24, in praise of Zeus: *ōrai te kath' hekaston etos ek peritropēs gēn tēn pasan eperchontai*. In the evidence *quails deorum natura sit* it is shown in Cicero, *Nat. d.* 2.19 (§49), how the sun causes the seasons: *ita ex quattuor temporum mutationibus omnium quae terra marique gignunter ignitia causaequae ducuntur*. Arius Didymus also speaks of the sun in Eusebius's *Praep. evang.* 15.15.7 (Diels, *Doxographi Graeci*, 465): it is taken by Cleanthes as the *hēgemonikon tou kosmou dia to megiston tōn astrōn hyparchein kai pleista symballesthai pros tēn tōn holōn dioikēsin, hēmeran kai eniauton poiounta kai tas allas ōras*. In Pseudo-Aristotle, *De mundo* 6.399a, we read of the "radiant sun" (*pamphaēs hēlios*) and its double course: *tē de tas tessaras hōras agōn tou etous*. In considering the world's orderly course, the same work reads: *tis de genoit' an apseudeia toiade, ēn tina phylattousin ai kalai kai gonimoi tōn holōn ōrai, therē te kai cheimōnas epagousai tetagmenōs* (5.397a). In the great and moving reckoning of all that can serve to infer an *effector* or *moderator* of the world, Cicero, in *Tusc.* 1.28 (§68), also mentions *commutationesque temporum quadrupertitas ad maturitatem frugum et ad temperationem corporum aptas*. Of course, the seasons too have their place in the evidence *pothen ennoian eschon theōn anthrōpoi*. This appears in Ps.-Plutarch as: *kai tetagmenōs hēmeran te kai nukta cheimōna te kai theros anatolas te kai dusmas* (scil. *horōntes; De placitis philosophorum* 1.6.10; from Aetius; Hermann Diels, *Doxographi Graeci* [Berlin: de Gruyter, 1929], 295). Compare also Plato, *Laws* 10.886a—"the beautiful ordering of the seasons" (*ta tōn hōrōn diakekosmēmena kalōs outōs*)—as evidence of the gods; *Symposium* 188a: the *sustasis* ("association") is full of both kinds of *eros*; *Philebus* 26b. Wisdom of Solomon 7:18 shows that use was made of the proof in Hellenistic Judaism: "the alternations of the solstices and the changes of the seasons" (*eidenai tropōn allagas kai metabolas kairōn*). *1 Clement* 20:9, in praise of the cosmic harmony ordained by God, shows that this proof passed into Christianity: "The seasons of spring and summer and autumn and winter give way in succession one to another in peace" (*kairoi earinoi kai therinoi kai metopōrinoi kai cheimerinoi en eirēnē metaparadidoasin allēlois*).

10. It is used in *BGU* 3.889.17, of the re-establishing of boundaries after the flood, and in *Inschriften von Priene*, edited by F. F. Hiller von Gärtringen (Berlin: Reimer, 1906), 42, II, 8, of the justification for drawing up boundaries. H. J. Cadbury, "Lexical Notes on Luke-Acts I," *JBL* 44 (1925) 219–27, refers to Galen, *Definitiones medicae* 2 (XIX, 349, Kühn): *horismos de legetai apo metaphoras tōn en tois chōriois horothesiōn* and ventures the reading (*horothesiōn*). But Cadbury prefers to take the *horothesiai* in the temporal sense and refer it, like *kairoi*, to the history of the nations and in the same sense, so that the subject would be the defining of the times of their habitation. As far as I can see, this

breaks down on the fact that *katoikia* ("habitation") must here be understood as corresponding to the *katoikein* that precedes, and thus refers, not to periods, but to places.

11. Compare Cicero: *vides habitari in terra raris et angustis in locis . . . (Republ.* 6.19 [§20]); *omnis enim terra quar colitur a vobis . . . parva quaedam insula est . . .* (6.20 [§21]); Seneca: *et terrarum orbem superne despiciens* (there follows a reference to the zones) *sibi ipse dixit: hoc est illud punctum, quod inter tot gentes ferro et igne dividitur? O quam ridiculi sunt mortalium termini! (Q. nat.* I, *praefatio,* 8); Pliny: *haec est material gloriae nostrae, haec sedes, hix honores gerimus, hix exercemus imperia (Nat. hist.* 2.174); etc.

12. Virgil: "By the gods' grace to heart-sick mortals given, and a path cleft between them" *(has inter mediamque duae mortalibus aegris munere concessae divom*; *Georgics* 1.237-238).

13. The Western reading (D, Irenaeus) "according to the boundaries of their habitation" *(kata horothesian tēs katoikias autōn)* is best understood in the light of this alternative. The variant reading establishes the historical meaning and renders the philosophical one impossible, for the seasons that God has established "according to the boundary of their habitation" are, of course, the historical epochs of the nations. I believe that the Western version of the text, which is not uniform, is connected with the particular destiny of the Acts of the Apostles (see my *A Fresh Approach to the New Testament and Early Christian Literature,* ILCK [New York: Scribner, 1936], 257–66). The fact that the version has been elaborated seems to me to be obvious in that it has made the joins (between tradition and the author's version) invisible (12:22; 14:7; 16:35), and in that questions are answered and motives supplied. Compare the appropriate observations in my "Style Criticism of the Book of Acts" in this volume (pp. 42–47). Of course the "Western" texts may, even so, have preserved old material. Therefore every important variant requires a renewed and unprejudiced investigation.

14. For *zētein* as the term for "investigating" and "examining" in Plato see, for example: "investigating the things beneath the earth and in the heavens" *(zētōn ta te hypo gēs kai ourania*; *Apol.* 19b); "Therefore, even now, I am still going about searching and investigating" *(taut' oun egō men eti kai nun periiōn zētō kai ereunō*; 23b); "contentiously rather than inquiring into the issue under discussion" *(philonikountas alla' ou zētountas to prokeimenon en tō logō*; *Gorgias* 457d; see also *Repub.* 499a; *Theaetetus* 201a); Marcus Aurelius: "searching through the discerning of signs" *(dia tekmarseōs zētountos*; 2.13.1); Plutarch "seek" and "investigation" *(zētein* and *zētēsis, De E apud Delphos* 385c. d).

15. Philo, "searching out the nature of the true God, even though the discovery may transcend all human ability" *(ameinon gar ouden tou zētein ton alēthē theon, kan hē euresis autou diapheugē dunamin anthrōpinēn*; *Spec.* 1.36). Nevertheless, according to 1.40, we should not cease from "the task of investigating his character, because even if we fail to make the discovery, the very search itself is intrinsically useful and an object of deserved ambition" *(zētēsis dia to tēn skpsin kai aneu tēs eureseōs kath' autēn tripothēton einai).* Compare also "those who seek and desire to find God" *(hoi gar zētountes kai epipothountes theon aneurein*; *Abr.* 87) and the seeking of the "being" *(on)* in *Post.* 15; and *Spec.* 1.345.

16. Gotthold Ephraim Lessing, *Theologische Streitschriften: Eine Duplik* (1778), I, at the end: "If God were to hold all truth in his right hand and in his left the only and eternally active urge to truth, even with the addition that I should err forever and ever . . . yet I should approach his left hand with humility and say: 'Give, Father! Pure truth is for you

alone!'"

17. Elsewhere, the seasons and the earth and its produce are mentioned jointly as proof of God's existence, as in Aratus's work, in the same poem of which the fifth verse is quoted in the Areopagus speech (17:28); in vv. 7-9, Zeus says when the earth is fit for ploughing and *hote dexiai hōrai kai phuta gurōsai kai spermata panta balesthai*. Compare *1 Clem.* 20:4—"The earth, bearing fruit in fulfillment of his will in its appropriate seasons, puts forth the food that abundantly supplies both humans and animals and all living things that are on it, making no dissension, neither altering anything he has decreed" (*gē kuophorousa kata to thelēma autou tois idiois kairois tēn panplēthē . . . anatellei trophēn*).

18. In *1 Clem.* 40:4, "the appointed times" (*tois prostetagmenois kairois*) takes up the expression "fixed times and seasons" (*hōrismenois kairois kai hōrais*), previously used in 40:2. On each occasion, regular times of sacrifice are meant.

19. See above, p. 186, n. 4.

20. Philo describes in *Post.* 15, how the greatest good results from the search (*zētēsis*) after the essence (*on*): "is utterly incomprehensible to any being, and also to be aware that he is invisible" (*katalabein hoti akatalēptos ho kata to einai theos panti kai auto touto idein hoti estin aoratos*).

21. Compare *Corp. Herm.* 5.2 *noēsin labein, idein kai labesthai autais tais chersi dunasai kai tēn eikona tou theou theasasthai* [similarly Norden; according to the edition of the *Hermetica* by W. Scott, 1924, the witnesses offer after *noēsin* either *idein* or *labein*, not both]; see also Norden, *Agnostos Theos*, 16–17. [Ed.] Dio Chrysostom, *Or.* 12.60, *elluthen timan kai therapeuein to theion prosiontas kai haptomenous meta peithous, . . .* —note in author's copy. [—H.G.]

22. Theodor Zahn has already referred in his commentary to Prov 30:26 and Homer *Odyssey* 87.459; *Die Apostelgeschichte des Lukas*, KNT 5 (Leipzig: Deichert, 1919-21).

23. The word *ktizein* ("create") is found frequently in the books of Ben Sira and the Wisdom of Solomon. And that itself is significant, for, in these books, the Greek mode of expression predominates.

24. Not only D and Irenaeus but the majority of texts, the so-called *koine*-revision, give the well-known reading "from one blood" (*ex henos aimatos*). This destroys the "striking-power" of the juxtaposition *ex henos—pan ethnos anthrōpōn*, and, for this reason, *aimatos* might be regarded as an addition. The question is, however, whether we simply have an innocent completion of *henos*, or whether there is a particular understanding of the passage underlying it. Since two other variants of this verse, *protetagmenous* and *kata horothesian*, seem to represent the historico-political interpretation, one might be led to suppose that this reading also points to the same interpretation: out of one blood—all peoples of the earth. But that is not a certain conclusion to be drawn. Also, it is not an Old Testament mode of expression, but one usual in Greek and also found in Josephus—see Johannes Behm, "*aima*," in *TDNT* (1964) 1.172–73.

25. The thought of Rom 5:12-21, in which the universality of sin (Adam) stands in juxtaposition to the universality of redemption (Christ), is far removed, for, as shown above, there is no mention of sin.

26. The expression "on all the face of the earth" (*epi pantos prosōpou tēs gēs*), on the other hand, obviously belongs to the Old Testament; see LXX Gen 8:9, *hudōr ēn epi panti prosōpō pasēs tēs gēs*; but also Luke 21:35, "for it will come upon all who dwell upon the face of the whole earth" (*epi pantas tous kathēmenous epi prosōpōn pasēs tēs gēs*). The

author evidently had complete command of Old Testament expressions; this is illustrated by "made" (*poiein*) in 17:24, 26; "heaven and earth" (*ouranou kai gēs*) in 17:24; "seek God" (*zētein ton theon*) in 17:27; and "he will judge the world in righteousness" (*krinein tēn oikoumenēn en dikaiosunē*) in 17:31. But the fact that, with the exception of 17:31, he makes such little use, and then only incidentally, of phrases found in the LXX shows how little the Old Testament influenced the content of his sermon.

[27.] Parallels to this optimism: Bileam to the army of Israel: *thaumazete toinun, ō makarios stratos, hoti tosoutos ex henos patros gegronate* (Josephus, *Ant.* 4.6.4 [§116])— note in author's copy. [—H.G.]

[28.] Dibelius deals on p. 179, in n. 37, with the objections raised by M. Pohlenz to this interpretation of Acts 17:26-27. [—H.G.]

29. Norden, *Agnostos Theos*, 31–56.

30. Richard Reitzenstein, "Die Areopagrede des Paulus," *Neue Jahrbücher für das klassischen Altertum* 31 (1913) 147, 394ff. [393–422]; Werner Wilhelm Jäger, *Göttingische gelehrte Anzeigen* 175 (1913) 606–10 [569–610]; Otto Weinreich, "Review of Norden, *Agnostos Theos*," *DLZ* (1913) 2953–54 [2949–64]; Harnack, *Ist die Rede des Paulus*; Peter Corssen, "Der Altar des unbek. Gottes," *ZNW* 14 (1913) 309–23; Theodor Birt, "*Agnōstoi theoi* und die Areopagrede des Apostels," *Rheinisches Museum für Philologie* 69 (1914) 342–92; Hans Theodor Plüss, *Festgabe für Hugo Blümner* (Zurich: Berichthaus, 1914) 36ff.; see also Martin Dibelius in *Wochenschrift für klassische Philologie* 32 (1915) 108–9; Otto Weinreich, *ARW* (1915) 1–52; Eduard Meyer, "Apollonios von Tyana und die Biographie des Philostratos" *Hermes* 52 (1917) 371–424; Theodor Zahn, *Die Apostelgeschichte*, 870–82; Wikenhauser, *Die Apostelgeschichte*, 369–90; Lake, *The Beginnings of Christianity*, 5.240–46.

31. Pausanias 1.1.4 (on the way from Phaleron to Athens), "altars of gods called unknown and to heroes and children of Thesus and Phalerus" (*brōmoi de theōn te onomazomenōn agnōstōn kai hērōōn kai paidōn tōn Thēseōs kai Phalērou*); Pausanias, 5.14.8 unknown gods (*agnōstōn theōn*) (Olympia).

32. "To the unknown gods" (*theois ag[nōstois?] Kapit[ōn] dadoucho[s]*)—altar inscription at Pergamon (Hugo Hepding, "Die Arbeiten zu Pergamon, 1908-09," II. Die Inschriften," *MDAIA* 35 [1910] 454–57; Adolf Deissman, *St. Paul: A Study in Social and Religious History*, trans. William E. Wilson [New York: Hodder and Stoughton, 1912] 287–91). [Ed.] See also P. W. Van der Horst, "The Altar of the 'Unknown God' in Athens (Acts 17, 23) and the Cult of 'Unknown Gods' in the Hellenistic and Roman Periods," in *ANRW* 2.18.2 (1989) 1426–56.

33. Tertullian, *Ad nationes* 2.9, "at Athens there was an altar with this inscription: 'To the Unknown Gods'" (*nam et Athenis ara est inscripta: ignotis deis*); and *Adv. Marc.* 1.9, "altars have been lavished on unknown gods; that, however, is the idolatry of Athens" (*invenio plane ignotis deis aras prostitutes, sed Attica idolatria est*); Jerome, *Commentary on Titus* 1:12 (7.707 Vallarsi), after the quotation of Acts 17:23: *inscripto autem area non ita erat, ut Paulus asseruit, "ignoto deo," sed ita: "Diis Asiae et Europae et Africae diis ignotis et peregrinis"*; Didymus-fragment in Mai's *Nova Bibliotheca Patrum* 4.2.139 on 2 Cor 10:5: *outō gar to Athēnēsin anakeimenon bōmō epigramma emphainon pollōn theōn noēma helkusas ho tauta graphōn metēnegken eis ton monon alēthinon theon.* . . .

34. Karl Bornhäuser suggests that the reference is to an altar to Yahweh; *Studien zur Apostelgeschichte* (Gütersloh: Bertelsmann, 1934), 143. In his opinion, the word "wor-

ship" (*eusebein*) indicates that the only God who can be meant is the one whom Paul considers as just!

35. Jessen, "*Agnōstoi theoi*," in Pauly-Wissowa, *Realenzyklopädie*, Suppl. 1.28ff.

36. A story of this kind is found in Herodotus 6.105, and tells how Pan complained of receiving too little attention from the people of Athens. Of the Christian writers, Isidor of Pelusium, in *Ep.* 4.69 (to Hero, *Migne graece* vol. 78, 1128) records the same story and another about a plague in Athens, in which no god gave any aid. *Ennoēsantes oun hoti estin isōs theos tis, hon autoi katelipon agepraston, ho ton loimon katapemmpsas*, if the Athenians had built a temple and an altar for an unknown god. Isho'dad (*Horae Semiticae*, X, p. 28; see below, p. 194, n. 64) records that the Athenians often did so, and tells the story of Pan (see above), but tells it as a story of an unknown demon; the altar, he says, was dedicated to the "unknown and hidden god."

37. The story is about the murder of Kylon's followers, who had fled to Athene, and about the plague that then came upon the city. The story is obviously very much older than Diogenes; see the mention of the purification in the *Athēnaiōn Politeia* of Aristotle 1.1 (Thalheim).

38. The account continues: *hothen eti kai nun estin eurein kata tous dēmous tōn Athēnaiōn bomous anōnumoue*—we do not hear what was on the altars. Theodor Birt, "*Agnōstoi theoi*" (1914) 355, thinks: *theōi*; but that can scarcely apply to the altars mentioned by Pausanis; in the accounts of them the word *agnōstos* is mentioned too regularly.

39. Norden has (1) traced the story of Timasion back to Philostratus's source, the book of a certain Damis (based on Philostratus, *Life of Apollonius of Tyanna* 6.3—the beginning of it); (2) asserted that the utterance by Apollonius was originally made in a speech delivered in Athens and was found to be in Apollonius's lost text *Peri thusiōn*; and (3) assumed that the "editor" of Acts had read this writing or that account by Damis. But it cannot be proved that the remark about the unknown demons came originally from "Damis." The naming of Athens is suggested by the mention of Hippolytus. [Dibelius's original judgments were more reserved: *Wochenschrift für klassische Philologie* 32 (1915) 108–9; see p. 190, n. 30.—H.G.] Then, however, it is improbable that the motif "unknown demons" was derived from the speech in Athens and the writing *peri thysiōn* which resulted from it.

40. The Old Testament, with the exception of the passage in Ps 49:2, does not speak of "world." As a result, *kosmos* ("world") is found in the LXX only in the books that are really Greek (Wisdom and the books of Maccabees).

41. Philo, too, uses the word to indicate idols (*Mos.* 1.303; 2.165, 168). But in the single application of the word to the sanctuary, the tabernacles (*Mos.* 2.88), we feel that it is the dualism which is being criticized—everything human is relative, what is real exists only with God: "a temple made by hands for the Father and Ruler of the universe" (*hieron cheiropoiēton kataskeuazontas tō patri kai hēgemoni tou pantos*). "Temples made by hands" (*naoi cheiropoiētoi*) are also mentioned in *Sibylline Oracles* 14.62.

42. Even here we can actually mention only an original Greek text: *Epistle of Jeremiah* 25:38 (the cultivation of idols); in Jud 11:17, "Your servant is indeed God-fearing and serves the God of heaven night and day" (*hē doulē sou theosebēs estin kai therapeuousa nuktos kai hēmeras ton theon tou ouranou*); and, finally, in Isa 54:17, "This is the heritage of the servants of the Lord" (*estin klēroromia tois therapeuousin kyrion*), the word is not used in its religious meaning (in the narrower sense of the word).

43. Compare Hermann Wolfgang Beyer, "*therapeia*," in *TDNT* (1965) 3.128–32. For the same ideas in Seneca compare above, p. 112.

44. Xenophon, *Memorabilia* 1.4.10, "Really . . . I do not disdain the godhead. But I think it is too great to need my service" (*outoi . . . hyperorō to daimonion, all' ekeino megaloprepesteron ēgoumai hē ōs tēs emēs therapeias prosdeisthai*).

45. Plato, *Eutyphro* 13a-d.

46. Philo, *Det.* 55: "piety, which consists in serving God, a virtue which consists in supplying the things which will be of use to the deity; for the deity is not benefited by anyone, inasmuch as he is not in need of anything, nor is it in the power of anyone to benefit a being who is in every way superior to himself. But, on the contrary, God himself is continually and unceasingly benefiting all things" (*tēn de eusebeian thou therapeian hyparchousan ou themis poristikēn eipein tōn ōphelēsontōn to theion. Ōpheleitai gar hyp' oudenos, ate mēte endees on mēte tiuos to en apasin autou kreitton pephykotos onēsai, tounantion de ta sympanta synechōs kai apaustōs ōphelei*). God's freedom from any kind of need is also mentioned previously in §54.

47. Hellenistic Judaism has made this demand completely its own. Numerous passages in Philo show to what extent he is aware of it; he also refers occasionally to Num 23:19: "God is not a human" (*ouch hōs anthrōpos ho theos; Sacr.* 94), with the additional comment "so that he completely transcends representation in human form" (*hina panta ta anthrōpologoumena hyperkypsōmen; Deus* 53) and exhorts, "You will take away therefore, O my mind, all things created, mortal, changeable, or unconsecrated from your conceptions regarding God—uncreated and immortal and unchangeable and holy and the only honorable one" (*apheleis oun ō psychē, pan genēton thnēton metablēton bebēlon apo ennoias tēs peri theou tou agenētou kai aphthartou kai atreptou kai hagiou kai monou markariou; Sacr.* 101). But Josephus also says that, at the dedication of the temple, Solomon "addressed God in words that he considered suitable to the divine nature and fitting for him to speak" (*epoiēsato logous pros ton theon, hous tētheia physei prepontas hypelambane; Ant.* 8.4.2 [§107]).

48. J. Geffcken, *Zwei griechische Apologeten*, Sammlung wissenschaftlicher Kommentare zu griechischen und römischen Schriftstellern (Leipzig: Teubner, 1907), 36–37.

49. Apuleius (*De Platone* 1.5): "needing nothing, entirely self-sufficient" (*nihil indigens, ipse conferens cuncta*). The passage quoted above in note 46 from *Det.* 55, gives an example from Philo; an example in a Christian writing is found in the *Praedicatio Petri* quoted in Clement of Alexandria's *Strom.* 6.39.3, "needing nothing nor bound by anything" (*anepideēs ou ta panta epideetai*).

50. Xenophanes according to Eusebius, *Praep. evang.* 1.8.4 (Hermann Diels, *Doxographi Graeci* [Berlin: Riemer, 1879], 580) of the gods: "none requires anything at all from anyone" (*epideisthai te mēdenos autōn mēdena mēd' holōs*). Parmenides (Diels, *Die Fragmente der Vorsokratiker* (Berlin: Weidman, 1903; English translation by Kathleen Freeman [Cambridge: Harvard Univ. Press, 1948] 18, B, 833) on the subject of "being" (*eon*): "for there is nothing he needs" (*esti gar ouk epideues*). Paraphrase of this passage is in the writings of Antiphon the Sophist (from Suidas; Diels, *Fragmente*, 80, B, 10): *dia touto oudenos deitai oute prosdechetai oudenos ti, all' apeiros kai adeētos.* According to Plato (*Timaeus* 34b), it is characteristic of a "fortunate god" (*eudaimōn theos*) that he is "bound by nothing else" (*oudenos heterou prosdeomenos*). Compare also Plutarch, *Comp. Arist. et Catonis* 4 (*Cato Maior,* 31, p. 354, F), *aprosdeēs men gar ho theos aplōs*; and *De Stoicorum repugnantiis* 1034, B, 1052, E (Zeno and Chrysippus);

Pseudo-Aristotle, *De mundo*, 6.398b *ouden gar epitechnēseōs autō dei kai hypēresias tēs par' heterōn, hōsper tois par' hēmin archousi tēs polucheirias dia tēn astheneian*; Lucian, *Cynicus*, 12, of the gods, "for they need nothing" (*outhenos gar deontai*). Compare also Diogenes Laertius 6.9.105, of the Cynics; Lucretius, *De rerum natura* 2.650 (Epicurean), Eusebius, *Praep. evang.* 6.13, of the neo-Pythagoreans and from the *Hermetica: Corp. Herm.* 6.1: *oute gar endeēs esti tinos, hina epithymēsas auto ktēsasthai kakos genētai*; Pseudo-Apuleius (*Asclepius* 41): *nihil enim deest ei qui ipse est omnia aut in eo sunt omnia.*

51. Heinrich Greeven, "*deomai,*" in *TDNT* (1964) 2.40-42.

52. *Det.* 54-56; see above, note 46. Even the difference between this passage and the Areopagus speech is significant. Thinking of Plato, Philo speaks of how piety is a service to God, if service is rightly understood; that is to say, not that it is of any use to God (for it is God himself who gives all things their use—it is the same antithesis which is mentioned in note 49), but in that men behave like slaves toward their master (here, however, there is a difference, see *Det*, §56, because the "masters" (*despotai*) are "in need of service" (*hypēresias endeeis*), but God "needs nothing" (*ou chreios*). But the Acts of the Apostles speaks of the religious service of God and then negates it by the reference to God's freedom from need. Thus we see that the interpretation of "service" (*therapeuein*) given above is the correct one. On the subject of God's freedom from need, compare also Philo, *Leg.* 1.44; *Cher.* 44, 119, 123; *Deus* 56-57.

53. Josephus, *Ant.* 8.4.3 (§111), "It is not possible for humans to give thanks to God through deeds for the benefits they have received, for the Deity needs nothing and is beyond any such requital" (*ergois men ou dunaton anthrōpois apodounai theō charin hyper hō eu peponthasin. Aprosdees gar to theion apantōn kai kreitton toiautēs*). With reference to this prayer of dedication of the temple compare note 47.

54. *1 Clement* 52:1: "he needs nothing at all; he desires nothing from anyone except to confess him" (*ouden oudenos chrēzei ei mēto exomologeisthai autō*); the *Praedicatio Petri* was quoted above (note 49) as an example of antithesis; compare also Aristides, 1.4: "he needs nothing, but all things need him" (*ei nihil opus esse, sed omnia eo egere*); 1.5: *ou chrēze ktl ... pantes de autou chrēzousin.*

55. *Ep. ad Diognetum*, 3.4, "For the one who made heaven and earth and everything within it and provides us all with what we need, cannot himself need any of these things that he supplies to them who imagine they are giving them to Him" (*ho gar poiēsas ton ouranon kai tēn gēn kai panta ta en autois kai pasin hēmin chorēgōn, hōn prosdeometha, oudenos an autos prosdeoito toutōn hōn tois oiomenois didonai parechei autos*).

56. We might think also of the Orphic hymn to Zeus, Fragment 21a (Kern), v. 5: "Zeus is the breath in everything; Zeus starts a fire without toil" (*Zeus pnoiē pantōn. Zeus akamatou pyros ormē*). By the usual derivation of the name Zeus from *zēn* (Plato, *Cratylus*, 396a; Aelius Aristides, *In Jovem*, 23), the tautology "lives and breathes" (*zōe kai pnoē*) could quite well develop from "Zeus breath/wind" (*Zeus pnoē*), but there is no example of it.

57. A proof is offered by *kai ge*, the reading of which we have most examples, for which we also have D with the error *kaite* (Γ became T). On the other hand, *kaitoi* occurs in AE, and there is also the reading *kaitoige* in א, among others—*quamvis*, gig, vulg, Irenaeus. But even this reading depends on an oversight, for how was the concessive clause to be interpreted?

58. We can see the difference between the current biblical ideas if we compare Acts 10:35: "but in every nation any one who fears him and does what is right is acceptable to him" (*all' en panti ethnei ho phoboumenos auton kai ergazomenos dikaiosunēn dektos autō estin*). There the interest is in the fact that salvation is not limited by national boundaries, an idea which has no place in the Areopagus speech. There the meaning is simply: "Every righteous person is pleasing to God" and not, as in Acts 17, "every person is related to God."

59. To see the difference we may compare the meaning of the forms of the names Zena and Dia in Plato, *Cratylus* 396a, b.: "Thus this god is correctly named, through whom all living beings have the gift of life" (*symbainei oun orthōs onomazesthai outos ho theos einai, di hon zēn aei pasi tois zōsin hyparchei*). Here, the vital "in" (*en*) of the Areopagus speech is missing. Compare also Adolf Deissmann, *Die neutestamentliche Formel "in Christo Jesu"* (Marburg: Elwert, 1892), 93ff.

60. Dio Chrysostom, *Or.* 12.27 (I, 162, v., Arnim).

61. Dio Chrysostom, *Or.* 12.28 [Ed.] See addendum p. 32, n. 1, from the same, *Or.* 12— marginal note in manuscript. [—H.G.]

62. Josephus, *Ant.* 8.4.2 (§108).

63. Norden, *Agnostos Theos,* 19–24, has collected passages that show that the Stoics regarded everything that has happened as "moved," but God as the one who, while not being "moved" himself, is the "mover." Especially characteristic: Chrysippus in Stobaeus, *Eclogae* 1.8.42, p. 106.8 (in Wachsmuth's edition; p. 260 in Heeren's edition), *kata ton chronon kineisthai te ekasta kai einai*. Philo. *Leg.* 1.6: what was created by us, *statai kai menei, hosa de epistēmē theou, peratōthenta palin kineitai*—*kineisthai* is thus a sign that God is the creator. Compare also Philo, *Cher.* 128; Lucan 9.580, "Jupiter is whatever lives, whatever moves" (*Jupiter est, quodcumque vides, quodcumque moveris* and, for the linking of *kineisthai* with *zēn*, Plato, *Timaeus* 37c, of the cosmic soul, "And when the father that engendered it perceived it in motion and alive, a thing of joy to the eternal gods, he too rejoiced" (*hōs de kinēthen auto kai zōn enoēsen tōn aidiōn theōn gegonos agalma ho gennēsas patēr, ēgasthē . . .*); for the linking of *zēn* with *einai*, Aelius Aristides, *In Jovem* 23: *zōēs te kai ousias ekastois estin aitios.*

64. Margaret Dunlop Gibson, *The Commentaries of Isho'dad of Merv, Bishop of Hadatha,* IV: *Acts of the Apostles* (1913), etc., with an introduction by J. Rendel Harris (*Horae Semiticae,* X, 1913). What follows above is found on p. 39 of the Syrian and p. 29 of the English text.

65. Here let us mention a reading which is found only in D (and in d), and which is usually glossed over by the commentaries. It takes *to kath' hēmeran* (d: *in diurnum*) as coming after *esmen.* I know no better explanation than that the words were written on the edge of a manuscript that was in several columns, with the intention that they should be added to the text of 17:11 (*to kath' hēmeran anakrinontes*), where they had been forgotten. The next transcriber undertook to add them, but did so incorrectly in 17:28, because this passage was found in the corresponding place in another column of the same page. A later transcriber then rectified the omission in 17:11 without noticing the mistake in 17:28. If we assume that it was a four-columned manuscript, 17:28 could in fact have been written in the same place in the fourth column where we read 17:11 in the first column (in the Sinaiticus, which is very closely written in four columns, the space between the two passages is even less, only 2-2/3 columns). If this theory is not accepted, then we must consider a correction of the words *tōn kath' hymas (poētōn)* to

tōn kath' hēmas (as in B), a correction that was wrongly read and, as a result, wrongly entered (as J. Rendel Harris writes in *Bulletin of the Bezan Club* 8 [1930] 6-7).

66. Concerning this grave of Zeus and the tendency to lie of the Cretans of which this grave gave evidence, see my commentary on Tit 1:12—Dibelius and Hans Conzelmann, *The Pastoral Epistles*, trans. Philip Buttolph and Adela Yarbro, Hermeneia (Philadelphia: Fortress Press, 1972).

67. This part of the translation is by Hugo Gressmann (Zahn translates "you are alive and stand firm") and is justified by the *essi gar aiei* (see above in the text) preserved by Chrysostom. The translation as a whole is taken from Lake and Jackson, *The Beginnings of Christianity*, 5.246–51.

68. J. Rendel Harris had already published an important parallel to it in "The Cretans Always Liars," *Expositor* 2 (1906) 305–17; and "A Further Note on the Cretans," *Expositor* 3 (1907) 332–37; compare his introduction to Mrs. Gibson's edition of Isho'dad, XII–XIII. The parallel is found in the Nestorian work called the Syrian *Gannat Busamé (Hortus Deliciarum)* and contains the passage reproduced above, but not the sentence about the "poets among the heathen."

69. Titus 1:12: "One of themselves, a prophet of their own, said, 'Cretans are always liars, evil beasts, lazy gluttons'" (*eipen tis ex autōn idios autōn prophētēs. Krētes aei pseustai, kaka thēria, gasteres argai*).

70. We can see from the continuation of the text given above how much was known by Isho'dad or his source: "thus the blessed Apostle Paul borrowed this saying from Minos: he now further borrowed 'we are of his race' from Aratus, a poet who wrote about God." Then follows a correct reproduction, partly translation, partly a summary of the contents, of Aratus's proem.

71. Chrysostom, XI, p. 744 (Montf.).

72. Callimachus, *In Jovem*, 8-9: *"Krētes aei pseustai" kai gar taphou, hō ana, seio*, and so on, as above.

73. Of course, we must take it for granted that the original hexameter in Acts 17:28 has been polished, but this was in accordance with "good tone" (Norden, *Agnostos Theos* [1913], 19, n.2). Lake, in *The Beginnings of Christianity* (1933), 5.250, introduces the attempts to reconstruct the verse: *en gar soi zōmen, kai kinumeth' ōde kai esmen* (J. Rendel Harris, *loc. cit.*); or *en soi gar zōmen kai kineomestha kai eimen* (A. B. Cook, *Zeus*, 3 vols. [Cambridge: Cambridge Univ. Press, 1914], 1.664). Certainly the words in Isho'-dad supposed to be by Minos cannot be turned into a complete line of hexameters. So it is still uncertain whether Isho'dad has quoted quite correctly.

74. Compare the passages in Dibelius and Conzelmann, *Pastoral Epistles*, on Tit 1:12.

75. Diogenes Laertius 1.10.112 (Loeb). According to this, "Minos and Rhadaman-thus" seems to be an independent poetic work; compare Zahn, *Apostelgeschichte*, 624, n. 94 (as against Diels, *Die Fragmente der Vorsokratiker* [1903], II, 12, 293, note).

[76.] Dibelius later renounced the theory of the quotation from Epimenides; see pp. 80–81. [—H.G.]

77. The D-text *hōsper kai tōn kath' hymas tines eirēkasin* (d: *sicut qui secundum vos sunt quidam*) seems to presuppose that *poiētai* was originally omitted. But perhaps the Greek text is a retranslation from Latin; this latter resulted, doubtless, because *tines tōn kath' hymas poiētōn* could not be rendered literally into Latin.

78. Lake, *The Beginnings of Christianity* (1933), 4.218, thinks *tines* refers to several poets, thus, perhaps, to Epimenides and Aratus, for it was not in accordance with liter-

ary convention that the word *tines* should be used to give a veiled reference to one only. But Philo writes in *Spec.* 1.48, "And some of your race, speaking with sufficient correctness, call them ideas" (*onomazousi d' autas ouk apo skopou tines tōn par' hymin ideas*)—and still means only Plato (he writes in the same way in *Spec.* 1.74, *hōs hoi poiētai phasi,* and means a Homeric expression). [Pseudo-Aristotle, *De mundo* 16, p. 397b, *tōn palaiōn . . . tines*; but the writer knows that it is about Thales. See Max Pohlenz, "Paulus und die Stoa", note 160 in his manuscript (see p. 179, n. 37) Thus into *tines* (Acts 17:28) we are entitled to read the reference to only one poet; the plural is due to literary convention and thus confirms an impression that the writer is conscious of his education. Contrast this with the non-literary manner in which the real Paul in 1 Cor 15:33 uses a verse by Menander, without knowing its origin and introducing it only by *mē planasthe.*

79. Callimachus, *Epigr.* 27, p. 54, in the small edition by Wilamowitz-Möllendorf: *Hēsiodou to t' aeisma kai ho tropos* is the beginning; the conclusion reads: *chairete leptai hrēsies, Arētou symbolon agrupniēs.*

80. Cleanthes, *In Jovem* 3-5 (*Stoicorum veterum fragmenta,* I, no. 537, Arnim). We have no certain information about a poet Timagenes, whom the Armenian Catena to Acts names here beside Aratus; compare Zahn, *Apostelgeschichte,* 625.

81. Harnack puts forward this view in *Ist die Rede des Paulus,* p. 24 n. 2.

82. The view is obviously pre-stoic; compare the allusion in Plato's *Timaeus* 40d, "and we must trust to those who have declared it aforetime, they being, as they affirmed, descendants of gods and knowing well, no doubt, their own forefathers" (*peisteon de tois eirēkosin emprosthen, ekgonois men theōn ousin, hōs ephasan, saphōs de pou pous ge autōn progonous eidosin.* Isho'dad of Merv writes in the commentary on Acts 17 that has already been mentioned, "and Plato and others say that souls are of the race of the gods."

83. Here, as in the case of individual examples of evidence in sections I and II, Ernst Hoffmann has substantially supported me with his advice.

84. Dio Chrysostom: *hōs agathoi te eien* (scil. *hoi theoi*) *kai philoien hēmas, ate dē xungeneis ontas autōn apo gar tō theōn ephē to tōn anthrōpōn einai genos, ouk apo Titanōn oud' apo Gigantōn* (*Or.* 30.26 [II, 310, v., Arnim]).

85. Seneca: *non sunt ad caelum elevandae manus nex exorandus aedituus, ut nos ad aurem simulacra, quasi magis exaudiri possimus, admittat: prope est a te deus, tecum est, intus est* (*Ep.* 41.1). Later we read in 41.2: *in unoquoque virorum bonorum . . . habitat deus.* Indeed, according to Seneca, this applies only to the good, that is, to the wise; but the wise man is not a supernaturally inspired being: he simply demonstrates what all men ought to be.

86. But this, too, leads to the idea of relationship; compare Seneca, *Ep.* 120.14, *mens dei, ex quo pars et in hoc pectus mortale defluxit.*

87. Seneca: *cum illa* (the vast realms above) *tetigit, alitur crescit ac velut vinculis liberatus in originem redit et hoc habet argumentum divinitatis suae, quod illum divina delectant; nec ut alienis sed ut suis interest* (*Q. nat.,* I, *praefatio,* 12)

88. Birt, "*Agnōstoi theoi,*" 368, has emphatically referred to this and the following passage.

89. We may even ask whether in this context *genos oun hyparchontes tou theou* the word *hyparchein* assumes a particular meaning. *Hyparchein* is more than *einai* and, as Ernst Hoffmann informs me, means to the Stoics and Pythagoreans the substantial

being: Diogenes Bab. (in Philodemus, *Piet.* 15.14; *Stoicorum veterum fragmenta,* III, p. 217, 33, Arnim) *ton kosmon graphei tō Dii ton auton hyparchein.* The idea of inherence, of which the *enyparchein* is characteristic, would then read: "since we now have our existence as the family of God." On the other hand, Luke has certainly entered *hyparchein* for a simple "to be" into the text of his source in five places in the Gospel (Luke 7:25; 8:41; 9:48; 11:13; 23:50). Thus we can simply conclude that it is in accordance with his style that he should have written *hyparchontes* instead of *ontes.*

90. Wisdom of Solomon 13:10: "But miserable, with their hopes set on dead things, are those who give the name 'gods' to the works of human hands, gold and silver fashioned with skill, and likenesses of animals, or a useless stone, the work of an ancient hand." Even the polemic in Philo, *Decal.* 66-75 and *Spec.* 1.21-22 is harsher than the Areopagus speech. Also characteristic of the speech is the absence of the polemical idea that the maker of the image ranks higher than the image itself (Wis 15:17; Philo, *Decal.* 69). Naturally, the struggle against images goes further in the writings of the Apologists: Aristides 13.1; Justin, *Ap.* 1.9.1; Athenagoras, *Suppl.* 23:1; Theophilus, *Ad Autol.* 2.2. But the question which is so important in the works of the Apologists, namely whether the images are actually the gods or whether they merely portray them, is evaded rather than dealt with in the words *to theion einai homoion* in the Areopagus speech (17:29).

91. *Hyperidōn* says more than *paridōn* (according to D): God wishes to erase the time that is past (d and Irenaeus: *despiciens*). It may be that the reading *paridōn* simply means "paying no attention to" and thus approaches nearer to the *paresis* of sins committed in the past (Rom 3:25). But it will be seen that there is really no connection between our passage and Romans 3.

92. D reads *andri Iēsou* ("a man, Jesus"). But D does not mention the name of Jesus in 17:18 at all. And again 17:18 suggested the rectification of the omission in 17:31. We can take it as a nicety of the text that, with deliberately careful intentions, the name Jesus is not mentioned in the speech itself—many other things, of course, which we should expect to find in a Christian sermon, are not mentioned either. The account in 17:18, however, comments upon it in advance. The D text thus presents a popular Christian version that supplies the name where the Christian expects it, but, on the other hand, omits it in the narrative of 17:18.

93. I do not think that we can agree here with Lake, *The Beginnings of Christianity* (1933), 4.219, who thinks that there is a reference here to the title "Son of Man." For characteristic of the belief in the Son of Man are the parousia upon the clouds of the heavens and his previous hiddenness. Neither is spoken of here. Moreover, we should expect the definite article if "man" (*anēr*) were intended to replace the title "Son of Man."

94. Paronomasia: *pantas pantachou* ("all [people] everywhere"; 17:30); tautology: *zōēn kai pnoēn* ("life and breath"; 17:25); alliteration: *pistin paraschōn pasin* ("he has given assurance to all"; 17:31).

95. Compare Birt, "*Agnōstoi theoi,*" 372n.

96. Curtius, "Paulus in Athen," 925.

97. The first passage to which Curtius refers in Phil 4:8, in fact, contains an enumeration of ideas from Hellenistic moral philosophy ("Paulus in Athens," 928): the one appearance in Paul of the word *aretē* ("goodness, excellence"), of the "natural, guiding motif in the Greek history of culture" (W. W. Jäger, *Paideia*, 25, English translation by Gilbert Highet 1939-43), is just as characteristic as the appearance of terms of a non-

Christian kind, such as *euphēmos* ("praiseworthy") and *prosphilēs* ("pleasing"); on this point, compare my commentary: *An die Thessalonicher I, II; An die Philipper*, 3d ed. HNT (Tübingen: Mohr/Siebeck, 1937).

98. Anton Fridrichsen submitted this proof in "Zur Auslegung von Röm 1,19f." *ZNW* 17 (1916) 159–68.

99. "From Heaven Came the Angel Throng."
  In the end you will surely win the day,
  For you have now become the family of God.

100. There are two reasons why the well-known description in the Epistle to the Romans (2:14-16) of the Gentiles who obey the law without knowing that they do so, does not belong here. In the first place, the actions of the Gentiles are good only relatively speaking, as is shown in 2:15, and are here cited only to shame the Jews; secondly, we are dealing not with natural theology but with natural ethics. Thanks to the leading of their hearts, the Gentiles know not of God, but of Good.

101. Here the subject is the "the one born of God" (*gegennēmenos ek theou*) who does not sin. In the continuation, we probably ought to read in the Latin Vulgate and two Greek minuscule manuscripts *hē gennēsis ek tou theou tērei auton* instead of *ho gennētheis ek theou*; see Harnack, *Die älteste griechische Kircheninschriften*, SDAW (Berlin: Reimer, 1915), 534ff. Then, according to this passage, the Christian is directly begotten by God.

102. Once more we refer to *protetagmenous* instead of *prostetagmenous*, and to *kata horothesian* in 17:26, also to the introduction of the name of Jesus in 17:31. [Ed.] On pp. 59 and 178, n. 35 Dibelius discusses points raised by Schmid, who seeks to show that the Areopagus speech conforms with the theology of the Pauline epistles; Wilhelm Schmid, "Die Rede des Apostels Paulus vor den Philosophen und Areopagiten in Athen," *Philologus* 95 (1942-43) 79–120. [–H.G.]

103. For this whole theme compare Walter Köhler, *Dogmengeschichte als geschichte des christlichen Selbstbewusstseins* (Zurich: Niehan, 1938), §§5, 13, 14. Ernst Hoffmann refers me to the fact that Nicholas of Cusa characteristically begins his text *De quaerendo Deum* with a reference to the *zētein* of the Areopagus speech.

104. *ē legein te ē akouein kainoteron*. Norden has given a host of examples of the comparative usage of "something new," and has furnished the corresponding proof for *legein ē akouein* as well (*Agostos Theos*, 334–35).

105. This is my attempt to render the apparently standard meaning of *spermologos*: it means one who picks up slick catchwords in the marketplace, in the same way that a crow picks up his food, and then makes out of them an apparently clever rigmarole; compare Eusthatius in Homer, *Od.* 5.490; and also Athenaeus, *Deipn.* 8.344c. The word can also mean simply "gossip" (Demosthenes 18.127, beside *peritrimm' agoras*). Compare also Norden, *Agnostos Theos*, 333; and especially Meyer, *Ursprung und Anfänge des Christentums*, 3.91n1.

106. Compare Acts 17:18 "he seems to be a preacher of foreign deities" (*xenōn daimoniōn dokei katangeleus einai* with Xenophon, *Memorabilia* 1.1.1: "Socrates is guilty of rejecting the gods acknowledged by the state and of bringing in strange deities" (*adikei Sōkratēs ous men hē polis nomizei theous ou nomizōn, hetera de kaina daimonia espherōn*). With reference to the use of *xena* ("foreign") instead of *kaina* ("strange, unheard of") see Norden, *Agnostos Theos*, 53n3.

107. Norden, *Agostos Theos*, 333.

108. Moreover, this also is not quite correct, for in Luke's Gospel the narrative is often stylized, and if, in Luke 1:5-80., the author has assumed the style of the old narratives, this is certainly not because he could not do otherwise but because he considered this style to be suitable. Thus there resulted the considerable difference in style between Luke 1:1-4 and what follows. Compare Harnack, *Mission und Ausbreitung des Christentums*, 4th ed. (Leipzig: Hinrichs, 1924), 104 [Ed.] see *The Mission and Expansion of Christianity in the First Three Centuries*, trans. and ed. James Moffatt (New York: Putnam, 1908).

109. If, as will be shown, we are not compelled to accept the theory that the Acts have been revised, then it is highly probably that the real name of the author was given in the first edition of the work, one not intended for a "canon." For we can hardly believe that both parts of the work should have expressly given the name of the person to whom it was dedicated, but carefully withheld the name of its author. But then we cannot see why the name of the author approved by the Church should not in this case have been the correct one, since it rested upon tradition.

[110.] The same subject is treated in detail on pp. 75–77.

111. A similar situation arises in the letters in Acts also: in the letter of the apostles and elders (15:26) we are given a characterization of Paul and Barnabas which does not correspond at all with the mood otherwise prevailing in Jerusalem; in the letter written by Lysias (23:30) instructions, about which we have heard nothing at all until then, are given to Paul's accusers.

112. Here again we can find a slight divergence between narrative and speech (see above, pp. 75–77); from the narrative we gain the impression that Jesus and the resurrection from the dead are the main themes of the proclamation. The speech mentions Jesus only at the end, does not give his name and, instead of hearing about the resurrection of the dead, we hear only about the resurrection of Jesus.

113. Ernst Curtius, *Stadtgeschichte von Athen* (Berlin: Weidmann, 1891), 262; *Sitzungsberichte der Berliner Akademie* (1893) 926–27.

114. W. M. Ramsey, *St. Paul, The Traveller and Roman Citizen* (London: Hodder & Stoughton, 1920), 199ff.; idem, *The Bearing of Recent Discovery on the Trustworthiness of the New Testament*, 2d ed. (London: Hodder & Stoughton, 1915), 101–5.

115. Compare Curtius, *Stadtgeschichte*, 167, 94.

116. Compare Cicero, *Nat. d.* 2.29 §74, *si quis dicat Atheniensium rem publicam consilio regi, desit illud "Arii pagi"*; and the most recent account in Lake, *The Beginnings of Christianity*, 4.212–13, where further literature is suggested.

117. I feel I ought once more to dwell briefly on this point (see above) in view of the fact that Karl Bornhäuser has explained the speech as one of defense before a court (*Studien zur Apostelgeschichte* [Gütersloh: Bertelsmann, 1934], 139–40). He interprets "took hold" (*epilabomenoi*; 17:19) as imprisonment, the questions in 17:19-20 as a trial (in which case however, the observation in 17:21 would be very much out of place). Curtius describes the whole scene as a preliminary hearing, as a result of which the assembly of Areopagus does not take up the accusation, otherwise Paul would have stood trial on the hill (*Stadtgeschichte*, 262–63).

118. Of course, "they took hold" (*epilabomenoi*) can mean violence, but not necessarily; and if an official arrest had been meant, the officials arresting Paul would have been named. Instead of this we read of a third person pl. "And they took hold . . .

brought" (*epilabomenoi te ... ēgagon*), which is not mentioned again. Who that is we are not told, but it is certainly no one commissioned by the court.

119. I owe it to a reference by Arnold von Salis that I can consider this possibility and so perhaps put an end to a premature conclusion that is generally adopted. Compare Walther Judeich, *Topographie von Athen*, 2d ed., HAW 3.2.2 (Munich: Beck, 1931), 299, and the illustration plate 13.

120. Several witnesses to the "Western" text, including D, say that this walk to the Areopagus took place only "after a few days." This addition is one of several made in the same group of texts; they have obviously arisen from consideration of the circumstances and thus present improvements that throw light on the subject. None would have omitted this note about time, whereas its insertion can be explained as arising out of a consideration of whether all this really did take place on the same day.

121. "Style Criticism of the Book of Acts." See above, pp. 35–36.

122. Harnack, *Luke the Physician*, trans. J. R. Wilkinson, CTL 23 (New York: Putnam, 1907), 19–60; idem, *The Date of the Acts and the Synoptic Gospels*, trans. J. R. Wilkinson, CTL 23 (New York: Putnam, 1911), 1–15.

123. In recent literature Albert Schweitzer, especially, has briefly but conclusively expounded this group of proofs; *The Mysticism of Paul the Apostle*, trans. William Montgomery (New York: Holt, 1931), 6–10.

124. Since, in the course of this examination, the passage 14:15-17 in the speech has constantly been referred to as the only parallel to the Areopagus speech that is to be found in the New Testament, it is appropriate here to compare the two. In Lystra also, Paul speaks to Gentiles, and this "speech" too, in spite of its brevity, stands out in the story on account of its more cultivated style: compare *en tais parōchēmenais geneais*, the litotes *ouk amartyron auton aphēken*, the onomatopoeia, and the alliteration *kairous karpophorous*. Again, in Acts 14, there occurs a solemn proclamation about God, and here too the evidence of God's existence is found in the ordering of nature, especially in the seasons of the year. But, on the whole, this "speech" in Lystra is nearer to the Septuagint than is the Areopagus speech. In contrast to 17:24, the proclamation about God does not contain the word "world" (*kosmos*), but is preached completely in Old Testament style (see Exod 20:11); the gods are described as "worthless" (*mataioi*; or *ta mataia*), as in 3 Kgs 16:2, 13, 26; 4 Kgs 17:15; Est 4:17; Jer 2:5; 8:19; 3 Macc 6:11. Admittedly there is a reference in 14:16 to the motif of ignorance in 17:30, but none to the revelation of salvation as having put an end to ignorance; that again is due to the situation, which required that what was new in the Christian preaching (introduced here by the word "bring good news" *euangelizesthai*) should be expounded right at the beginning in contrast to the Gentile deification of men. The most original element is the exposition in 14:17. Here, as elsewhere (see above, pp. 97–98), in the course of giving evidence of God, the seasons of the year are mentioned. Linked with them here is rain or, possibly, rather, the rainy seasons, which are perhaps more appropriate to the idea of a fruitful ordering of the year. This is suggested by Cadbury, "Lexical Notes," 219–21; in support of the suggestion he quotes Luke's partiality for doublets of the same meaning. *Trophē kai euphrosunē* is perhaps also a doublet of this kind. And this may again be occasioned by the LXX, which, in several passages, makes *euphrosunē* refer to eating and drinking (Jdt 12:13; Eccl 9:7; Sir 9:10; 31:28), and in Ps 4:8, taking food is paralleled with receiving *euphrosunē* (*edōkas euphrosunēn eis tēn kardian mou. Apo kairou sitou kai oinou kai elaiou autōn eplēthunthēsan*; compare also Isa 25:6 *piontai euphrosunēn*).

It seems that it is only by this usage of language that we can explain the combination which is so striking elsewhere, according to which God has filled the hearts of men with "food and gladness," that is (completely in harmony with Old Testament thought), has made their hearts glad with eating and drinking. But in the Stoic proof of God these ideas, of different origin, are arranged thus: God revealed himself by a purposeful ordering of human life; men were therefore able to recognize him.

125. This beginning of a story which was originally independent is, in fact, still clearly perceptible. The itinerary that underlies the story of the journey (see above, pp. 123–25) has in 14:6 reported the journey through the towns of Lycaonia and, after mentioning the station Lystra, has already mentioned the next station, Derbe. Now, from 14:8 onwards, Luke inserts the story of the lame man in Lystra; thus he must refer the reader back once more to the station before the last. The text supplied by D, which is always concerned to make "seams" invisible, has quite logically omitted the words "in Lystra" (*en Lystrois*) in 14:8.

126. This verse 17:32, which does not once mention the mocking words, is so colorless that it admits of little attempt at explanation. We should therefore be ill-advised to see in 17:18 a reference to the Stoics and Epicureans. Moreover, the desire expressed by some listeners to hear Paul again should be regarded as a way out of an embarrassing situation, rather than as a serious promise, for Paul does not take it up.

127. Compare Carl Munzinger, *Paulus in Korinth: Neue Wege zum Verständnis des Urchristentums* (Heidelberg: Evangelischer, 1908), 79–80: "But he felt that this failure in Athens was his own fault. . . . He now knew . . . how he should not preach. He did not need, however, to think of a new way . . . ; he returned immediately to his old and proved method of preaching." Holzner declares that Paul says after the Areopagus speech: "In future I shall speak no more of Greek wisdom, but of Christ only, and of the foolishness of the cross"; *Paulus: Sein Leben und Seine Briefe* (Freiburg: Herder, 1937), 198.

128. I shall not deal with the questions as to whether the itinerary was the work of the same author and whether the "we" was already in the text of this source or added when the Acts was written, since the answers to these questions do not affect my examination.

129. In the presentation of the apostle's first missionary activities (Acts 13–14), other words are used with the meaning of sermon: "the word of God" (*logos tou theou*) in Cyprus (13:7), "speak" (*lalein*) in Iconium (14:1), "bring good news" (*euangelizesthai*) in Lystra and Derbe (14:7, 21). But the first phrase is found within an independent story (of the sorcerer), and *euangelizesthai* is a favorite word with Luke, so, perhaps, inserted by him; at any rate, these words cannot with certainty be derived from the itinerary.

130. The first proof of the existence of a Christian community in Athens is given by the letter from Dionysius of Corinth (about 170) to the community; this letter is mentioned by Eusebius in *Hist. eccl.* 4.23.2. The reference to the bishops Publius and Quadratus (4.23.3) may not be relied upon, since our Areopagite Dionysius is also named in the same context (contrary to all probability, as far as can be seen from Acts 17) as the first bishop of Athens.

131. We might perhaps think that, in 17:19-20, a sentence has been used out of the itinerary. That would explain why "May we know what this new teaching is which you present?" (*dunametha gnōnai tis hē kainē autē hē hypo sou laloumenē didachē*) is once more followed by "we wish to know" (*boulometha oun gnōnai*). Or, in the sentences which follow directly upon the speech, we could suppose that there are passages from

the itinerary, "some scoffed, but others said . . . , but some of them joined" (*hoi men ech-leuazon, hoi de eipan . . . , tines de andres kollēthentes*). But these are only speculations. We must restrict ourselves to taking only the two sentences mentioned above as belonging to the itinerary, because their language and subject-matter make it probable that they do in fact belong to it.

132. We have to choose an offensive expression of this kind in order to make clear the real associations it would have for Paul's listeners. Our word "cross" is too strongly suggestive of sanctity. It is only when the word cross (1 Cor 1:18) is brought home to our minds as a gallows that we can understand why it scandalized the Jews and was foolishness to the Gentiles.

8. PAUL IN ATHENS

[1.] For a full analysis, see chap. 7. [—H.G.]

[2.] For reference to Epimenides, see Diogenes Laertius 1.10.110. [—H.G.]

[3.] The last three paragraphs are from the revised version of this essay that appeared in English in *Research and Progress* 6/1 (Jan–Feb 1940) 3–7. The 1939 version was a bit shorter and less developed at the end. In the German edition and earlier version of this translation, Greeven put the more developed ending in a footnote instead of replacing the older version, as I have done here.

9. THE APOSTOLIC COUNCIL

[1.] There is also something on this subject in the *Wochenschrift für klassischen Philologie* 36 (1919) 5ff., and in *TLZ* 59 (1934) 247. [—H.G.]

2. The β-text mentions appropriately in v. 6 that the crowd is present (paving the way for v. 12); it lets Peter speak, filled with the Holy Spirit (preparation for v. 28?), and the elders agree with Peter's speech. This and the well-known ethical interpretation of the Apostolic Decree detract from rather than adding to the seriousness of the dispute.

3. At least Julius Wellhausen gives expression to what is astonishing about it: "having recourse to the conversion of Cornelius, which took place long ago, but remained completely forgotten and had no further effect"; *Kritische Analyse der Apostelgeschichte*, AKGWG 15 (Berlin: Weidman, 1914), 27.

4. I stand by the opinion I expressed twenty years ago in my volume that a book which bore the name of a particular person to whom it was dedicated cannot have been published without the author's name being made known, and that the tradition concerning Luke as the author is therefore to be taken seriously; *A Fresh Approach to the New Testament and Early Christian literature* (New York: Scribner, 1936), 63–64.

5. I intend to prove elsewhere [see chap. 10] that these passages do not belong to the original story of Cornelius.

[6.] "Paul n'aurait pas mieux dit"; Alfred Loisy, *Les Actes des Apôtres* (Paris: Nourry, 1920).

7. "And all the assembly kept silence" (*Esigēsen de pan to plēthos*)—we must make the following observations on this connecting-link, which has called forth so many conjectures from the commentators: (1) As a comparison with v. 13 shows, the words really mean very little; they are not intended to emphasize either that the opposition can say

nothing further (Wendt), or that no agreement was reached (Bauernfeind). (2) The β-text, which inserts the elders' agreement with the speech, simply wants to rectify the failure to comment on the way in which it was received. The insertion therefore signifies very little. (3) When we see how little Luke is concerned here with "correct" narrative and how many questions he leaves open, we shall take the fact that he here mentions the crowd, which was not mentioned in v. 6, simply as an example of how carelessly he tells his story here, where something quite different is important to him, and we shall not conclude that there were various sources.

8. Bauernfeind speaks of "grievous abbreviation."

9. The mention in the legend about Peter (12:17) belongs to this old story, which originated in tradition. We may take as proof of this the conclusion of the narrative "he went to another place," which is to be understood as the disinterested conclusion to the legend, but which would sound very odd in a continuous record.

10. The emphasis is on *kērussein* ("proclaim"), which is a much stronger word then *anaginōskein* ("read"): Moses is preached *kata polin* ("in every city"); obviously, the reference is especially to the Dispersion, where he is "proclaimed" in this way. But the words "without our assistance" are not included.

11. James Hardy Ropes suggested a similar interpretation in "Acts xv.21," *JBL* 15 (1896) 75–81. The suggestion was then taken up by Lake and Cadbury in *The Beginnings of Christianity*, 4.177–78.

12. It is usual to take this point as an argument against Luke's authorship: A man who was so close to Paul would "surely" have questioned him about events in the Apostolic Council. This view does not take into account that: (1) people of that time and of that position in society did not behave toward one another as if they were reporters; (2) at that time, Luke had no plans to be a writer; and (3) even if he had been informed, Luke obviously ascribed less importance to reproducing accounts of this critical event than to emphasizing his main theme.

13. I shall not examine the text in detail, but merely observe that, contrary to the opinion I held previously, I do not consider the omission of *kai pniktou* ("and strangled") or *pniktōn* in the β-text as original, since the express mention of "strangled" beside "blood" is not superfluous (finally, compare Bauernfeind). The omission of *pniktou* is then explained by the process of moral interpretation that is characteristic of the β-text.

14. I refer once more to my analysis of the story of Cornelius. [Compare chap. 10.]

15. The D-text of v. 5, which omits *ois oude* ("to them not") can hardly be genuine, since its origin is to be understood thus: it was desired to remove the analouthon, just as Marcion, the Peshitta and others had already endeavored to do in omitting *ois* ("to them"). But, even if the D-text had been genuine, it still could not have referred to the circumcision of Titus; for if Titus had retained for life the mark of the covenant of Israel that would certainly not have been a giving-way by Paul *pros hōran* ("for a moment").

10. THE CONVERSION OF CORNELIUS

1. See *A Fresh Approach to the New Testament and Early Christian Literature*, ILCK (New York: Scribner, 1936), 64–66. [Ed.] See also chap. 3 above.

2. Bauernfeind has given a careful discussion of them in *Kommentar und Studien zur Apostelgeschichte*, edited by Volker Mitelmann, WUNT 22 (Tübingen: Mohr/Siebeck, 1980).

3. Bauernfeind, *Kommentar und Studien*, on 11:15: a relic of pre-Lukan tradition which, instead of the speech in 10:34ff., contains only a brief, significant comment.

4. When, in 11:16, Peter quotes words of Jesus which are found only in Acts, there, however, in a proleptic sense, this also points to a linking-up which originated with the author. Alfred Loisy realized this, while Julius Wellhausen, *Kritische Analyse der Apostelgeschichte*, AKGWG 15 (Berlin: Weidmann, 1914), 20, finds the meaning "obscure."

5. Compare Dibelius, *From Tradition to Gospel*, trans. Bertram Lee Woolf (New York: Scribner, 1965) 16–17.

6. We are certainly dealing with pre-Lukan formulae that have nothing to do with the situation. This is indicated by the word *arxamenos* ("beginning"), which is no longer declined, but has become "frozen" in the nominative; the word is also used in the same sense in Acts 1:22, and we meet it elsewhere in formal phrases (Luke 23:5; 24:47). Moreover, the two verses 10:36 and 10:37 read as if they were actually parallels: "The word (which) he sent to the children of Israel, preaching good news of peace by Jesus Christ . . . ," and "you know the word which was proclaimed throughout all Judaea. . . ." Even this could be explained if we were to take it that rival versions of the same theme were erroneously thought to co-exist. At any rate, *humeis oidate* ("You know," 10:36) is striking. Nothing justifies our assuming that Cornelius "knows" anything.

7. This phrase also disposes of the somewhat rationalistic view of Jacquier: *"Il semble que Pierre n'aurait pu parler ainsi s'il y avait eu dans le récipient des animaux purs et des impurs. Il pouvait tuer un animal pur."* In this case the visionary's horror at the profane mingling of clean and unclean is not taken into consideration. Perhaps the Latin translation of Acts 10:13-15—which Augustine preserved in *Contra Faustum* 31.3; see Joseph Zycha, *Sancti Aureli Augustini*, Corpus scriptorum ecclesiasticorum latinorum 25, parts 1 & 2 (Vindobonae: Tempsky, 1891), 758—also seeks to satisfy this rationalistic idea. In it the voice from heaven is made to say: "Peter, slay all that you see in the cage and eat it"; see Friedrich Blass, *Acta Apostolorum, sive, Lucae ad Theophilum liber alter: secundam formam quae videtur Romanum* (Leipzig: Teubner, 1896), XXII, and 32.

8. On the whole, this result coincides with that of Bauernfeind, who, however, arrives at it in a completely different way. He takes the beginning of Peter's sermon (10:35) to be a pre-Lukan "stereotyped watchword," thinks it contradicts 10:28, therefore removes this verse and the adjoining ones and, *for this reason*, also rejects the vision. That completely uncertain element, the "stereotyped watchword," is made the point of departure here, and the inferences are therefore doubtful. Bauernfeind only partially excludes Peter's justification.

[9.] For the meaning of the speeches in the Cornelius narrative compare also pp. 64–65.

10. It is characteristic, however, that the whole of this neutral expression, which simply means that someone else began to speak (compare 15:13), has been invested by the commentators with specific interpretations: "itaque antea non tacuerant" (Blass); "the opposition which had previously been raised against Paul and the people of Antioch subsided after this speech by Peter" (Hans Hinrich Wendt, *Die Apostelgeschichte*, KEKNT 3 [Göttingen: Vandenhoeck & Ruprecht, 1913]); "this means not only that the

opposition became silent, but also that there was no agreement . . ." (Bauernfeind, *Kommentar und Studien zur Apostelgeschichte*).

11. As is well known, the introduction given in the "Western" text is far more precise than the one in the usual text. The "Western" text describes the intruders as Pharisees; it makes Paul expressly oppose them, so that they finally order Paul and Barnabas to travel to the apostles and elders in Jerusalem and to submit to arbitration there. This "sharper" interpretation should now have made itself felt in the way in which the discussion is presented, but there is no sign of this at all. The only special contributions made by D and its dependents to the account of the discussion are the observations that Peter spoke "in the (Holy) Spirit" and that the elders agreed with him. Editors making this latter comment obviously wanted to fill out the somewhat abrupt form of 15:12.

12. It is not only Irenaeus (*Haer.* 3.12.14) who does not retain Acts 15:12 (he is concerned only with the speeches in Acts). But the renderings found in the *Didasc. syr.* 24 (Achelis, TU NF 10:2, pp. 124–32) and *Apos. Const.* 6.12 also reject Acts 15:21b.

13. "V. 12, as it stands, cannot have originated with Luke. The absence of detailed speeches by Paul and Barnabas, which would not, in itself, be remarkable, is only noticed at all because longer utterances are ascribed to Peter and James"; Martin Sorof, *Die Entstehung der Apostelgeschichte: Eine kritische Studie* (Berlin: Nicolai, 1890), 98. The superfluity of 15:12 and 15:4 "proves that both of them" (Barnabas and Paul) "are really only embellishment and that v. 12 did not belong to the original account"; Erwin Preuschen, *Die Apostelgeschichte*, HNT (Tübingen: Mohr/Siebeck, 1912).

14. We should have to assume that 15:1-5 is the beginning of an account, the remained of which has been lost, but that 15:6-18 is a separate account. But the principal question, of "Why Cornelius, why not Paul?" would remain unanswered.

15. We should have to suppose that Paul's dispute had in fact been settled by recollecting the case of Cornelius; but the Epistle to the Galatians provides decisive evidence against this in the fact that nothing at all is said there about Cornelius.

16. The question is simply whether with the Apostolic Decree the account returns to the point of the dispute; it may be that, historically, the decree does not belong here at all.

17. This is what Bauernfeind does (see note 8 above). Out of his justifiably high valuation of the "stereotyped watchword" in 10:35, he unjustifiably deduces that this "battle-cry" had a central position in the story of Cornelius in its pre-Lukan form, and indeed was perhaps formulated by Peter himself. "But it is very remarkable that these decisive and exonerating words in Luke are prepared for, or rather anticipated by a much less weighty sentence of the same meaning" (10:28b). This less "weighty sentence" is therefore said to be of editorial origin. But if we attribute both verses to Luke's own work, 10:38b can certainly be understood as the knowledge derived from the vision, 10:35 as a truth commonly known.

18. This has already been seen by Johannes Weiss, *Über die Absicht und den literarischen Character der Apostelgeschichte* (Göttingen: Vandenhoeck & Ruprecht, 1897), 18: "According to the detail given in the story in 10:2, Cornelius is a proselyte, but no attention is paid to this fact in the context of the whole story"—although the term "proselyte" here is an exaggeration.

19. Perhaps this insertion and modification of the original story explains why Peter is twice described as reflecting upon the vision: 10:17 "Now while Peter was greatly puzzled about what to make of the vision that he had seen" (*hôs de en heautô diêporei ho*

Petros, ti an eiê to horama ho eiden); and 10:19 "While Peter was still thinking about the vision" (*tou de Petrou dienthumoumenou peri tou horamatos*).

20. Bauernfeind, *Kommentar und Studien*.

21. The reverse is true in Luke's version; see p. 147.

11. THE TEXT OF ACTS

[1.] In general see: Ernst Haenchen and Peter Weigandt, "The Original Text of Acts?" *NTS* 14 (1967–68) 469–81; A. F. J. Klijn, *A Survey of the Researches into the Western Text of the Gospels and Acts* (Utrecht: Kemink, 1949); idem, *A Survey of the Researches into the Western Text of the Gospels and Acts: Part Two 1949–1969*, NovTSup 21 (Leiden: Brill, 1969); idem, "In Search of the Original Text of Acts," in *Studies in Luke-Acts: Essays Presented in Honor of Paul Schubert*, 2d ed., edited by Leander E. Keck and J. Louis Martyn (Minneapolis: Fortress Press, 1980), 103–10; Bruce M. Metzger, *The Text of the New Testament: Its Transmission, Corruption, and Restoration*, 3d ed. (New York: Oxford Univ. Press, 1992); Walter Thiele, "Ausgewählte Beispiele zur Charakterisierung des 'westlichen' Textes der Apostelgeschichte," *ZNW* 56 (1965) 51–63.

[2.] Codex D is the fifth-century Codex Bezae (Cantabrigiensis) in the Cambridge University Library. See Eldon J. Epp, *The Theological Tendency of Codex Bezae Cantabrigiensis in Acts*, SNTSMS 3 (Cambridge: Cambridge Univ. Press, 1966).

3. Compare chap. 4 above.

4. I speak of Luke as the author of Acts. For my reasons see above, especially p. 157.

[5.] See Bruce M. Metzger, *A Textual Commentary on the Greek New Testament*, 4th ed. (New York: United Bible Societies, 1994), 267–69.

[6.] See ibid, 335.

7. Compare p. 113–14.

[8.] This is a seventh-century collation of earlier manuscripts. As Haenchen describes it: "In 616 Thomas of Harkel, at Enaton Monastery near Alexandria, collated the text translated from Greek in 506 by Philoxenus with three old MSS in the case of the Gospels and, in the case of Acts with one, which contained a Western text"; Ernst Haenchen, *The Acts of the Apostles: A Commentary*, trans. Bernard Noble et al. (Oxford: Blackwell, 1971), 51 n3. See also A. Hilgenfeld, "Thomas von Heraklea und die Apostelgeschichte," *ZWTh* 43 (1900) 401–22; and Paul Harb, "Die heraklensische Übersetzung des Neuen Testaments: Neue Handschriftenfunde," *OrChr* 64 (1980) 36–74.

[9.] It is unclear if Dibelius is referring to the Greek marginal reading of the Herakleian Syriac.

[10.] For the three variant versions of 15:34 see Metzger, *Textual Commentary*. Metzger agrees with Dibelius in omitting the verse.

11. The Acts passage listed in Goodspeed's edition of the Apologists are not quotations; we have here no more than similarity of material. Concerning Marcion, see Adolf von Harnack, *Marcion: The Gospel of the Alien God*, trans. John E. Steely and Lyle D. Bierma (Durham, N.C.: Labyrinth, 1990).

[12.] Note that the syntax of this verse appears four different sequences in the Greek, Syriac, Latin, and Coptic witnesses, and a fifth in the Armenian. See Metzger, *Textual Commentary*. See Matthew Black, "The Holy Spirit in the Western Text of Acts," in *New*

Testament Textual Criticism, Its Significance for Exegesis: Essays in Honour of Bruce M. Metzger, edited by Eldon Jay Epp and Gordon D. Fee (Oxford: Clarendon, 1981), 159–70.

13. F. J. Foakes-Jackson and Kirsopp Lake, editors, *The Beginnings of Christianity,* 5 vols. (London: Macmillan, 1933), 4.9.

14. Ibid., 4.53.

15. Metzger disagrees with Dibelius since the connecting particle is missing; see Metzger, *Textual Commentary,* 287.

16. James Hardy Ropes in Foakes-Jackson and Lake, *The Beginnings of Christianity,* 3.237.

17. See p. 137.

Bibliography

Works of Martin Dibelius in English

1934   *From Tradition to Gospel.* Translated by Bertram Lee Woolf. London: Nicholson & Watson. (Reprinted: Greenwood, S.C.: Attic, 1982. German eds. 1919, 1933)

1935   *Gospel Criticism and Christology.* London: Nicholson & Watson. (Lectures given at King's College, London, in October 1934; German included as part of *Botschaft und Geschichte: Gesammelte Aufsätze.* Vol. 1: *Zur Evangelienforschung,* 1953)

1936   *A Fresh Approach to the New Testament and Early Christian Literature.* ILCK. New York: Scribner. (German ed. 1926)

1939   *The Message of Jesus Christ: The Tradition of the Early Christian Communities Restored and Translated into German.* ILCK. Translated by Frederick C. Grant. New York: Scribner. (German ed. 1935)

1940   *The Sermon on the Mount.* New York: Scribner. (The Schaffer Lectures given at Yale Divinity School, 1937)

1949   *Jesus.* Translated by Charles B. Hedrick and Frederick C. Grant. Philadelphia: Westminster. (German ed. 1939)

1953   *Paul.* Edited and completed by Werner Georg Kümmel. Translated by Frank Clarke. London: Longmans, Green. U.S. ed. Philadelphia: Westminster, 1962. (German ed. 1951)

1956   *Studies in the Acts of the Apostles.* Edited by Heinrich Greeven. Translated by Mary Ling. New York: Scribner. (German ed. 1951)

1972   *The Pastoral Epistles: A Commentary on the Pastoral Epistles.* Revised by Hans Conzelmann. Translated by Philip Buttolph and Adela Yarbro. Edited by Helmut Koester. Hermeneia. Philadelphia: Fortress Press. (German eds. 1931, 1955)

1975   "The Initiation in Apuleius and Related Initiatory Rites." In *Conflict at Colossae: A Problem in the Interpretation of Early Christianity, Illustrated by Selected Modern Studies,* edited and translated by Fred O. Francis and Wayne A. Meeks, 61–121. Rev. ed. SBS 4. Missoula, Mont.: Scholars. (German ed. 1917)

1976   *James: A Commentary on the Epistle of James*. Revised by Heinrich Greeven. Translated by Michael A. Williams. Edited by Helmut Koester. Hermeneia. Philadelphia: Fortress Press. (German ed. 1921; 11th German ed. 1964)

Major Works in German

1906   *Die Lade Jahves: Eine religionsgeschichtliche Untersuchung*. FRLANT 7. Göttingen: Vandenhoeck & Ruprecht.

1909   *Die Geisterwelt im Glauben des Paulus*. Göttingen: Vandenhoeck & Ruprecht.

1911   *An die Thessalonicher I, II; An die Philipper.* HNT. Tübingen: Mohr/Siebeck.

1911   *Die urchristliche Überlieferung von Johannes dem Täufer.* FRLANT 15. Göttingen: Vandenhoeck & Ruprecht.

1912   *An die Kolosser; Epheser; An Philemon.* HNT. Tübingen: Mohr/Siebeck.

1913   *Die Brief Paulus.* Vol. 2: *Die neun kleine Briefe.* HNT. Tübingen: Mohr/Siebeck. (Combines the 1911 and 1912 vols., while adding the Pastorals; these were divided again in later editions.)

1917   *Die Isisweihe bei Apuleius und verwandte Initiationsriten.* SHAW.PH. Heidelberg: Winter. (ET 1975)

1919   *Die Formgeschichte des Evangeliums.* 1st ed. Tübingen: Mohr/Siebeck. (See 2d ed. 1933)

1921   *Der Brief des Jakobus.* KEKNT 15. Göttingen: Vandenhoeck & Ruprecht. (Later editions revised by Heinrich Greeven; ET 1976)

1923   *Der Hirt des Hermas.* HNT 4 (Supplementary Volume). Tübingen: Mohr/Siebeck.

1925   *Geschichtliche und übergeschichtliche Religion im Christentum.* Göttingen: Vandenhoeck & Ruprecht. (See 2d ed. 1929)

1926   *Geschichte der urchristlichen Literatur.* 2 vols. SG 934, 935. Berlin: de Gruyter. (See ET 1936; rev. German ed. 1975)

1927   *An die Kolosser; Epheser; An Philemon.* 2d rev. ed. HNT 12. Tübingen: Mohr/Siebeck.

1928   *Urchristentum und Kultur: Rektoratsrede gehalten bei der Stiftungsfeier der Universität am 22. November, 1927.* Heidelberger Universitätsreden 2. Heidelberg: Winter.

1929   *Evangelium und Welt.* Göttingen: Vandenhoeck & Ruprecht. (2d ed. of *Geschichtliche und übergeschichtliche Religion im Christentum*, 1925)

1931   "Literatur zur Formgeschichte des Neuen Testaments ausserhalb den Evangelien." *TRu* 3 (1931) 207–42.

1931   *Die Pastoralbriefe.* 2d ed. HNT 13. Tübingen: Mohr/Siebeck. (See 3d rev. ed., 1955; ET 1972)

1932   *Jungfrauensohn und Krippenkind: Untersuchungen zur Geburtsgeschichte Jesu im Lukas-evangelium.* SHAW.PH 1931/32. Heidelberg: Winter.

1933   *Die Formgeschichte des Evangeliums.* 2d ed. Tübingen: Mohr/Siebeck. (ET 1965)

1933   *Das soziale Motiv im Neuen Testament.* Genf: Forschungsabteilung des oekumensichen Rates.

1935   *Die Botschaft von Jesus Christus: Die alte Überlieferung der Gemeinde in Geschichten, Sprüchen und Reden.* Tübingen: Mohr/Siebeck. (ET 1939)

1937　　*An die Thessalonicher I, II; An die Philipper.* 3d ed. HNT. Tübingen: Mohr/Siebeck.

1939　　*Die Hauptfragen der Synoptikerkritik: Eine Auseinandersetzung mit R. Bult-mann, M. Dibelius und ihrer Vorgängern.* BFCT 40. Gütersloh: Bertelsmann.

1939　　*Jesus.* SG 1130. Berlin: de Gruyter. (See 3d ed., 1960; ET 1949)

1939　　*Paulus auf dem Aeropag.* SHAW.PH 1938/39. Heidelberg: Winter.

1941　　*Paulus und die Mystik.* Munich: Reinhard.

1949　　*Die Reden der Apostelgeschichte und die antike Geschichtsschreibung.* SHAW.PH 1949. Heidelberg: Winter.

1951　　*Aufsätze zur Apostelgeschichte.* Edited by Heinrich Greeven. FRLANT 60. Göttingen: Vandenhoeck & Ruprecht. (ET 1956)

1951　　*Paulus.* Edited and completed by Werner Georg Kümmel. SG 1160. Berlin: de Gruyter. (ET 1953)

1953　　*Botschaft und Geschichte: Gesammelte Aufsätze.* Vol. 1: *Zur Evangelien-forschung.* In collaboration with Heinz Kraft. Edited by Günther Bornkamm. Tübingen: Mohr/Siebeck.

1955　　*Die Pastoralbriefe.* 3d ed. Revised by Werner Georg Kümmel. HNT 13. Tübingen: Mohr/Siebeck. (See 2d ed. 1931; ET 1972)

1956　　*Botschaft und Geschichte: Gesammelte Aufsätze.* Vol. 2: *Zum Urchristentum und zur hellenistischen Religionsgeschichte.* In collaboration with Heinz Kraft. Edited by Günther Bornkamm. Tübingen: Mohr/Siebeck.

1960　　*Jesus.* 3d ed. with Afterword by Werner Georg Kümmel. SG 1130. Berlin: de Gruyter. (See 1st ed. 1939; ET 1949)

1975　　*Geschichte der urchristlichen Literatur.* Edited by Ferdinand Hahn. ThBü 58. Munich: Kaiser. (Rev. in accordance with the English ed. in 1936; 1st ed. 1926.)

Assessments of Dibelius and His Work

Anonymous. "Dibelius, Martin." In *Evangelische Kirchenlexikon: Kirchlich-theologisches Handwörterbuch,* edited by H. Brunotte and O. Weber, 1:934. 2d ed. 4 vols. Göttingen: Vandenhoeck & Ruprecht, 1955–61.

Anonymous. "Dibelius, Martin." In *New Catholic Encyclopedia,* edited by L. A. Bushinski, 4:733–34. 2d ed. Detroit: Thomson Gale, 2003.

Anonymous. "Dibelius, Martin." In *Oxford Dictionary of the Christian Church,* edited by E. A. Livingstone, 478, 3d ed.. New York: Oxford Univ. Press, 1997.

Bartsch, Hans Werner. "Martin Dibelius." *ZdZ* 2 (1948) 13–15.

Bringeland, Hans. "Dibelius, Martin." In *Dictionary of Biblical Interpretation,* edited by John H. Hayes, 2:296–97. Nashville: Abingdon, 1999.

Dibelius, Martin. "Dibelius, Martin." In *Die Religionswissenschaft der Gegenwart in Selbstdarstellungen,* edited by Erich Stange, 5:1–37. 5 vols. Leipzig: Meiner, 1929.

Fridrichsen, Anton. *Bibliographia Dibeliana atque Bultmanniana.* Coniectanea Neotestamentica 8. Uppsala: Seminarium Neotestamenticum, 1944.

Gasque, W. Ward. "The Influence of Martin Dibelius." In *A History of the Interpretation of the Acts of the Apostles,* 201–50. Grand Rapids: Eerdmans, 1975. (Reprinted Peabody, Mass.: Hendrickson, 1989)

Geiser, Stefan. *Verantwortung und Schuld: Studien zu Martin Dibelius.* Hamburger theologischer Studien 20. Münster: Lit, 2000.

Genthe, Hans Jochen. *Kleine Geschichte der neutestamentliche Wissenschaft*, 240–43, 260–61. Göttingen: Vandenhoeck & Ruprecht, 1977.

Greeven, Heinrich. "Martin Dibelius." *FAB* 2 (1948) 26–31.

Jornod, Jean-Pierre. "Trois critiques allemands du 20ᵉ siècle face aux synoptiques: essai comparatif sur les méthodes critiques d'Heitmüller, Bultmann et Dibelius." Thèse bach. theol., Genf 1950.

Kümmel, Werner Georg. "Dibelius, Martin." In *Theologische Realenzyclopädie*, edited by Gerhard Krause und Gerhard Müller, 8:726–29. Berlin: de Gruyter, 1981.

———. "Martin Dibelius als Theologe." *TLZ* 74 (1949) 129–40.

———. *The New Testament: The History of the Investigation of Its Problems*, 263–66, 330–34, 380–83. Translated by S. McLean Gilmour and Howard C. Kee. Nashville: Abingdon, 1972.

Ludolphy, Ingetraut. "Dibelius, Martin." In *The Encyclopedia of the Lutheran Church*, edited by Julius Bodensieck, 1:704. 3 vols. Minneapolis: Augsburg, 1965.

Merk, Otto. "Dibelius, Martin." In *Religion in Geschichte und Gegenwart*, 4th ed., edited by Hans Dieter Betz, 2:834. Tübingen: Mohr/Siebeck, 1998.

Neill, Stephen, and Tom Wright. *The Interpretation of the New Testament, 1861-1986*. Oxford: Oxford Univ. Press, 1988.

Preisker, Herbert. "Martin Dibelius z. Gedächtnis." *FF* 24 (1948) 191–92.

Rusche, Helga. "Dibelius, Martin." In *Lexikon für Theologie und Kirche*, edited by Walter Kasper, 3:205. Freiburg: Herder, 1995.

Select Bibliography on the Book of Acts

1. COMMENTARIES

Barrett, C. K. *A Critical and Exegetical Commentary on the Acts of the Apostles.* 2 vols. International Critical Commentary. Edinburgh: T. & T. Clark, 1994–98.

Bruce, F. F. *The Acts of the Apostles: The Greek Text with Introduction and Commentary.* 3d ed. Grand Rapids: Eerdmans, 1990.

Conzelmann, Hans. *Acts of the Apostles.* Translated by James Limburg et al. Edited by Helmut Koester. Hermeneia. Philadelphia: Fortress Press, 1987. German rev. ed. 1972.

Dunn, James D. G. *The Acts of the Apostles.* Epworth Commentaries. Peterborough: Epworth, 1996.

Eckey, Wilfried. *Die Apostelgeschichte: Der Weg des Evangeliums von Jerusalem nach Rom.* 2 vols. Neukirchen-Vluyn: Neukirchener, 2000.

Fitzmyer, Joseph A. *The Acts of the Apostles.* AB 31. New York: Doubleday, 1998.

Gaventa, Beverly Roberts. *The Acts of the Apostles.* ANTC. Nashville: Abingdon, 2003.

Gonzalez, Justo L. *Acts: The Gospel of the Spirit.* Maryknoll, N.Y.: Orbis, 2001.

Haenchen, Ernst. *The Acts of the Apostles: A Commentary.* Translated by Bernard Noble and Gerald Shinn. Edited by R. McL. Wilson. Philadelphia: Westminster, 1971. 16th German ed. 1977.

Jervell, Jacob. *Die Apostelgeschichte.* KEKNT 3. Göttingen: Vandenhoeck & Ruprecht, 1998.

Johnson, Luke Timothy. *The Acts of the Apostles.* SacPag 5. Collegeville, Minn.: Liturgical, 1992.

Kee, Howard Clark. *To Every Nation under Heaven: The Acts of the Apostles.* NTC. Harrisburg, Pa.: Trinity, 1997.

Krodel, Gerhard A. *Acts.* ACNT. Minneapolis: Augsburg, 1986.

Lüdemann, Gerd. *Early Christianity according to the Traditions in Acts: A Commentary.* Translated by John Bowden. Minneapolis: Fortress Press, 1989. German ed. 1987.

Mussner, Franz. *Die Apostelgeschichte.* NEBKNT 5. Würzburg: Echter, 1984.

Pesch, Rudolf. *Die Apostelgeschichte.* 2 vols. EKKNT 5. Neukirchen-Vluyn: Neukirchener, 1986.

Roloff, Jürgen. *Die Apostelgeschichte.* NTD 5. Göttingen: Vandenhoeck & Ruprecht, 1981.

Schille, Gottfried. *Die Apostelgeschichte des Lukas.* THKNT 5. Berlin: Evangelische Ver-
laganstalt, 1983.

Schmithals, Walter. *Die Apostelgeschichte des Lukas.* ZBK. Neues Testament 3.2. Zurich:
Theologischer Verlag, 1982.

Schneider, Gerhard. *Die Apostelgeschichte.* 2 vols. HTKNT 5. Freiburg: Herder, 1980–82.

Spencer, F. Scott. *Acts.* Readings. Sheffield: Sheffield Academic, 1997.

Talbert, Charles H. *Reading Acts: A Literary and Theological Commentary on the Acts of
the Apostles.* New York: Crossroad, 1997.

Taylor, Justin. *Les Actes des deux Apôtres.* Volume 5: *Commentaire historique (Act. 9,1—
18,22).* EBib 23. Paris: Lecoffre, 1994.

Weiser, Alfons. *Die Apostelgeschichte.* 2 vols. ÖTKNT 5/1-2. Gütersloh: Gütersloher,
1981–85.

Witherington, Ben III. *The Acts of the Apostles: A Socio-Rhetorical Commentary.* Grand
Rapids: Eerdmans, 1998.

Zahn, Theodor. *Die Apostelgeschichte des Lukas.* 2 vols. KNT 5/1-2. Leipzig: Deichert,
1919–21.

Zmijewski, Josef. *Die Apostelgeschichte.* RNT. Regensburg: Pustet, 1994.

2. MONOGRAPHS AND ARTICLES

Arlandson, James Malcolm. *Women, Class, and Society in Early Christianity: Models
from Luke-Acts.* Peabody, Mass.: Hendrickson, 1997.

Avemarie, Friedrich. *Die Tauferzählungen der Apostelgeschichte: Theologie und
Geschichte.* WUNT 139. Tübingen: Mohr/Siebeck, 2002.

Barrett, C. K. *Luke the Historian in Recent Study.* Facets. Philadelphia: Fortress Press,
1970.

Bartchy, S. Scott. "Community of Goods in Acts: Idealization or Social Reality?" In *The
Future of Early Christianity: Essays in Honor of Helmut Koester,* edited by Birger A.
Pearson, 309–18. Minneapolis: Fortress Press, 1991.

Bonz, Marianne Palmer. *The Past as Legacy: Luke-Acts and Ancient Epic.* Minneapolis:
Fortress Press, 2000.

Bovon, François. *L'Oeuvre de Luc: Etudes d'exégèse et de theologie.* LD 130. Paris: Cerf,
1987.

Brawley, Robert L. *Centering on God: Method and Message in Luke-Acts.* LCBI. Louisville:
Westminster John Knox, 1990.

Bruce, F. F. "The Speeches in Acts—Thirty Years After." In *Reconciliation and Hope: New
Testament Essays on Atonement and Eschatology Presented to L. L. Morris on His 60th
Birthday,* edited by Robert Banks, 53–68. Grand Rapids: Eerdmans, 1974.

Cadbury, Henry J. *The Book of Acts in History.* New York: Harper, 1955.

———. *The Making of Luke-Acts.* 2d ed. London: SPCK, 1958.

Cassidy, Richard J. *Society and Politics in the Acts of the Apostles.* Maryknoll, N.Y.: Orbis,
1987.

———, and Philip J. Scharper, editors. *Political Issues in Luke-Acts.* Maryknoll, N.Y.:
Orbis, 1983.

Chance, J. Bradley. *Jerusalem, the Temple, and the New Age in Luke-Acts.* Macon, Ga.:
Mercer, 1988.

Conzelmann, Hans. "The Address of Paul on the Areopagus." In Keck and Martyn 1980:217–30.

D'Angelo, Mary Rose. "'Knowing how to preside over his own household': Imperial Masculinity and Christian Asceticism in the Pastorals, Hermas, and Luke-Acts." In *New Testament Masculinities*, edited by Stephen D. Moore and Janice Capel Anderson, 241–71. Semeia Studies 45. Atlanta: Society of Biblical Literature, 2003.

Downing, F. Gerald. "Common Ground with Paganism in Luke and in Josephus." *NTS* 28 (1982) 546–59.

Dupont, Jacques. *The Salvation of the Gentiles: Essays on the Acts of the Apostles*. Translated by John R. Keating. New York: Paulist, 1979.

Elliger, Winfried. *Paulus in Griechenland: Philippi, Thessaloniki, Athen, Korinth*. 2d ed. SBS 92/93. Stuttgart: Katholisches Bibelwerk, 1990.

Epp, Eldon J. "The Ascension in the Textual Tradition of Luke-Acts." In *New Testament Textual Criticism: Its Significance for Exegesis: Essays in Honour of Bruce M. Metzger*, edited by Eldon J. Epp and Gordon D. Fee, 131–45. Oxford: Clarendon, 1981.

———. *The Theological Tendency of Codex Bezae Cantabrigiensis in Acts*. SNTSMS 3. Cambridge: Cambridge Univ. Press, 1966.

Esler, Philip F. *Community and Gospel in Luke-Acts: The Social and Political Motivations of Lucan Theology*. SNTSMS 57. Cambridge: Cambridge Univ. Press, 1987

Fletcher-Louis, Crispin T. H. *Luke-Acts: Angels, Christology, and Soteriology*. WUNT 2/94. Tübingen: Mohr/Siebeck, 1997.

Foakes-Jackson, F. J., and Kirsopp Lake, editors. *The Beginnings of Christianity: Acts of the Apostles*. 5 vols. London: Macmillan, 1919–33.

Garrett, Susan R. *The Demise of the Devil: Magic and the Demonic in Luke's Writings*. Minneapolis: Fortress Press, 1989.

Gasque, W. Ward. *A History of the Interpretation of the Acts of the Apostles*. Peabody, Mass.: Hendrickson, 1989. Reprint of 1975 ed.

Gowler, David B. *Host, Guest, Enemy, and Friend: Portraits of the Pharisees in Luke and Acts*. ESEC 2. New York: Lang, 1991.

Grässer, Erich. *Forschungen zur Apostelgeschichte*. WUNT 137. Tübingen: Mohr/Siebeck, 2001.

Hedrick, Charles W. "Paul's Conversion/Call: A Comparative Analysis of the Three Reports in Acts." *JBL* 100 (1981) 415–32.

Hemer, Colin J. *The Book of Acts in the Setting of Hellenistic History*. WUNT 49. Tübingen: Mohr/Siebeck, 1989.

Hengel, Martin. *Acts and the History of Earliest Christianity*. Translated by John Bowden. Minneapolis: Fortress Press, 1980. German ed. 1979.

Hill, Craig C. *Hellenists and Hebrews: Reappraising Division within the Earliest Church*. Minneapolis: Fortress Press, 1992.

Horn, Friedrich Wilhelm, editor. *Das Ende des Paulus: Historische, theologische und literaturgeschichtliche Aspekte*. BZNW 106. Berlin: de Gruyter, 2001.

Jervell, Jacob. *The Theology of the Acts of the Apostles*. NTT. Cambridge: Cambridge Univ. Press, 1996.

———. *The Unknown Paul: Essays on Luke-Acts and Early Christian History*. Minneapolis: Augsburg, 1984.

Johnson, Luke Timothy. *Sharing Possessions: Mandate and Symbol of Faith*. OBT. Philadelphia: Fortress Press, 1981.

Keck, Leander E., and J. Louis Martyn, editors. *Studies in Luke-Acts*. Philadelphia: Fortress Press, 1980 [1966].

Kee, Howard Clark. *Good News to the Ends of the Earth: The Theology of Acts*. Philadelphia: Trinity, 1990.

Klauck, Hans-Josef. *The Religious Context of Early Christianity*. Translated by Brian McNeil. Minneapolis: Fortress Press, 2003.

———. *Magic and Paganism in Early Christianity: The World of the Acts of the Apostles*. Translated by Brian McNeil. Minneapolis: Fortress Press, 2003.

Klein, Günter. "Der Synkretismus als theologisches Problem in der ältesten christlichen Apologetik." *ZTK* 64 (1967) 40–82. Reprinted in idem, *Rekonstruktion und Interpretation: Gesammelte Aufsätze zum Neuen Testament*, 262–301. BEvT 50. Munich: Kaiser, 1969.

Korn, Manfred. *Die Geschichte Jesu in veränderter Zeit: Studien zur bleibenden Bedeutung Jesu im lukanischen Doppelwerk*. WUNT 2/51. Tübingen: Mohr/Siebeck, 1993.

Kremer, Jacob, editor. *Les Actes des Apôtres: Traditions, Rédaction, Théologie*. BETL 48. Gembloux: Duculot, 1979.

Lampe, Peter. *From Paul to Valentinus: Christians in Rome in the First Two Centuries*. Translated by Michael Steinhauser. Minneapolis: Fortress Press, 2003.

Lentz, John Clayton Jr. *Luke's Portrait of Paul*. SNTSMS 77. Cambridge: Cambridge Univ. Press, 1993.

Lin, Szu-Chuan. *Wundertaten und Mission: Dramatische Episoden in Apg 13–14*. Europäische Hochschulschriften 23/623. Frankfurt: Lang, 1998.

Löning, Karl. "Das Evangelium und die Kulturen: Heilsgeschichtliche und kulturelle Aspekte kirchlicher Realität in der Apostelgeschichte." In *ANRW* 2.25.3 (1985) 2604–46.

———. "Das Gottesbild der Apostelgeschichte im Spannungsfeld von Frühjudentum und Fremdreligion." In *Monotheismus und Christologie: Zur Gottesfrage im hellenistischen Judentum und im Urchristentum*, edited by Hans-Josef Klauck, 88–117. QD 138. Freiburg: Herder, 1992.

MacDonald, Dennis R. *Does the New Testament Imitate Homer? Four Cases from the Acts of the Apostles*. New Haven: Yale Univ. Press, 2003.

Maddox, Robert. *The Purpose of Luke-Acts*. FRLANT 126. Göttingen: Vandenhoeck & Ruprecht, 1982.

Marguerat, Daniel. *The First Christian Historian: Acts of the Apostles*. Translated by Ken McKinney et al. SNTSMS 121. Cambridge: Cambridge Univ. Press, 2002. French ed. 1999.

Marshall, I. Howard, and David Peterson. *Witness to the Gospel: The Theology of Acts*. Grand Rapids: Eerdmans, 1998.

Matson, David Lertis. *Household Conversion Narratives in Acts: Pattern and Interpretation*. JSNTSup 123. Sheffield: Sheffield Academic, 1996.

Matthews, Christopher R. *Philip: Apostle and Evangelist—Configurations of a Tradition*. NovTSup 105. Leiden: Brill, 2002.

Matthews, Shelly. *First Converts: Rich Pagan Women and the Rhetoric of Mission in Early Judaism and Christianity*. Contraversions. Stanford: Stanford Univ. Press, 2001.

Moessner, David P., editor. *Luke the Interpreter of Israel*. Vol. 1: *Jesus and the Heritage of Israel: Luke's Narrative Claim upon Israel's Legacy*. Harrisburg, Pa.: Trinity, 1999.

Mount, Christopher. *Pauline Christianity: Luke-Acts and the Legacy of Paul*. NovTSup 104. Leiden: Brill, 2002.

Nave, Guy D. Jr. *The Role and Function of Repentance in Luke-Acts*. SBLAB 4. Atlanta: Society of Biblical Literature, 2002.

Neagoe, Alexandru. *The Trial of the Gospel: An Apologetic Reading of Luke's Trial Narratives*. SNTSMS 116. Cambridge: Cambridge Univ. Press, 2002.

Neirynck, F. "Miracle Stories in the Acts of the Apostles: An Introduction." In *Les Actes des Apôtres: Traditions, Rédaction, Théologie*, edited by J. Kremer, 169–213. BETL 48. Gembloux: Duculot, 1979.

Neyrey, Jerome H. "Benefaction, Providence, and Theodicy: God in the Acts of the Apostles." In idem, *Render to God: New Testament Understandings of the Divine*, 82–106. Minneapolis: Fortress Press, 2004.

———, editor. *The Social World of Luke-Acts: Models for Interpretation*. Peabody, Mass.: Hendrickson, 1991.

Niklas, Tobias, and Michael Tilly, editors. *The Book of Acts as Church History: Text, Textual Traditions, and Ancient Interpretations*. BZNW 120. Berlin: de Gruyter, 2003.

Omerzu, Heike. *Der Prozess des Paulus: Eine exegetische und rechtshistorische Untersuchung der Apostelgeschichte*. BZNW 115. Berlin: de Gruyter, 2002.

Pervo, Richard I. *Luke's Story of Paul*. Minneapolis: Fortress Press, 1990.

———. *Profit with Delight: The Literary Genre of the Acts of the Apostles*. Philadelphia: Fortress Press, 1987.

Plümacher, Eckhard. *Lukas als hellenistischer Schriftsteller: Studien zur Apostelgeschichte*. SUNT 9. Göttingen: Vandenhoeck & Ruprecht, 1972.

Pokorný, Petr. *Theologie der lukanischen Schriften*. FRLANT 174. Göttingen: Vandenhoeck & Ruprecht, 1998.

Porter, Stanley E. *The Paul of Acts: Essays in Literary Criticism, Rhetoric, and Theology*. WUNT 115. Tübingen: Mohr/Siebeck, 1999. Reprinted, Peabody, Mass.: Hendrickson, 2001.

Reimer, Andy M. *Miracle and Magic: A Study in the Acts of the Apostles and the* Life of Apollonius of Tyana. JSNTSup 235. London: Sheffield Academic, 2002.

Robinson, James M. "Acts." In *The Literary Guide to the Bible*. Edited by Robert Alter and Frank Kermode. Cambridge, Mass.: Belknap, 1987.

Rosenblatt, Marie-Eloise. *Paul the Accused: His Portrait in the Acts of the Apostles*. Zacchaeus Studies. Collegeville, Minn.: Liturgical, 1995.

Schreiber, Stefan. *Paulus als Wundertäter: Redaktionsgeschichtliche Untersuchungen zur Apostelgeschichte und den authentischen Paulusbriefen*. BZNW 79. Berlin: de Gruyter, 1996.

Seim, Turid Karlsen. *The Double Message: Patterns of Gender in Luke-Acts*. Nashville: Abingdon, 1994.

Skinner, Matthew L. *Locating Paul: Places of Custody as Narrative Settings in Acts 21–28*. SBLAB 13. Atlanta: Society of Biblical Literature, 2003.

Soards, Marion L. *The Speeches in Acts: Their Content, Context, and Concerns*. Louisville: Westminster John Knox, 1994.

Soffe, Grahame. "Christians, Jews, and Pagans in the Acts of the Apostles." In *Pagan Gods and Shrines of the Roman Empire*, edited by Martin Henig and Anthony King, 239–56. Oxford University Committee for Archaeology Monograph 8. Oxford: Oxford University Committee for Archaeology, 1986.

Spencer, F. Scott. *The Portrait of Philip in Acts: A Study of Roles and Relations*. JSNTSup 67. Sheffield: Sheffield Academic, 1992.

Stegemann, Ekkehard W., and Wolfgang Stegemann. *The Jesus Movement: A Social History of Its First Century.* Translated by O. C. Dean Jr. Minneapolis: Fortress Press, 1999.

Stegemann, Wolfgang. *Zwischen Synagoge und Obrigkeit: Zur historischen Situation der lukanischen Christen.* FRLANT 152. Göttingen: Vandenhoeck & Ruprecht, 1991.

Stehlan, Rick. *Paul, Artemis, and the Jews in Ephesus.* BZNW 80. Berlin: de Gruyter, 1996.

———. *Strange Acts: Studies in the Cultural World of the Acts of the Apostles.* BZNW 126. Berlin: de Gruyter, 2004.

Stenschke, Christoph W. *Luke's Portrait of Gentiles Prior to Their Coming to Faith.* WUNT 2/108. Tübingen: Mohr/Siebeck, 1999.

Sterling, Gregory E. "'Athletes of Virtue': An Analysis of the Summaries in Acts (2:41-47; 4:32-35; 5:12-16)." *JBL* 113 (1994) 679–96.

———. *Historiography and Self-definition: Josephos, Luke-Acts, and Apologetic Historiography.* NovTSup 64. Leiden: Brill, 1992.

Talbert, Charles H. *Literary Patterns, Theological Themes, and the Genre of Luke-Acts.* SBLMS 20. Missoula, Mont.: Scholars, 1974.

———. *Reading Luke-Acts in Its Mediterranean Milieu.* NovTSup 107. Leiden: Brill, 2003.

———, editor. *Luke-Acts: New Perspectives from the Society of Biblical Literature Seminar.* New York: Crossroad, 1984.

———, editor. *Perspectives on Luke-Acts.* Edinburgh: T. & T. Clark, 1978.

Tannehill, Robert C. *The Narrative Unity of Luke-Acts: A Literary Interpretation.* Vol. 2: *The Acts of the Apostles.* Foundations and Facets. Minneapolis: Fortress Press, 1990.

Thompson, Richard P., and Thomas E. Phillips, editors. *Literary Studies in Luke-Acts: Essays in Honor of Joseph B. Tyson.* Macon, Ga.: Mercer Univ. Press, 1998.

Thornton, Claus-Jürgen. *Der Zeuge des Zeugen: Lukas als Historiker der Paulusreisen.* WUNT 56. Tübingen: Mohr/Siebeck, 1991.

Thurston, Bonnie. *Spiritual Life in the Early Church: The Witness of Acts and Ephesians.* Minneapolis: Fortress Press, 1993.

Tyson, Joseph B. *Images of Judaism in Luke-Acts.* Columbia, S.C.: Univ. of South Carolina Press, 1992.

———, editor. *Luke-Acts and the Jewish People: Eight Critical Perspectives.* Minneapolis: Augsburg, 1988.

Verheyden, J., editor. *The Unity of Luke-Acts.* BETL 142. Leuven: Peeters, 1999.

Walaskay, Paul W. *"And So We Came to Rome": The Political Perspective of St. Luke.* SNTSMS 49. Cambridge: Cambridge Univ. Press, 1983.

Wildhaber, Bruno. *Paganisme populaire et prédication apostolique: D'après l'exégèse de quelques séquences des Actes: Eléments pour une théologie lucanienne de la mission.* Le monde de la Bible. Geneva: Labor et Fides, 1987.

Wilson, Stephen G. *The Gentiles and the Gentile Mission in Luke-Acts.* SNTSMS 23. Cambridge: Cambridge Univ. Press, 1973.

———. *Leaving the Fold: Apostates and Defectors in Antiquity.* Minneapolis: Fortress Press, 2004.

———. *Luke and the Law.* SNTSMS 50. Cambridge: Cambridge Univ. Press, 1983.

———. *Related Strangers: Jews and Christians, 70–170 C.E.* Minneapolis: Fortress Press, 1995.

Winter, Bruce W., editor. *The Book of Acts in Its First Century Setting.* 6 vols. Grand Rapids: Eerdmans, 1993–.

Witherington, Ben III, editor. *History, Literature, and Society in the Book of Acts*. Cambridge: Cambridge Univ. Press, 1996.

Woods, Edward J. *The "Finger of God" and Pneumatology in Luke-Acts*. JSNTSup 205. Sheffield: Sheffield Academic, 2001.

Index of Authors

Editor's note: Dates (whenever available) have been supplied for authors of earlier generations in order to provide historical context.

Index of Ancient Sources

Romans

1 Corinthians

2 Corinthians

Galatians